more
HEALTHY
ONE DISH
COOKING

more HEALTHY ONE DISH COOKING

SOUPS • SALADS • LIGHT MEALS • STIR-FRIES
CURRIES AND STEWS • BAKES AND ROASTS

Reader's Digest

Shredded pork with Thai lime dressing, page 176

Contents

Chicken and raspberry salad with lime vinaigrette, page 58

More Healthy One-Dish Cooking gives you more than 180 well-balanced, one-dish meal ideas, all of which maximise flavour and nourishment, and minimise fuss and the washing up. Some recipes are cooked in just one pot, while others involve a little preparation before you bring the ingredients all together in a single dish. From hearty soups and stews, tempting roasts and oven-bakes, creamy risottos and satisfying pasta dishes to speedy stir-fries, salads, nutritious sandwiches and healthy pizzas, there are dishes for all tastes and occasions.

All the recipes in *More Healthy One-Dish Cooking* are designed to provide a healthy balance of energy and nutrients, while restricting saturated fats, salt and added sugars. Most contain less than 30 g of total fat and a maximum of 8 g of saturated fat per serving. Most also have no more than 900 mg of sodium per serving, apart from a handful, such as pizzas, where the recipe we provide is far less salty than would normally be the case. If you have any health concerns, we recommend that you omit all salt from the recipes in this book.

You'll find that, in general, the recipes use fresh ingredients over packaged or processed foods, and whole grains over refined grains. They also make generous use of fruit and vegetables, which will help you to reach the daily recommended intake of two serves of fruit and five serves of vegetables.

The Editors

Eat well, eat healthily

Healthy eating is all about variety in the right proportions – plenty of fruit and vegetables and slowly digested carbohydrates, a little good-quality protein and low-fat dairy. Restrict foods that are high in saturated fats, salt and sugar.

Carbohydrates

At least half of your daily energy should come from carbohydrates, such as bread, pasta, rice, cereals, pulses and starchy vegetables and fruit. They provide half the kilojoules as the same weight of fat. Ideally, go for wholegrain, unrefined varieties, which are rich in fibre and contain higher levels of nutrients, such as B group vitamins. Also, most are a good source of slowly digested carbohydrate, which provide the body with slow-release energy that will keep you satisfied for longer.

Glycaemic index

Carbohydrate foods have a ranking of 1–100, known as the Glycaemic Index (GI). This ranking indicates how quickly the carbohydrate in a particular food is broken down by the body and released as glucose into the bloodstream compared with the same quantity of pure glucose.

The lower a food's GI, the more slowly it is digested and the lower the rise in blood glucose. For a steady release of energy that will help keep you satisfied for longer and help to avoid fluctuating energy levels, choose low- or medium-GI carbohydrate foods, such as pasta, noodles, long-grain and basmati rice, oats, pulses, wholegrain breads and most types of fruit.

Vegetables and fruit

Choose at least five serves of vegetables and salad a day. Vegetables have practically no fat and are packed with many vitamins, minerals and other anti-oxidant nutrients that help to protect against illness. They also provide vital dietary fibre, which is essential for a healthy digestion. Try to eat a wide variety, as each type of vegetable contains different combinations of nutrients. One serve means one cup of salad or half a cup of cooked vegetables.

Two serves of fruit a day will boost your intake of fibre, vitamin C, beta-carotene and anti-oxidants. One serve is equal to one medium or two small pieces of fruit. Fresh juices are nutritious but can be high in kilojoules, so don't overdo it – it is better to eat whole fruit and vegetables and quench your thirst with water.

Variety in vegetables and fruit

✤ Green leafy vegetables are the best source of folate – a deficiency causes weakness, loss of appetite, forgetfulness, insomnia and anaemia. They are also the richest source of vitamin K, essential for healthy bones, and calcium.

✤ Orange, yellow and red vegetables and fruit, such as carrots, capsicums (bell peppers), sweet potatoes (kumara), strawberries and mangoes, are rich in vitamin C, beta-carotene and other powerful anti-oxidants that are thought to help fight against cancer, heart disease, cataracts, arthritis and general ageing.

✤ Avocado is rich in beneficial oils and anti-oxidants, with good amounts of vitamin C, folate and vitamin E.

✤ Onions, garlic and others of the onion family contain allicin, a phytochemical believed to help lower blood cholesterol and stimulate the immune system. They are rich in anti-oxidants, and garlic has a natural antibacterial effect.

✤ Tomatoes are an excellent source of vitamin C and also lycopene, another powerful anti-oxidant.

✤ Berries are one of the best known sources of anti-oxidants, and also have good amounts of fibre and vitamin C.

✤ Brassicas, including cabbage, brussels sprouts, cauliflower, broccoli, kale and swede, provide plenty of fibre. They are also star anti-oxidant performers as well as being a good source of vitamin C, folate and minerals.

Protein

Meat, poultry, fish, dairy, eggs, tofu, pulses and nuts contain protein, which is essential for growth and cell repair. Protein also provides minerals such as iron, zinc and magnesium, and B vitamins (B_{12} is found only in sources of animal protein). The body doesn't require a huge amount of protein; for optimum health, women should eat about 46 g and men 64 g a day.

Protein foods can be high in fat so choose lean meat and meat products, trim visible fat and remove the skin from poultry. Eat fish at least once a week: all fish are low in fat, including oily fish, such as trout, sardines and salmon. Fish and seafood are rich in omega-3 fatty acids (especially oily fish), which are believed to help to reduce the risk of heart disease.

Pulses are naturally low in fat, as is tofu, made from soybeans. Rich sources of plant protein, they are also valuable for their soluble fibre, B vitamins, minerals and heart-friendly phytonutrients. Try to eat lentils, beans or peas at least twice a week.

Nuts, although high in fat and kilojoules, contain mainly the 'healthier' unsaturated type of fat.

Dairy

Milk, yogurt and cheese are all excellent sources of calcium, needed for strong bones and teeth, blood clotting, muscle contraction and a healthy nervous system. Dairy foods are particularly important for young children, for adolescent girls – to prevent osteoporosis later in life – and for women in general. As dairy products can be high in saturated fat, try to choose low- or reduced-fat varieties where possible. However, if you are feeding young children under the age of two years, use full-fat versions to provide them with sufficient energy.

Aim to include 2–3 portions of dairy foods each day. A portion could include: a glass of milk; a small tub of yogurt; 125 g (4 oz) cottage cheese; or a matchbox-sized piece of cheddar cheese.

the total cholesterol level as well as the 'bad' LDL cholesterol level when they displace saturated fats in the diet.

Polyunsaturated fats lower the total and 'bad' LDL cholesterol in the blood and reduce the risk of heart disease. Certain polyunsaturated fatty acids (known as essential fatty acids) must be supplied by food. There are two groups of these: omega-3 fats, primarily found in the fats of fish, particularly deep sea oily fish; and omega-6 fatty acids from common vegetable oils, such as safflower, sunflower, maize, cottonseed and grapeseed; nuts such as walnuts, Brazil nuts and pine nuts; and polyunsaturated margarines. Aim to eat a little of the omega-6 fats, but concentrate more on the omega-3 fats – both groups are essential for good health.

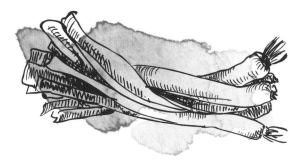

Fats

A small amount of the right kind of fat is essential for a healthy diet, providing valuable fat-soluble vitamins and essential fatty acids. Some fat also makes food taste good. However, no more than one-third of your daily kilojoule intake should come from fat. Fats can be divided into three main groups.

Saturated fats are found mainly in fat on meat, dairy foods, deli meats such as bacon and sausages, and in commercial shortenings used in biscuits, snacks and other processed foods. Coconut and palm oil are also high in saturated fats. They raise both the total cholesterol level and the 'bad' LDL cholesterol level. A high intake of these fats increases the level of cholesterol in the blood, which in turn raises the risk of heart disease and some cancers. Eating less saturated fat is one of the most important things you can do for your heart. Dietary guidelines recommend reducing saturated fats to less than 10 per cent of the total kilojoules consumed.

Mono-unsaturated fats are particularly high in olive, canola, macadamia and peanut (groundnut) oils, most nuts and avocados. These fats lower

Salt

A small amount of sodium (available from foods or salt) is needed for healthy body function, but most people in the developed world eat far too much salt. Overconsumption can lead to health problems, such as high blood pressure and an increased risk of heart disease, stroke and kidney failure.

The National Health and Medical Research Council has set the recommended dietary intake (RDI) for sodium at 920 mg/day, with an upper limit of 2300 mg. Eating processed, fast and ready-made foods, and adding salt to your food all contribute to overconsumption. There is also 'hidden' salt in bread, cheese, cured meats and smoked fish. Other high-salt foods include many condiments and canned foods, so always check the label and buy salt-reduced versions if they are available.

How much should you eat?

Daily guidelines for nutrients are based on average energy (kilojoule or calorie) requirements, depending on age, gender and activity levels. These figures are based on the intakes for an average adult man or woman. These figures are appropriate for those who are not overweight or completely sedentary. Those who are overweight should aim to reduce these levels by 25 per cent, indicated in parentheses.

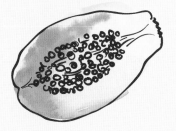

Food group	Women	Men
Kilojoules	8000 (6000)	10,000 (7500)
Calories	2000 (1500)	2500 (1875)
Carbohydrate	260-275 g (185-205 g)	310-340 g (230-255 g)
Fruit	2 serves	2 serves
Vegetables	5 serves	5 serves
Protein	46 g	64 g
Total fat (maximum)	64 g (40 g)	80 g (60 g)
of which saturates	20 g (16 g)	27 g (20 g)
Fibre	25 g	30 g
Sodium (maximum)	2300 mg (or 5 g salt)	2300 mg (or 5 g salt)

Sugar

Added sugars contain no vitamins, minerals or fibre, and simply provide the body with empty kilojoules. Pure glucose has a GI ranking of 100 and may cause rapid fluctuations in blood glucose. However, a small amount of sugar adds to the enjoyment of food, so you can include occasional sweet foods as part of a well-balanced diet, as long as you don't overdo it.

Remember that fruit contains fructose (a natural fruit sugar) and fruit or fruit juice can often be used for sweetening dishes rather than using added sugar. There is an added benefit in using fruit, as the fibre slows down the rate at which its sugar is released into the bloodstream.

You could also try some of the low-GI alternatives to sugar, such as maple syrup, pure floral honey or agave syrup. The latter is the juice of a spiky desert plant, concentrated to make a sweet, mild-flavoured syrup that releases its energy slowly.

A boost for one-dish meals

The recipes in this book have been designed to be complete lunch or dinner dishes, served with good bread or a simple salad. But you may want to boost the recipe to provide a more substantial meal.

Boosting carbs

Adding filling carbohydrates – especially those low-GI carbohydrates that are broken down slowly and keep blood glucose steady – will stretch a recipe further and keep you feeling fuller for longer. It is also one of the best ways to stretch a meal for lots of hungry people.

❧ **Beans and lentils** are a high-fibre carbohydrate option. Mashed or crushed, they make a nutritious alternative to mashed potatoes.

❧ **Bread** is the simplest accompaniment, and is best freshly baked or served warm. Pita, grain, rye and real sourdough breads are better GI choices than white or many wholemeal (whole-wheat) bread.

❧ **Burghul** (bulgur or cracked wheat) is a delicious alternative to rice, with a wholesome, nutty flavour. Enjoy it plain, or tossed with a little olive oil and lemon juice, and plenty of chopped fresh herbs.

❧ **Couscous** goes particularly well with saucy stews and casseroles (called tagines in North Africa, where couscous is a staple).

❧ **Pasta and noodles** come in all shapes, sizes and flavours and are a perfect low-fat accompaniment. For those following a wheat-free diet, choose rice noodles, soba noodles (made from buckwheat) and wheat-free varieties of pasta.

❧ **Potatoes** are a versatile accompaniment. Steam baby potatoes and toss with olive oil, lemon zest and fresh mint, or make a warm salad of boiled new potatoes with a vinaigrette dressing and chopped fresh herbs. Boil two to three root vegetables such as carrots, swede, parsnips, celeriac, potatoes or sweet potatoes (kumara), then mash with yogurt and chives. Mash potato with cannellini beans for a low-GI mash.

❧ **Quinoa** is a high-protein grain that originated in South America. Unlike most other plant grains, it is a good source of complete protein. This low-GI grain is also high in fibre.

❧ **Rice** is great with stews, casseroles, curries and stir-fries. Wholegrain varieties, such as brown or wild rice (not a true rice but a grain), are healthy options.

Enhancing flavour

Make the most of herbs, spices and other seasonings. They'll bring a whole new flavour dimension to your cooking that may mean you are able to use less salt than you've used previously.

❧ **Herbs** Fresh robust herbs, such as rosemary, thyme, sage, oregano and bay leaves, are particularly good in slow-cooked dishes, such as casseroles and stews, as well as marinades and stuffings. They are usually added at the start to mellow their flavour and often removed before serving.

Tender herbs, such as chives, mint, tarragon, dill, basil, chervil, parsley and coriander (cilantro), have a much fresher flavour than the robust herbs. They are usually added to dishes at the last minute, as prolonged cooking generally spoils their flavour.

❧ **Spices** Spices add fragrant scents and exotic flavours to a wide range of dishes. Buy them in small quantities and whole if possible, to be ground when required, to retain their freshness. A mortar and pestle or an electric coffee or spice grinder is ideal for grinding your own. Store in airtight containers, in a cupboard, away from direct heat and sunlight, and use within six months.

Pepper complements all savoury dishes with its warm, pungent taste, and brings out the flavour of other ingredients. For a spicy kick, use dried red chilli flakes, chilli powder or chilli seasoning blends. Paprika is far milder, with a sweet, earthy aroma, and is ideal for stews and sauces.

Warm spices impart an aromatic flavour to dishes. They include coriander, cumin, star anise and turmeric, and are usually included early in the cooking process to allow their flavours to mellow. Cinnamon, ginger, cardamom, nutmeg and other sweet spices add fragrant, spicy undertones to stews and simmered dishes.

Don't forget to make the most of the fresh aromatics - garlic, onion, lemongrass and ginger.

Just add fibre

Many health experts say that the average adult should aim to consume 25–30 g of dietary fibre a day. It's not difficult to achieve this. Here are some ideas:

❧ Eat two serves of fruit and five serves of vegetables every day.

❧ Eat porridge or muesli with fruit and nuts for breakfast.

❧ Snack on fruit and nuts.

❧ Choose low-GI grainy, soy and linseed, rye or real sourdough breads.

❧ Pack in the pulses: try adding lentils to soups and sauces; add chickpeas to salads or serve them as a side dish.

Healthy homemade stock

Commercial liquid stock, or stock powder or cubes, quickly increases the sodium level of a dish. It's worth shopping for the salt-reduced versions of stock, or using half commercial stock, half water. But better still is the stock that you make yourself.

Beef, veal or lamb stock

Makes About 1.5 litres   **Time** 3¼ hours

1 kg (2 lb) meat bones (beef, veal or lamb)
2 sprigs fresh thyme
2 sprigs fresh parsley
1 large bay leaf
2 onions, roughly chopped
2 celery stalks, roughly chopped
2 carrots, roughly chopped
6 black peppercorns

Place the bones in a stockpot or large saucepan and add 8 cups (2 litres) water, or enough to cover the bones. Bring to a boil, skimming off the scum as it rises to the surface.

Tie together the thyme, parsley and bay leaf, and add to the pan with the onions, celery, carrots and peppercorns. Cover and gently simmer for 2–3 hours.

Cool slightly, then strain the stock into a large heatproof bowl through a sieve, discarding the solids. Leave to cool, then chill. Skim any fat from the surface before using the stock.

Per 1 cup (250 ml)
119 kJ, 29 kcal, 2 g protein, 1 g fat (<1 g saturated fat), 2 g carbohydrate (1 g sugars), <1 g fibre, 37 mg sodium

Chicken stock

Makes About 1.5 litres   **Time** 1¼ hours

1 chicken carcass or the bones from 4 chicken pieces (or fresh chicken wings, browned first)
1 onion, roughly chopped
1 large carrot, roughly chopped
1 celery stalk, roughly chopped
1 large bay leaf
6 black peppercorns

Break up the chicken carcass or bones and put them in a stockpot or large saucepan with the onion, carrot, celery, bay leaf and black peppercorns, and pour in 8 cups (2 litres) water.

Bring to a boil over high heat, then reduce the heat until the liquid is gently simmering. Cover the pan and leave to bubble for 1 hour.

Cool slightly, then strain the stock into a large heatproof bowl through a sieve, discarding the solids. Leave to cool, then chill. Skim any fat from the surface before using the stock.

Per 1 cup (250 ml)
158 kJ, 38 kcal, 3 g protein, 2 g fat (<1 g saturated fat), 1 g carbohydrate (<1 g sugars), <1 g fibre, 19 mg sodium

Vegetable stock

Makes About 1.75 litres   **Time** 1¼ hours

15 g (½ oz) butter

250 g (8 oz) leeks, roughly chopped

250 g (8 oz) onions, roughly chopped

1 large bay leaf

4 sprigs fresh thyme

4 sprigs fresh parsley

250 g (8 oz) carrots, roughly chopped

150 g (5 oz) celery, roughly chopped

5 black peppercorns

Melt the butter in a stockpot or large saucepan over medium heat. Stir in the leeks and onions. Reduce the heat to low, cover and cook for 20 minutes without lifting the lid.

Tie the herbs together and add to the pan with the carrots, celery, peppercorns and 8 cups (2 litres) water. Increase the heat and slowly bring to a boil, skimming off any scum as it rises to the surface. Reduce the heat to low as soon as the water boils, and simmer for 35 minutes.

Cool slightly, then strain the stock into a large heatproof bowl through a sieve, discarding the solids. Leave to cool, then chill.

Per 1 cup (250 ml)
138 kJ, 33 kcal, <1 g protein, 2 g fat (1 g saturated fat), 3 g carbohydrate (3 g sugars), 2 g fibre, 39 mg sodium

Fish stock

Makes About 1 litre   **Time** 50 minutes

1 kg (2 lb) trimmings from white fish (skin, bones, and heads without gills)

1 onion, thinly sliced

4 sprigs fresh parsley

2 bay leaves

2 carrots, thinly sliced

2 celery stalks, thinly sliced

4 black peppercorns

Rinse the fish trimmings well and put them in a stockpot or large saucepan. Add the onion, parsley, bay leaves, carrots, celery, black peppercorns and 5 cups (1.25 litres) water. Bring to a boil, then reduce the heat and gently simmer for 30 minutes, skimming off the scum as it rises to the surface.

Cool slightly, then strain the stock into a large heatproof bowl through a sieve, discarding the solids. Leave to cool, then chill.

Per 1 cup (250 ml)
116 kJ, 28 kcal, 4 g protein, <1 g fat (<1 g saturated fat), 2 g carbohydrate (1 g sugars), <1 g fibre, 31 mg sodium

Putting stock to good use

❧ Stock will not thicken while it is cooking, but a well-concentrated meat or chicken stock should gel once it has cooled. Any solidified fat can then be scraped off the top for a lower-fat stock.

❧ Stock should be cooled then kept, covered, in the refrigerator for 4 days (2 days for fish stock) or in the freezer for up to 3 months (2 months for fish stock). If you intend to freeze the stock, it is best to remove the fat, then rapidly boil the liquid to get a concentrated stock. Frozen stock can be defrosted or rehydrated straight from frozen, but should be simmered for at least 10 minutes. It can also be diluted.

❧ You can freeze reduced, concentrated stock in ice-cube trays. The frozen stock cubes can then be packed in a freezer bag and used individually.

❧ Add frozen stock cubes to hot liquids in soups and stews, and they will melt almost instantly.

❧ Use fresh, raw or cooked bones to make meat stock, plus any lean meat scraps. Trim any fat or fatty skin from meat or bones before using in the stock. For a richer stock, first roast the bones at 230°C (450°F/Gas 8) for 40 minutes.

❧ Chicken stock can be made with the leftovers from a roasted chicken – it makes for a great base.

❧ Fish trimmings (the head, skin and bones) from any white fish with a good flavour can be used. Oily fish are not suitable for making stock as they give it a strong, fatty flavour.

❧ Make a shellfish stock using prawn (shrimp), lobster or mussel shells, instead of fish trimmings.

Chicken noodle soup, page 39

Soups

A hearty soup is one of the simplest, most nourishing and versatile of dishes. Fresh seasonal produce, simmered in a nutritious stock with carbohydrates and protein, is perfect for a midweek dinner or weekend lunch.

Seafood noodle bowl

Serves 4

Preparation
20 minutes

Cooking
10 minutes

Per serving
*1056 kJ, 252 kcal,
29 g protein, 2 g fat
(<1 g saturated fat),
29 g carbohydrate
(3 g sugars), 1 g fibre,
601 mg sodium*

3 cups (750 ml) salt-reduced fish or chicken stock (pages 14–15)

2 teaspoons salt-reduced soy sauce

4 spring onions (scallions), chopped

2.5 cm (1 inch) piece fresh ginger, grated

1 lemongrass stem, white part only, thinly sliced (optional)

225 g (8 oz) thick firm white fish fillets, such as blue-eye or hake, skin removed, cut into chunks

125 g (4 oz) scallops, without roe, thickly sliced

175 g (6 oz) peeled cooked prawns (shrimp)

200 g (7 oz) bok choy, thinly sliced

300 g (10 oz) wok-ready udon (rice) noodles

1 Put the stock, soy sauce, spring onions, ginger and lemongrass, if using, in a large saucepan. Bring to a boil.

2 Add the fish and return to a boil. Add the scallops, reduce the heat and gently simmer for 1 minute.

3 Stir in the prawns, bok choy and udon noodles. Cook until the prawns are heated through and the noodles are cooked. Serve immediately.

Instead of the prawns and scallops, use cooked and shelled pipis or clams (vongole) and mussels.

Red lentil soup

Onions, garlic, ginger and turmeric are all rich in anti-oxidants, but the real star of this recipe is turmeric. Curcumin, the active ingredient found in turmeric, has been shown to have anti-inflammatory effects and is currently the subject of research that is investigating its potential to reduce the risk of some cancers and dementia.

2 tablespoons olive oil

1 red onion, diced

3 cloves garlic, crushed

5 cm (2 inch) piece fresh turmeric, peeled and chopped, or 1¼ tablespoons ground turmeric

3 cm (1¼ inch) piece fresh ginger, peeled and chopped

1 cup (250 g) red lentils

2½ cups (625 ml) salt-reduced chicken or vegetable stock (pages 14-15)

fresh coriander (cilantro) leaves, to garnish

1 Heat the oil in a large saucepan over low heat. Add the onion, garlic, turmeric and ginger, and gently cook, stirring occasionally, for 10 minutes.

2 Add the lentils and stock. Bring to a boil, then reduce the heat to a simmer and cook, covered, for 20 minutes, until the lentils are soft. Add some extra stock or water if the soup becomes thick or too dry.

3 Purée the soup using a stick blender, food processor or upright blender. Ladle into bowls and serve garnished with coriander leaves.

Serves 2

Preparation
10 minutes

Cooking
35 minutes

Per serving
2374 kJ, 567 kcal, 37 g protein, 22 g fat (3 g saturated fat), 60 g carbohydrate (8 g sugars), 20 g fibre, 816 mg sodium

Spelt and tomato soup

1 tablespoon olive oil

1 onion, finely diced

100 g (3½ oz) cracked spelt

2 teaspoons tomato paste
(concentrated purée)

600 ml (21 fl oz) salt-reduced
vegetable stock (page 15)

400 ml (14 fl oz) no added
salt or sugar tomato juice
or tomato passata (puréed
tomatoes)

1 teaspoon mixed dried
herbs

pinch of sugar

pinch of salt

freshly ground black pepper

2 tablespoons sunflower
seeds

2 tomatoes, seeded and diced

2 tablespoons crème fraîche
or light sour cream

2 tablespoons snipped
fresh chives

1 Heat the oil in a saucepan over medium heat. Cook the onion for 5 minutes, until translucent. Add the spelt and tomato paste, and cook for 1 minute.

2 Add the stock and tomato juice or passata. Stir in the mixed dried herbs and sugar, then season with salt and freshly ground black pepper. Bring to a boil, then reduce the heat, cover and simmer for about 10 minutes.

3 Meanwhile, toast the sunflower seeds in a dry frying pan. Remove from the pan and coarsely chop.

4 Purée the soup with a stick blender. Stir in the diced tomatoes and briefly return to a boil. Taste and season with salt and pepper.

5 Ladle the soup into four bowls and swirl 2 teaspoons of the crème fraîche or sour cream through each serving. Serve topped with the sunflower seeds and chives.

Serves 4

Preparation
15 minutes

Cooking
20 minutes

Per serving
*1040 kJ, 249 kcal,
7 g protein, 13 g fat
(4 g saturated fat),
31 g carbohydrate
(10 g sugars), 5 g fibre,
808 mg sodium*

This soup can also be prepared using barley or burghul (bulgur) instead of the spelt.

Fry 100 g (3½ oz) prawns (shrimp) in 1 tablespoon oil for 2 minutes, then season with salt and black pepper. Divide among the soup bowls before serving.

Pea and pesto soup

Serves 4

Preparation
10 minutes

Cooking
10 minutes

Per serving
727 kJ, 174 kcal,
12 g protein, 9 g fat
(1 g saturated fat),
12 g carbohydrate
(4 g sugars), 9 g fibre,
187 mg sodium

750 g (1½ lb) frozen peas

4 spring onions (scallions), trimmed

1 tablespoon lime juice

2½ tablespoons pesto

pinch of salt

freshly ground black pepper

Top the soup with shaved
parmesan or pecorino cheese,
or some fresh basil leaves.

1 Bring 4 cups (1 litre) water to a boil in a large saucepan. Add the peas and spring onions. Cover and return to a boil, then reduce the heat and simmer for 5 minutes.

2 Remove and discard the spring onions. Take out and reserve about 1 cup (150 g) of the peas.

3 Add the lime juice and 1 tablespoon of the pesto to the mixture in the pan. Using a stick blender, purée the soup, then stir in the reserved peas and season with salt and freshly ground black pepper. Briefly reheat the soup.

4 Ladle the soup into serving bowls and serve topped with the remaining pesto.

Minted asparagus and pea soup

200 g (7 oz) asparagus spears

1 tablespoon olive oil

2 French shallots (eschalots), chopped

175 g (6 oz) potatoes, chopped

1 cup (150 g) frozen peas

$2\frac{1}{2}$ cups (625 ml) salt-reduced vegetable stock (page 15)

1 sprig fresh mint

pinch of salt

freshly ground black pepper

$\frac{1}{3}$ cup (90 g) thick (Greek-style) yogurt

$\frac{1}{4}$ cup (40 g) pine nuts, toasted

1 Snap off any woody ends from the asparagus spears at the point where they break easily. Cut off and reserve the tips. Roughly chop the remainder.

2 Heat the oil in a large saucepan and add the shallots, chopped asparagus and potatoes. Cover and cook over medium heat, stirring occasionally, for 6-8 minutes, until tender. Set aside a handful of peas and add the remainder to the pan with the stock and mint. Cook for a further few minutes until the potatoes are tender.

3 Cool slightly, then purée the soup in a food processor or blender. Return to the pan and season with salt and freshly ground black pepper.

4 Cook the asparagus tips and reserved peas in a saucepan of boiling water for 2 minutes, then drain.

5 Bring the soup to a boil, then stir in the asparagus tips and peas. Ladle the soup into serving bowls and top each serving with 1 tablespoon yogurt and some pine nuts.

Serves 4

Preparation
20 minutes

Cooking
15 minutes

Per serving
891 kJ, 213 kcal, 7 g protein, 14 g fat (3 g saturated fat), 14 g carbohydrate (6 g sugars), 4 g fibre, 812 mg sodium

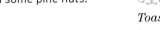

Toast the pine nuts by placing them in a small, dry frying pan over medium–high heat, and tossing frequently for 1 minute, until light golden.

Don't be tempted to rush the cooking of the onions – gently caramelising them is essential to achieve a sweetly mellow flavour.

Adding some white wine with the stock will enhance the final flavour.

Onion soup

Serves 4

Preparation
10 minutes

Cooking
55 minutes

Per serving
*1778 kJ, 425 kcal,
19 g protein, 19 g fat
(8 g saturated fat),
45 g carbohydrate
(19 g sugars), 6 g fibre,
855 mg sodium*

1 tablespoon olive oil

1 tablespoon (20 g) butter

1.25 kg (2½ lb) brown (yellow) onions, halved and thinly sliced

2 teaspoons soft brown sugar

1 tablespoon plain (all-purpose) flour

3 cups (750 ml) salt-reduced beef or chicken stock (page 14)

1 baguette, cut into 12 slices

¾ cup (100 g) grated gruyère

1 Heat the oil and butter in a large saucepan until the butter melts. Add the onions and cook over medium-low heat, stirring occasionally, for 15 minutes. Increase the heat to medium and cook for a further 20 minutes, until the onions are golden brown. Stir in the sugar and flour, mixing well. Pour in the stock and 3 cups (750 ml) water, stirring constantly until well combined. Bring to a boil, then reduce the heat and simmer for 15 minutes, until the mixture is slightly thickened.

2 Just before serving, preheat the grill (broiler) to high. Toast the baguette slices on both sides until lightly golden. Sprinkle with the cheese, then briefly grill until the cheese has melted.

3 Ladle the soup into warmed bowls. Top each with three toasts and quickly serve before the bread goes soggy.

Creamy sweet potato and asparagus soup

750 g (1½ lb) asparagus spears

250 g (8 oz) white or orange sweet potatoes (kumara), diced

2 teaspoons olive oil

1 onion, halved and thinly sliced

1 cup (250 ml) salt-reduced chicken stock (page 14)

½ teaspoon dried marjoram

¼ teaspoon cayenne pepper

pinch of salt

¾ cup (180 ml) skim milk

1 Trim the asparagus spears, reserving the trimmings. Cut the spears into short lengths. Bring 2½ cups (625 ml) water to a boil in a saucepan. Add the asparagus tips and cook for 2 minutes to blanch. Remove with a slotted spoon and set aside for garnish.

2 Add the sweet potatoes to the boiling water and cook for 10 minutes, until just tender. Remove with a strainer or slotted spoon. Add the asparagus trimmings, reduce to a simmer, cover and cook for 10 minutes. Strain the liquid to give 2 cups (500 ml) and discard the asparagus trimmings.

3 Heat the oil in a saucepan and cook the onion over medium-low heat for 7 minutes, until light golden. Stir in the reserved cooking liquid, the chicken stock, remaining uncooked asparagus, marjoram, cayenne pepper and salt, and bring to a boil. Reduce the heat until simmering, cover and cook for 6 minutes, until the asparagus is tender.

4 Cool slightly, then transfer the mixture to a blender or food processor with the sweet potatoes. Purée the soup, then return to the saucepan and stir in the milk. Cook for 2 minutes, until heated through. Serve the soup garnished with the reserved asparagus tips.

Serves 4

Preparation
15 minutes

Cooking
40 minutes

Per serving
523 kJ, 125 kcal, 9 g protein, 3 g fat (<1 g saturated fat), 16 g carbohydrate (10 g sugars), 4 g fibre, 345 mg sodium

Prepare asparagus by holding each spear with both hands, close to the base, then gently bending the stalk until it snaps. The stalk should break where the tough part begins. Store the trimmed spears, standing in cold water and covered with plastic wrap, for up to 4 days in the refrigerator.

Potato and leek soup with croutons

Using starchy potatoes will give the soup a creamier texture. For a lovely green hue and a vitamin boost, process the soup with some chopped fresh flat-leaf (Italian) parsley.

Serves 4

Preparation
15 minutes

Cooking
30 minutes

Per serving
*1527 kJ, 365 kcal,
12 g protein, 15 g fat
(2 g saturated fat),
44 g carbohydrate
(7 g sugars), 6 g fibre,
808 mg sodium*

¼ cup (60 ml) olive oil

3 slices bread, crusts removed, cut into cubes

1 brown (yellow) onion, chopped

2 leeks, white part only, sliced

2 cloves garlic, crushed

4 large potatoes, about 750 g (1½ lb) in total, cut into cubes

4 cups (1 litre) salt-reduced chicken or vegetable stock (pages 14-15)

ground white pepper, to taste

1 Preheat the oven to 200°C (400°F/Gas 6). Line a baking tray with baking (parchment) paper. Pour half the olive oil into a bowl, add the bread cubes and toss until well coated. Spread the bread cubes over the tray and bake for 10-15 minutes, until the croutons are light golden brown. Leave to cool.

2 Meanwhile, heat the remaining olive oil in a large saucepan over medium heat. Sauté the onion and leeks for 4-5 minutes, until soft.

3 Add the garlic and cook for 1 minute, then add the potatoes, stock and 2 cups (500 ml) water. Bring to a boil, then reduce the heat and simmer for 20-25 minutes, until the vegetables are soft.

4 Purée the soup using a stick blender or food processor. Season with ground white pepper, then ladle into warmed bowls and top with the croutons.

Fry some chopped bacon with the onion and leeks. Alternatively, fry some thin slices of prosciutto until crisp, then crumble over the top of the soup.

Chunky fish soup

Serves 4

Preparation
15 minutes

Cooking
25 minutes

Per serving
631 kJ, 151 kcal,
19 g protein, 5 g fat
(1 g saturated fat),
8 g carbohydrate
(3 g sugars), 2 g fibre,
539 mg sodium

pinch of saffron threads

2 teaspoons extra virgin
olive oil

60 g (2 oz) bacon, rind
removed and chopped

1 small boiling (waxy) potato
(e.g. long white), scrubbed
and finely diced

100 g (3½ oz) parsnips,
finely diced

2 celery stalks, finely chopped

1 small onion, finely chopped

1 bay leaf

1 strip of finely pared
lemon zest

pinch of salt

freshly ground black pepper

3 cups (750 ml) salt-reduced
fish stock (page 15)

250 g (8 oz) skinless firm
white fish fillet, cut into
bite-sized pieces

4 spring onions (scallions),
finely chopped

1 Put the saffron threads in a small frying pan over medium heat and stir until they just begin to give off their aroma. Immediately tip onto a small plate and set aside.

2 Heat the oil in a large non-stick saucepan over medium heat, add the bacon and cook, stirring, for 2 minutes. Add the potato, parsnips, celery and onion. Gently cook for 1 minute, stirring frequently.

3 Add the saffron threads, bay leaf and lemon zest, and season with salt and freshly ground black pepper. Pour in the fish stock and slowly bring to a boil. Reduce the heat to medium-low, half cover the pan and simmer, stirring occasionally, for about 8 minutes, until the vegetables are almost tender when pierced with the tip of a knife.

4 Lay the fish pieces on top of the vegetables. Reduce the heat to low and tightly cover the pan. Simmer the soup for 7–8 minutes, until the fish flakes easily and all the vegetables are tender. Remove and discard the bay leaf and lemon zest.

5 Ladle the soup into bowls, sprinkle with the chopped spring onions and serve immediately.

Potatoes do not contain as much vitamin C as some other vegetables, but they are still an important source of vitamin C because of the large quantity normally eaten.

Celery was originally grown as a medicinal herb, only being used as a cooked vegetable and salad ingredient in the late 17th century. Green celery has beta-carotene, which the body converts into vitamin A.

Curried beetroot and apple soup

1 tablespoon olive oil

15 g (½ oz) butter

250 g (8 oz) beetroot (beets), peeled and roughly chopped

2 sweet apples, peeled and cut into chunks

1 large red onion, chopped

1 tablespoon mild curry powder

2 cups (500 ml) salt-reduced vegetable stock (page 15)

pinch of salt

freshly ground black pepper

⅓ cup (90 g) light sour cream or crème fraîche

2 hard-boiled (hard-cooked) eggs, roughly chopped

Serves 4

Preparation
15 minutes

Cooking
20 minutes

Per serving
1023 kJ, 244 kcal, 7 g protein, 15 g fat (6 g saturated fat), 22 g carbohydrate (20 g sugars), 5 g fibre, 774 mg sodium

Instead of curry powder, try using 2 teaspoons grated horseradish from a jar or 1 teaspoon wasabi (Japanese horseradish) paste.

1 Heat the olive oil and butter in a large saucepan over medium heat. Stir in the beetroot, apples and red onion. Cover and cook for 10 minutes, shaking the pan occasionally to prevent sticking. Stir in the curry powder and gently cook for 5 minutes.

2 Stir in half the vegetable stock, then purée the soup in a food processor or blender.

3 Return the soup to the pan and stir in the remaining vegetable stock. Season with salt and freshly ground black pepper, and slowly bring to a boil.

4 Ladle the soup into bowls, swirl 1 tablespoon sour cream or crème fraîche into each serving and scatter with the egg pieces.

Lentil soup

This quick lentil and vegetable soup makes a nourishing winter lunch or simple dinner. Lentils are a GI 'superfood', providing hunger-satisfying protein, soluble fibre and low-GI carbohydrate. Silverbeet (Swiss chard) can replace the baby spinach if you like.

1 tablespoon olive oil

1 large brown (yellow) onion, finely chopped

1 large carrot, finely diced

1 large potato, finely diced

2 celery stalks, finely diced

4 cups (1 litre) salt-reduced chicken or vegetable stock (pages 14-15)

2 x 400 g (14 oz) cans lentils, rinsed and drained

¼ cup (60 ml) lemon juice

100 g (3½ oz) baby spinach leaves, shredded

1 Heat the olive oil in a large saucepan over medium heat. Sauté the onion, carrot, potato and celery for 10 minutes, until just tender.

2 Pour in the stock and 4 cups (1 litre) water. Bring to a boil, then reduce the heat to medium-low and simmer for 15 minutes, until the vegetables are soft.

3 Stir in the drained lentils and lemon juice, and cook for 3-4 minutes, until the lentils are heated through. Stir in the spinach and ladle into warmed serving bowls.

Serves 4-6

Preparation
10 minutes

Cooking
30 minutes

Per serving
618 kJ, 148 kcal,
10 g protein, 4 g fat
(<1 g saturated fat),
17 g carbohydrate
(6 g sugars), 5 g fibre,
815 mg sodium

For a thrifty soup, soak 1 cup (185 g) dried green lentils in water overnight, then drain. Make the soup as directed, cooking the lentils for 30 minutes, until tender.

Dried red lentils can also be used instead of green lentils; add them straight to the soup and cook for about 15 minutes.

Mushroom broth with herb croutons

Serves 6

Preparation
10 minutes

Cooking
20 minutes

Per serving
668 kJ, 159 kcal,
5 g protein, 10 g fat
(2 g saturated fat),
12 g carbohydrate
(2 g sugars), 4 g fibre,
705 mg sodium

¼ cup (60 ml) extra virgin olive oil

1 small onion, finely chopped

1 small bulb fennel, finely chopped

1 clove garlic, chopped

500 g (1 lb) mixed fresh mushrooms, roughly chopped

1 litre (4 cups) boiling water

1 tablespoon vegetable stock (bouillon) powder

8 thin slices ciabatta

2 tablespoons chopped fresh parsley

2 tablespoons chopped fresh mint

pinch of salt

freshly ground black pepper

1 Heat 2 tablespoons of the olive oil in a large saucepan over high heat. Cook the onion and fennel, stirring often, for 5 minutes, until slightly softened. Stir in the garlic and mushrooms. Cook, stirring frequently, for 5 minutes.

2 Pour in the boiling water and stir in the stock powder. Return to a boil, then reduce the heat and simmer for 10 minutes.

3 Meanwhile, preheat the grill (broiler). Lightly brush the ciabatta slices on both sides with the remaining oil and toast them for about 1 minute on each side, until golden. Cut the bread into cubes and place in a bowl. Add the parsley and mint, and toss well.

4 Season the soup with salt and freshly ground black pepper. Ladle the soup into bowls and serve topped with the herb croutons.

Mushrooms are a useful source of the B vitamins B_6, folate and niacin, as well as copper. In Asian cultures, mushrooms are renowned for their ability to boost the immune system and the Chinese have put them to medicinal use for over 6000 years.

Carrot, orange and fetta soup

1 tablespoon olive oil

1 onion, finely chopped

4 carrots, finely chopped

1 clove garlic, crushed

2¹/₂ cups (625 ml) salt-reduced vegetable stock (page 15)

juice of 1 small orange

2 tablespoons chopped fresh tarragon, plus extra leaves, to garnish

freshly ground black pepper

¹/₂ cup (80 g) crumbled fetta

Serves 4

Preparation
10 minutes

Cooking
20 minutes

Per serving
623 kJ, 149 kcal,
5 g protein, 10 g fat
(4 g saturated fat),
10 g carbohydrate
(9 g sugars), 2 g fibre,
887 mg sodium

1 Heat the oil in a large saucepan and cook the onion, carrots and garlic over medium heat for 5 minutes, until softened but not browned.

2 Add the stock, orange juice and half the chopped tarragon, and bring to a boil. Reduce the heat, cover and gently simmer for 6–8 minutes, until all the vegetables are tender.

3 Cool slightly, then spoon out and reserve about a quarter of the vegetables. Process the remainder of the soup in a food processor or blender until almost smooth, but still with some texture. Season with freshly ground black pepper.

4 Return the soup to the pan with the reserved vegetables and heat until boiling. Ladle the soup into bowls and top each serving with some crumbled fetta. Sprinkle with the remaining chopped tarragon and the whole leaves, and a little freshly ground black pepper.

This soup freezes well. Prepare it to the end of step 3, add the reserved vegetables and cool quickly. Freeze for up to 1 month.

Serve the soup with some toasted crusty bread spread with olive tapenade.

Turning soup into a meal

Some soups make a hearty meal. Others need an extra 'something' – a bit of protein, a carbohydrate element or something fresh and green – to round them out. Here are a few creative suggestions for you to try.

Easy carb ideas

❧ Add cooked pasta to your hot soup. Any type is fine, but you may want to break up long pasta. Cook the pasta separately first so it doesn't absorb too much of the liquid in the soup.

❧ Stir some left-over cooked rice into the soup. Brown rice is particularly good as it keeps its shape and texture.

❧ Add rice noodles, such as flat rice stick noodles or rice vermicelli. First soak them in boiling water for 5 minutes, then drain and add to the hot soup.

Add a dollop of sour cream, crème fraîche or low-fat thick (Greek-style) yogurt, or a final swirl of basil or sun-dried tomato pesto.

Carbs and crunch

Hummus fingers

Toast some thinly sliced **pide (Turkish flat bread)** under a hot grill (broiler) until golden brown on both sides. Spread generously with **hummus** and drizzle with a little **extra virgin olive oil.**

Tapenade toasts

Toast slices of **sourdough bread** under a hot grill (broiler) until golden on both sides. Spread with some **tapenade (olive paste)** and top with sliced **tomato.**

Ricotta and pesto bites

Cut a **baguette** into 1 cm (½ inch) slices and toast under a hot grill (broiler) until golden on both sides. Spread with some **pesto** and **fresh ricotta,** then cook until the ricotta is lightly golden.

Crunchy croutons

Cut or tear **day-old bread** into 2 cm (³⁄₄ inch) pieces. Heat 1 cm (½ inch) **olive oil** in a small frying pan over medium-high heat. Fry the bread until crisp and golden brown, then drain on paper towels. Alternatively, spread the bread on a baking tray, spray with a little olive oil and bake in a 190°C (375°F/Gas 5) oven for 5-10 minutes, until crisp and golden.

Fresh and fabulous

Leafy greens should be included in a meal whenever possible, and you can always serve a simple salad before or after your soup. Another way to increase the green quotient is to add some chopped English spinach, silverbeet (Swiss chard), kale or mustard greens to the hot soup; they will cook quickly in the heat. A squeeze of lemon or lime juice will help your body to absorb the iron present in leafy greens, and will also add a fresh flavour burst.

Easy greens

Asian greens

Add some chopped Asian greens to the soup. The stems take a little longer to cook, so chop them separately and briefly cook before adding the leaves.

Broccoli

Broccoli is full of goodness. Chop it into small florets and cook for only about 5 minutes in the soup, so it still has some texture.

Greens

Some greens can be added at the table to simply wilt into the hot soup, rather than having to be cooked. Try a good handful of chopped or baby rocket (arugula), watercress sprigs or baby spinach leaves.

Fresh herbs

Think of fresh herbs as salad leaves, rather than something to be added in tiny pinches. Herbs such as flat-leaf (Italian) parsley, basil, coriander (cilantro) and chervil will add lovely fresh flavours, either alone, or even in a mixture.

Protein power

❧ Canned beans, lentils and chickpeas add a satisfying, nutritious element to any meal. Stir them directly into the soup to heat through, or make a quick accompanying salad by combining them with chopped spring onions (scallions), tomatoes and baby spinach leaves, drizzled with extra virgin olive oil and a little red wine vinegar or lemon juice.

❧ Eggs can be added to soups in many ways. You could chop up boiled eggs to sprinkle on top of your soup, or cook them omelette-style and cut into strips or small pieces. Alternatively, add a lightly beaten raw egg to the hot soup in a thin stream, stirring constantly – the egg will cook as it hits the hot liquid.

❧ Canned tuna is a great pantry stand-by, and comes in convenient individual-serve sizes. Drain the tuna and stir it into soup at the last minute, to gently heat through.

❧ Chopped ham, shredded left-over chicken, or any type of left-over cooked meat can be added to soup. Cut the meat into small pieces and add it to your hot soup just before serving – it will heat through quickly.

❧ Serve your soup sprinkled with a little grated firm cheese such as cheddar or parmesan, or try crumbling a soft cheese such as fetta, ricotta or even a mild blue over the soup and topping it with some freshly ground black pepper.

Chunky vegetable and pasta soup

Serves 4

Preparation
10 minutes

Cooking
30 minutes

Per serving
*869 kJ, 207 kcal,
7 g protein, 10 g fat
(1 g saturated fat),
22 g carbohydrate
(8 g sugars), 5 g fibre,
410 mg sodium*

2 tablespoons olive oil

1 bay leaf

1 onion, finely chopped

1 carrot, diced

1 celery stalk, diced

1 clove garlic, crushed

1 yellow capsicum (bell pepper), diced

100 g (3$^{1}/_{2}$ oz) mushrooms, chopped

1 parsnip, diced

410 g (15 oz) can chopped tomatoes

2 cups (500 ml) hot salt-reduced chicken or vegetable stock (pages 14–15)

75 g (2$^{1}/_{2}$ oz) wholemeal (whole-wheat) spaghetti

grated parmesan, to serve

Frozen vegetables are great for everyday meals, saving time on shopping and preparation. There is a wide variety of mixtures, some with celery, capsicums (bell peppers) and mushrooms, as well as the usual carrots, peas and beans. Cook fresh onion and garlic, then add some frozen mixed vegetables in step 2 in place of the fresh ingredients. Reduce the cooking time by about 5 minutes.

1 Heat the oil in a large saucepan over high heat. Add the bay leaf, onion, carrot, celery and garlic, reduce the heat to low, then cover and cook for 2 minutes.

2 Stir in the capsicum and mushrooms, cover and cook for 2 minutes. Add the parsnip and tomatoes, then pour in the hot stock and bring to a boil. Reduce the heat and simmer, covered, for 20 minutes, until the vegetables are tender.

3 Snap the spaghetti into 4 cm (1$^{1}/_{2}$ inch) pieces and stir into the soup. Bring back to a boil, then reduce the heat and simmer for 5 minutes, until the pasta is tender.

4 Remove the bay leaf, ladle the soup into bowls and serve sprinkled with grated parmesan.

Piquant cod chowder

2 sprigs fresh parsley

2 sprigs fresh thyme

1 bay leaf

7.5 cm (3 inch) celery stalk

410 g (15 oz) can chopped tomatoes

3 cups (750 ml) salt-reduced fish stock (page 15)

1/3 cup (80 ml) medium cider

1 large onion, chopped

400 g (14 oz) boiling (waxy) potatoes (e.g. long white), cut into large chunks

250 g (8 oz) carrots, thickly sliced

250 g (8 oz) zucchini (courgettes), thickly sliced

250 g (8 oz) green beans, cut into short lengths

1 yellow or red capsicum (bell pepper), sliced

pinch of salt

freshly ground black pepper

500 g (1 lb) cod fillet, skin removed, cut into large pieces

2 tablespoons finely chopped fresh parsley

1 tablespoon snipped fresh chives

finely shredded zest of 1 lemon

1 Tie the parsley, thyme and bay leaf with the celery to make a bouquet garni. Put the bouquet garni in a large saucepan. Add the tomatoes and their juice, the stock, cider and onion. Stir to combine, then bring to a boil. Reduce the heat to low, half cover the pan and simmer for 15 minutes.

2 Add the potatoes and carrots. Increase the heat to medium and cook, covered, for 15 minutes, until the vegetables are almost tender. Stir in the zucchini, beans and capsicum, and simmer, covered, for 5 minutes, until all the vegetables are tender. Discard the bouquet garni.

3 Season with salt and freshly ground black pepper, then add the cod to the simmering broth. Cover and gently cook for 3–5 minutes, until the fish is opaque, just firm and flakes easily. Do not allow the broth to boil rapidly or the fish will overcook and start to break up.

4 Make a garnish by combining the parsley, chives and lemon zest. Ladle the fish and vegetables into warmed bowls, then add the broth. Sprinkle the garnish over the top and serve at once.

Serves 4

Preparation
20 minutes

Cooking
40 minutes

Per serving
1085 kJ, 259 kcal, 31 g protein, 2 g fat (<1 g saturated fat), 28 g carbohydrate (13 g sugars), 9 g fibre, 472 mg sodium

The green beans are a good source of fibre and they provide valuable amounts of folate. The zucchini provide niacin and vitamin B$_6$.

Chicken and vegetable steamboat

Serves 4

Preparation
20 minutes

Cooking
15 minutes

Per serving
*1766 kJ, 422 kcal,
37 g protein, 8 g fat
(2 g saturated fat),
50 g carbohydrate
(4 g sugars), 7 g fibre,
896 mg sodium*

500 g (1 lb) boneless, skinless chicken breast, cut into thin strips

$^1/_2$ teaspoon Chinese five-spice

1 tablespoon light soy sauce

1 celery stalk, thinly sliced

3 cm (1$^1/_4$ inch) piece fresh ginger, peeled and chopped

1 clove garlic, thinly sliced

1 lemongrass stem, white part only, or 1 strip of lemon zest

2$^1/_2$ cups (625 ml) salt-reduced chicken stock (page 14)

1 large red capsicum (bell pepper), cut into chunks

250 g (8 oz) baby corn

200 g (7 oz) broccolini, cut into florets

2 spring onions (scallions), thinly sliced

200 g (7 oz) fresh or wok-ready rice noodles

250 g (8 oz) bok choy, quartered lengthwise

*Instead of noodles, you
can use Chinese dumplings
(pot-stickers) or won tons
from Chinese and Asian
supermarkets. There are
several types, with different
fillings. Follow the packet
instructions for serving
portions and cooking.*

1 Put the chicken in a bowl. Add the Chinese five-spice and soy sauce. Mix well, then set aside.

2 Combine the celery, ginger, garlic, lemongrass or lemon zest, stock and 3$^1/_2$ cups (875 ml) water in a large saucepan. Bring to a boil, then reduce the heat, cover and simmer for 5 minutes.

3 Add the chicken to the pan, then add the capsicum, baby corn and broccolini. Return to a boil and simmer for 3 minutes, until the chicken is cooked and the vegetables are just tender.

4 Add the spring onions and noodles, gently stir to combine, then return to a boil. Lay the bok choy over the top and simmer for about 2 minutes, until the bok choy leaves are wilted and the noodles are hot and cooked.

5 Take the pan to the table and serve, ladling the cooked ingredients into warmed bowls with a little of the broth. Ladle out the last of the broth at the end of the meal.

Chicken noodle soup

2 teaspoons olive oil

1 small brown (yellow) onion, diced

1 carrot, diced

1 celery stalk, diced

400 ml (14 fl oz) salt-reduced chicken stock (page 14)

85 g (3 oz) packet 2-minute noodles

1 cup (175 g) shredded or chopped cooked chicken meat

chopped fresh parsley, to garnish

1 Heat the oil in a saucepan over medium heat and cook the onion, carrot and celery for 5 minutes, until tender. Pour in the chicken stock and 2 cups (500 ml) water, and bring to a boil.

2 Break up the noodles while still in the packet, then add to the soup with the chicken. Cook for 2 minutes, until the noodles are tender and the chicken is heated through.

3 Ladle the soup into bowls and serve sprinkled with chopped parsley.

Serves 2

Preparation
15 minutes

Cooking
10 minutes

Per serving
*1645 kJ, 393 kcal,
29 g protein, 18 g fat
(6 g saturated fat),
28 g carbohydrate
(5 g sugars), 5 g fibre,
878 mg sodium*

Add a pinch of mixed dried Mediterranean herbs with the stock.

Instead of 2-minute noodles, use rice noodles, vermicelli, egg noodles or udon noodles, and flavour the soup with South-East Asian herbs and spices, such as fresh ginger, fresh chilli and coriander (cilantro).

Capsicum and tomato soup with egg and chilli

The anti-oxidant lycopene in tomatoes gives them their wonderful rich colour. As a rich source of potassium, tomatoes can help to regulate blood pressure, reducing the risk of stroke.

Serves 4

Preparation
10 minutes

Cooking
25 minutes

Per serving
1046 kJ, 250 kcal,
11 g protein, 19 g fat
(3 g saturated fat),
9 g carbohydrate
(8 g sugars), 2 g fibre,
678 mg sodium

¼ cup (60 ml) olive oil

1 onion, chopped

1 celery stalk, diced

2 red capsicums (bell peppers), diced

410 g (15 oz) can chopped tomatoes

600 ml (21 fl oz) hot salt-reduced chicken stock (page 14)

pinch of salt

freshly ground black pepper

4 eggs

1 spring onion (scallion), finely chopped

pinch of dried red chilli flakes

1 Heat 1 tablespoon of the oil in a large saucepan over high heat. Cook the onion, celery and capsicums for 30 seconds, until sizzling. Reduce the heat to medium-high, cover and cook, shaking the pan occasionally, for 5 minutes, until the vegetables are softened.

2 Add the tomatoes and stir in the hot stock. Bring to a boil, then reduce the heat, cover and simmer the soup for 15 minutes. Season the soup with salt and freshly ground black pepper.

3 Heat the remaining 2 tablespoons oil in a large frying pan over medium-high heat. Break in the eggs and cook for 1-2 minutes, until the whites are set but the yolks are still soft.

4 Ladle the soup into four bowls. Float an egg on each portion and sprinkle with the chopped spring onion and the chilli flakes.

For a meaty soup, slice 100 g (3½ oz) chorizo and add it to the soup at the end of step 2 to warm through while the eggs are frying.

For a complete meal in a bowl, add ⅓ cup (50 g) miniature pasta shapes in step 2 during the final 5 minutes of cooking.

Low-fat laksa

Serves 4

Preparation
10 minutes

Cooking
20 minutes

Per serving
2263 kJ, 541 kcal,
40 g protein, 17 g fat
(8 g saturated fat),
55 g carbohydrate
(7 g sugars), 5 g fibre,
880 mg sodium

250 g (8 oz) dried cellophane noodles (Chinese vermicelli)

2 tablespoons laksa paste

3 cups (750 ml) salt-reduced chicken stock (page 14)

200 ml (7 fl oz) low-fat coconut milk

1 lemongrass stem, white part only, bruised

500 g (1 lb) skinless salmon fillets, cut into small chunks

500 g (1 lb) bok choy, coarsely chopped

1 tablespoon lime juice

3 cups (270 g) bean sprouts, trimmed

1/2 cup (15 g) fresh coriander (cilantro) leaves

lime wedges, to serve

1 Cook the noodles in a saucepan of boiling water for 3 minutes, until tender. Drain well and set aside.

2 Combine the laksa paste with the stock, coconut milk and 1 cup (250 ml) water in a large saucepan. Add the lemongrass stem and bring to a boil. Reduce the heat to medium-low and simmer for 10 minutes.

3 Add the salmon and simmer for 2–3 minutes, until the salmon flakes easily when tested with a fork. Add the bok choy and lime juice, and cook for 2 minutes, until the bok choy has wilted.

4 Divide the noodles and bean sprouts among four bowls and pour the soup over the top. Sprinkle with the coriander and serve immediately, with the lime wedges on the side for squeezing over.

Substitute the salmon with prawns (shrimp) or thinly sliced chicken breast and add an extra 2–3 minutes to the cooking time. Use rice vermicelli instead of cellophane noodles if you prefer.

Herb-scented ham and pea soup

1 tablespoon extra virgin olive oil

1 onion, chopped

1 small carrot, diced

2 cloves garlic, sliced

1 leek, white part only, chopped

1 celery stalk, diced

2 tablespoons chopped fresh parsley

1 potato, diced

100 g (3$\frac{1}{2}$ oz) lean boiled or baked ham, diced

3$\frac{1}{4}$ cups (500 g) shelled fresh or frozen peas

$\frac{1}{2}$ teaspoon dried herbes de Provence, or to taste

2 cups (500 ml) salt-reduced vegetable stock (page 15)

3 large lettuce leaves, finely shredded

freshly ground black pepper

2 tablespoons cream

Serves 4

Preparation
15 minutes

Cooking
50 minutes

Per serving
*969 kJ, 231 kcal,
14 g protein, 11 g fat
(4 g saturated fat),
19 g carbohydrate
(8 g sugars), 9 g fibre,
818 mg sodium*

Green peas are a good source of the B vitamins B$_1$, B$_5$ and niacin, and they provide useful amounts of folate and vitamin C. As a good source of soluble fibre, they are beneficial for those with high cholesterol levels.

1 Heat the oil in a large saucepan over low heat. Add the onion, carrot, garlic, leek, celery, parsley, potato and ham. Stir well, then cover the pan, reduce the heat and sweat the vegetables, stirring occasionally, for 30 minutes, until they are softened.

2 Add the peas, herbes de Provence, vegetable stock and 2 cups (500 ml) water, and bring to a boil. Reduce the heat to medium-high and cook until the peas are just tender, about 10 minutes for fresh peas or 5 minutes for frozen. Add the lettuce and gently cook for a further 5 minutes.

3 Purée half to two-thirds of the soup in a blender, then stir the purée back into the rest of the soup. Alternatively, use a stick blender to partly purée the soup in the pan. Gently reheat the soup, if necessary. Taste and season with freshly ground black pepper.

4 Ladle the soup into warmed bowls. Swirl a little cream into each portion and serve at once.

Golden lentil soup

This velvety soup owes its rich colour to a combination of lentils, parsnips and carrots. With dry sherry and a horseradish-flavoured cream adding to the flavour, it makes a hearty, warming meal when served with chunks of crusty bread.

Serves 6

Preparation
15 minutes

Cooking
1 hour 20 minutes

Per serving
910 kJ, 217 kcal,
7 g protein, 8 g fat
(5 g saturated fat),
24 g carbohydrate
(13 g sugars), 6 g fibre,
881 mg sodium

1¹/₂ tablespoons (30 g) butter

1 large onion, finely chopped

500 g (1 lb) parsnips, cut into small cubes

350 g (12 oz) carrots, cut into small cubes

²/₃ cup (160 ml) dry sherry

¹/₃ cup (90 g) red lentils

4 cups (1 litre) salt-reduced vegetable stock (page 15)

pinch of salt

freshly ground black pepper

2 teaspoons grated horseradish, from a jar

¹/₂ cup (125 g) light sour cream

snipped fresh chives, to serve

Omit the grated horseradish, if you prefer, and simply add a spoonful of light sour cream or crème fraîche to the soup before serving.

1 Melt the butter in a large saucepan over low heat. Add the onion, then stir well, cover the pan and sweat the onion for 10 minutes, until softened. Stir in the parsnips, carrots and sherry. Bring to a boil, cover and gently simmer for 40 minutes.

2 Stir in the lentils, stock and 1 cup (250 ml) water, and season with salt and freshly ground black pepper. Bring to a boil, then reduce the heat, cover and simmer for 15-20 minutes, until the lentils are tender.

3 Purée the soup using a stick blender or upright blender. Gently reheat the soup until boiling, adding a little stock or water if it is too thick.

4 Stir the horseradish into the sour cream. Ladle the soup into warm bowls and top each portion with a spoonful of the horseradish mixture. Scatter snipped chives over the top and sprinkle with freshly ground black pepper.

Japanese miso soup

Shiitake mushrooms, ginger and a stock made with dried kombu seaweed bring rich savoury flavours to this broth, which is quick and easy to make. With delicate tofu and slightly peppery watercress, the resulting soup is ideal for a light lunch. Add soba noodles for a more substantial soup.

1 packet dried kombu (kelp) or other dried or roasted seaweed, about 25 g (1 oz)

1 tablespoon sake, Chinese rice wine or dry sherry

2 teaspoons caster (superfine) sugar

$^{1}/_{2}$ teaspoon finely grated fresh ginger

2 tablespoons white miso paste

4 spring onions (scallions), diagonally sliced

6 fresh shiitake mushrooms, thinly sliced

100 g (3$^{1}/_{2}$ oz) tofu, diced

100 g (3$^{1}/_{2}$ oz) trimmed watercress

1 Put the kombu in a saucepan and pour in 4 cups (1 litre) water. Slowly bring to a boil, then remove from the heat and cover the pan. Set aside for 5 minutes. Use a slotted spoon to remove the kombu.

2 Stir the sake, rice wine or sherry, sugar and ginger into the broth and bring back to a boil. Reduce the heat, then stir in the miso paste until it dissolves completely.

3 Add the spring onions, mushrooms, tofu and watercress. Cook very gently, stirring, for 2 minutes without allowing the soup to boil.

4 Ladle the soup into small bowls and serve at once.

Serves 4

Preparation
10 minutes, plus 5 minutes soaking

Cooking
10 minutes

Per serving
344 kJ, 82 kcal, 5 g protein, 2 g fat (<1 g saturated fat), 10 g carbohydrate (5 g sugars), 5 g fibre, 532 mg sodium

Research suggests that the humble soybean is a disease-fighting powerhouse. Soybeans and their products, such as tofu and miso paste, contain compounds called phyto-oestrogens. Growing evidence suggests that a diet rich in phyto-oestrogens can help to protect against breast and prostate cancer, heart disease and osteoporosis.

Beef pho

This Vietnamese noodle soup with beef is traditionally served with accompaniments such as fresh herbs, chilli or lime, which guests add to the hot steaming soup as they like. This soup is so satisfying it can easily be served as a main course.

400 ml (14 fl oz) salt-reduced beef stock (page 14)

1 teaspoon grated fresh ginger

1 cinnamon stick

2 star anise

2 green cardamom pods, bruised

½ teaspoon coriander seeds, toasted

2 teaspoons fish sauce

200 g (7 oz) dried rice vermicelli

200 g (7 oz) sirloin steak, trimmed and thinly sliced

To serve

4 cups (120 g) fresh coriander (cilantro) leaves

2½ cups (50 g) fresh Vietnamese mint

1 cup (90 g) bean sprouts, trimmed

1 long red chilli, seeded and sliced

1 lime, cut into wedges

⅓ cup (80 ml) hoisin sauce

1 Combine the beef stock, ginger, cinnamon stick, star anise, cardamom pods, coriander seeds and fish sauce in a large saucepan or stockpot with 6 cups (1.5 litres) water and bring to a boil. Reduce the heat to low and simmer for 10–15 minutes, until aromatic.

2 Meanwhile, soak the noodles according to the packet instructions. Drain well and set aside.

3 Strain the stock, discarding the spices, then return to the pan and bring back to a boil. Add the steak and simmer for 5 minutes, until the meat is cooked.

4 Divide the noodles among serving bowls, pile the steak on top and ladle over the hot stock.

5 Serve the pho with the coriander, mint, bean sprouts, chilli, lime wedges and hoisin sauce passed separately so that guests can help themselves.

Serves 4

Preparation
15 minutes

Cooking
25 minutes

Per serving
1190 kJ, 284 kcal, 16 g protein, 4 g fat (1 g saturated fat), 45 g carbohydrate (1 g sugars), 2 g fibre, 883 mg sodium

Beef is a great source of protein. Choose lean cuts of steak and make sure they are trimmed of fat before slicing.

Quinoa salad with asparagus, page 70

Salads

Substantial salads are the ultimate in healthy one-dish meals. Prepared from a wide variety of foods, they offer a wonderful range of flavours, colours and textures, as well as maximum vitamins and minerals.

Soft-boiled eggs on lettuce hearts with parsley cream

Serves 4

Preparation
20 minutes

Cooking
10 minutes

Per serving
*846 kJ, 202 kcal,
12 g protein, 15 g fat
(7 g saturated fat),
6 g carbohydrate
(4 g sugars), <1 g fibre,
383 mg sodium*

4 large eggs

4 butter (Boston) lettuces

1 tablespoon trout caviar

mustard cress, to serve

Parsley cream

150 g (5 oz) low-fat thick
(Greek-style) yogurt

$\frac{1}{4}$ cup (60 ml) reduced-fat
cream

2 teaspoons capers, rinsed
and finely chopped

2 teaspoons lemon juice

pinch of salt

freshly ground white pepper

1–2 tablespoons finely
chopped fresh parsley

1 Cook the eggs in a saucepan of boiling water until soft-boiled, about 7 minutes. Immediately rinse the eggs in cold water, then set aside until ready to peel.

2 Meanwhile, twist the pale inner heart from each lettuce as a single piece. If needed, wash and shake dry in a clean tea towel (dish towel). Reserve the outer leaves for use in other dishes. Halve each lettuce heart lengthwise and then remove the stalk base. Arrange two halves on each serving plate or in glass bowls.

3 To make the parsley cream, beat the yogurt with the cream, then stir in the capers and lemon juice. Season with salt and freshly ground white pepper. Stir in the parsley.

4 Peel the eggs, halve lengthwise and place each half onto a lettuce heart. Drizzle the parsley cream over the salads and top with the trout caviar. Snip the mustard cress with kitchen scissors directly over each serving.

*Use 100 g (3½ oz) sliced smoked
salmon for the garnish instead
of the trout caviar.*

Instead of frying and slicing the steaks, arrange 400 g (14 oz) thinly sliced roast beef on the salad.

Beef and mixed leaf salad

150 g (5 oz) mixed salad leaves

1 small red onion, halved and sliced

2 beef rump (round) steaks, about 200 g (7 oz) each

1 tablespoon sunflower or vegetable oil

$^1/_2$ cup (125 ml) reduced-fat cream

3 teaspoons salt-reduced soy sauce

pinch of garlic powder

Mustard vinaigrette

$^1/_4$ cup (60 ml) sunflower or vegetable oil

$^1/_4$ cup (60 ml) white balsamic vinegar

1 teaspoon wholegrain mustard

1 To make the vinaigrette, put the oil, vinegar and mustard in a screw-top jar, and shake well to combine.

2 Combine the salad leaves and onion in a bowl. Add the vinaigrette and toss to coat, then divide the salad among four serving plates.

3 Heat a non-stick frying pan over medium–high heat. Brush the steaks with the oil, then cook for 3 minutes on each side. Transfer to a plate and loosely cover with foil.

4 Add the cream to the pan, then stir in the soy sauce and garlic powder. Gently simmer, stirring, for 2 minutes, until the sauce has thickened. Remove from the heat.

5 Stir any juices that the steaks have released into the sauce. Slice the steaks into strips and arrange on top of the salad. Drizzle with the sauce and serve immediately.

Serves 4

Preparation
20 minutes

Cooking
10 minutes

Per serving
1602 kJ, 383 kcal, 24 g protein, 30 g fat (8 g saturated fat), 5 g carbohydrate (5 g sugars), <1 g fibre, 206 mg sodium

Spicy burghul and pumpkin salad

Tomato, burghul and fetta salad

Add ³⁄₄ **cup (130 g) burghul (bulgur)** and **2 teaspoons dried oregano** to a saucepan containing **1 cup (250 ml) boiling salt-reduced vegetable stock** (page 15). Cover, reduce the heat to its lowest setting and leave to cook for 10 minutes. Combine ¹⁄₄ **cup (60 ml) red wine vinegar**, ¹⁄₄ **cup (60 ml) olive oil**, **2 tablespoons water**, a **pinch of salt** and **freshly ground black pepper** in a bowl. Fluff the burghul with a fork and add to the bowl along with **300 g (10 oz) diced cucumber**, **300 g (10 oz) diced tomato**, **1 thinly sliced onion** and **6 diced, pickled baby capsicums (bell peppers)**. Toss well, season with **pepper**, and sprinkle with **1 cup (150 g) crumbled fetta.**

Spicy burghul and pumpkin salad

⅓ cup (80 ml) olive oil

400 g (14 oz) pumpkin (winter squash), peeled and cut into small cubes

¾ cup (130 g) burghul (bulgur)

1 cup (250 ml) salt-reduced vegetable stock (page 15)

1-1½ tablespoons harissa paste

⅓ cup (80 ml) lemon juice

1 tablespoon tomato paste (concentrated purée)

pinch of salt

200 g (7 oz) jar pickled baby capsicums (bell peppers), drained and cut in half

4 spring onions (scallions), thinly sliced

⅔ cup (30 g) coarsely chopped fresh coriander (cilantro)

⅓ cup (20 g) coarsely chopped fresh mint

1 Heat half the oil in a saucepan over medium heat. Add the pumpkin and cook for 1-2 minutes, until browned and starting to soften.

2 Add the burghul and stock, and stir in 1 tablespoon of the harissa paste. Return to a boil. Cover the saucepan, reduce the heat to its lowest setting and leave the burghul and pumpkin to cook for 10 minutes.

3 Meanwhile, combine the lemon juice and tomato paste in a large bowl. Whisk in the remaining oil and add salt to taste. Add the capsicum halves, spring onions, coriander and mint to the bowl.

4 Fluff the burghul and pumpkin mixture with a fork and leave to cool briefly. Gently fold through the herb mixture. Add harissa to taste. Serve warm or leave to cool.

Serves 4

Preparation
20 minutes

Cooking
15 minutes

Per serving
1555 kJ, 372 kcal, 7 g protein, 24 g fat (3 g saturated fat), 31 g carbohydrate (8 g sugars), 7 g fibre, 616 mg sodium

Combine ¾ cup (200 g) natural (plain) yogurt, 2 tablespoons lemon juice and 1 crushed clove garlic with some salt and pepper. Serve the yogurt with the salad.

Harissa is a fiery north African paste made from dried chillies, garlic, cumin, caraway seeds and tomato paste.

Beetroot, rocket and goat's cheese salad

Serves 4

Preparation
10 minutes

Cooking
Nil

Per serving
1197 kJ, 286 kcal,
6 g protein, 26 g fat
(8 g saturated fat),
7 g carbohydrate
(7 g sugars), 3 g fibre,
445 mg sodium

$1^{3}/_{4}$ cups (60 g) wild rocket (arugula)

420 g (15 oz) can or jar baby beetroot (beets)

1 large avocado, diced

75 g ($2^{1}/_{2}$ oz) goat's cheese

$1^{1}/_{2}$ tablespoons extra virgin olive oil

3 teaspoons white wine vinegar

pinch of salt

freshly ground black pepper

When handling beetroot, it's a good idea to wear gloves to prevent your hands from getting stained.

Instead of using goat's cheese, you can use halved bocconcini (fresh baby mozzarella balls) or crumbled fetta.

1 Arrange the rocket around a shallow serving bowl.

2 Drain the baby beetroot well, then cut them into halves or quarters.

3 Arrange the beetroot and avocado over the rocket, then crumble the goat's cheese over the top.

4 Whisk the olive oil with the vinegar and season with salt and freshly ground black pepper. Drizzle over the salad and serve.

Tuna, chickpea and egg salad

420 g (15 oz) can tuna in springwater, well drained, flaked

400 g (14 oz) can chickpeas, rinsed and drained

4 gherkins (pickles), finely chopped

4 radishes, thinly sliced

1 large celery stalk, thinly sliced

1 tablespoon baby capers, rinsed and squeezed dry

1 tablespoon chopped fresh dill

4 hard-boiled (hard-cooked) eggs, cut into quarters

2 tablespoons fresh chervil or fresh small flat-leaf (Italian) parsley leaves

Dressing

1½ tablespoons extra virgin olive oil

2 tablespoons orange juice

1 tablespoon red wine vinegar

1 teaspoon dijon mustard

freshly ground black pepper

1 To make the dressing, combine the oil, orange juice, vinegar and mustard in a small jug and whisk well. Season with freshly ground black pepper.

2 Put the tuna, chickpeas, gherkins, radishes, celery, capers and dill in a large bowl. Pour the dressing over the salad and gently toss to combine.

3 Divide the salad among four serving bowls and top with the egg quarters. Serve sprinkled with the chervil or parsley leaves.

Serves 4

Preparation
15 minutes

Cooking
Nil

Per serving
1282 kJ, 306 kcal, 32 g protein, 16 g fat (4 g saturated fat), 10 g carbohydrate (2 g sugars), 3 g fibre, 430 mg sodium

This high-protein salad is also high in beneficial fats from the tuna and olive oil, as well as providing good amounts of fibre and anti-oxidants.

Duck salad

Serves 2

Preparation
10 minutes

Cooking
15 minutes

Per serving
1490 kJ, 356 kcal,
9 g protein, 32 g fat
(8 g saturated fat),
10 g carbohydrate
(9 g sugars), 2 g fibre,
316 mg sodium

1 small duck breast

pinch of salt

freshly ground black pepper

1 cup (30 g) watercress sprigs

1 cup (30 g) shredded
radicchio

1 red apple, thinly sliced

2 spring onions (scallions),
diagonally sliced

1 tablespoon olive oil

2 teaspoons white wine
vinegar

1 Preheat the oven to 190°C (375°F/Gas 5).

2 Heat a non-stick ovenproof frying pan over medium-low heat. Season the duck with salt and freshly ground black pepper, and place in the pan, skin side down. Cook for 6-8 minutes, until the skin is crisp and most of the fat has rendered. Turn and cook the other side for 1 minute.

3 Transfer the pan to the oven and cook the duck for a further 6 minutes for medium, until done to your liking. Set the duck aside to rest for a few minutes, then slice it.

4 Combine the watercress, radicchio, apple, spring onions and duck slices in a serving bowl.

5 Whisk together the oil and vinegar, and season with salt and pepper. Pour the dressing over the salad, gently toss together and serve.

Chicken and soba noodle salad

¾ cup (180 ml) salt-reduced chicken stock (page 14)

2 cloves garlic, crushed

½ teaspoon ground ginger

¼ teaspoon dried red chilli flakes

375 g (13 oz) boneless, skinless chicken breast

300 g (10 oz) dried soba (buckwheat) noodles

250 g (8 oz) green beans, halved

2 carrots, cut into thin matchsticks

1 tablespoon salt-reduced soy sauce

3 teaspoons peanut (groundnut) or vegetable oil

1½ tablespoons dark brown sugar

2 cups (150 g) finely shredded cabbage

1 Combine the stock, garlic, ginger and chilli flakes in a large frying pan and bring to a boil. Reduce to a simmer, add the chicken, cover and cook for 5 minutes. Turn and cook the chicken for a further 5 minutes, until cooked through. Transfer the chicken to a plate, reserving the cooking liquid. When the chicken is cool enough to handle, cut or shred it into pieces.

2 Meanwhile, cook the noodles in a large saucepan of boiling water for 6 minutes, until al dente. Add the beans and carrots for the last minute of cooking. Drain well.

3 Whisk the soy sauce, oil, sugar and reserved cooking liquid in a large bowl. Add the shredded chicken, noodles, beans, carrots and cabbage, tossing to combine. Serve at room temperature or chilled.

Serves 4

Preparation
20 minutes

Cooking
15 minutes

Per serving
2055 kJ, 491 kcal, 32 g protein, 10 g fat (3 g saturated fat), 64 g carbohydrate (10 g sugars), 6 g fibre, 384 mg sodium

Chicken and raspberry salad with lime vinaigrette

Serves 4

Preparation
15 minutes

Cooking
10 minutes

Per serving
1855 kJ, 443 kcal,
38 g protein, 31 g fat
(5 g saturated fat),
4 g carbohydrate
(3 g sugars), 2 g fibre,
407 mg sodium

30 g (1 oz) pine nuts

1 green lettuce, such as butter (Boston) lettuce, leaves separated

⅓ cup (90 g) raspberries

1 tablespoon olive oil

2 boneless, skinless chicken breasts

pinch of salt

freshly ground black pepper

Lime vinaigrette

2 tablespoons lime juice

1 teaspoon raspberry vinegar

1 teaspoon finely grated lime zest

½ teaspoon sugar

large pinch of salt

50 ml (1¾ fl oz) olive oil

1 Toast the pine nuts in a dry frying pan. Remove from the pan and set aside to cool.

2 Divide the lettuce among four serving plates and arrange the raspberries on top.

3 To make the lime vinaigrette, combine the lime juice with the vinegar, lime zest, sugar and salt. Whisk in the olive oil.

4 Heat the oil in a frying pan over medium heat. Season the chicken with salt and freshly ground black pepper. Sauté for 3-4 minutes on each side, until the chicken is cooked through. Remove from the pan and briefly cool, then slice crosswise.

5 Divide the chicken slices among the salads. Drizzle the lime vinaigrette over each serving and lightly toss. Sprinkle with the pine nuts and serve immediately.

You can use slivered almonds instead of the pine nuts. Lemon juice and zest can also be used in place of lime.

If you are pressed for time, use smoked turkey or smoked chicken breast.

Green salad with raspberry dressing

Prepare the lettuce as described in the main recipe and place in a large bowl. In a separate bowl, stir **50 g (1³⁄₄ oz) thawed frozen raspberries, 1 teaspoon raspberry vinegar, 1 tablespoon white balsamic vinegar, 1 teaspoon dark balsamic vinegar, ¹⁄₂ teaspoon sugar** and a **pinch of salt** together. Whisk in ¹⁄₃ **cup (80 ml) vegetable oil**. Toss the salad with the dressing. Arrange **toasted pine nuts or slivered almonds** and some **fried chicken breast** on the salad, if desired.

Chicken and raspberry salad with lime vinaigrette

Asian pork salad

Serves 4

Preparation
20 minutes

Cooking
Nil

Per serving
*1109 kJ, 265 kcal,
16 g protein, 9 g fat
(3 g saturated fat),
28 g carbohydrate
(6 g sugars), 2 g fibre,
890 mg sodium*

100 g (3½ oz) dried rice vermicelli

300 g (10 oz) Chinese barbecued pork (char siu), thinly sliced

100 g (3½ oz) Asian salad greens

1 red or yellow capsicum (bell pepper), thinly sliced

⅓ cup (10 g) fresh coriander (cilantro) leaves

⅓ cup (7 g) fresh mint leaves

1 tablespoon pink pickled ginger, chopped (optional)

Dressing

1½ tablespoons salt-reduced soy sauce

1 tablespoon rice vinegar

2 teaspoons lime juice

1 teaspoon sesame oil

1 small red chilli, seeded and finely chopped

1 Soak the vermicelli according to the packet instructions. Drain well, then cut into shorter lengths, if preferred.

2 To make the dressing, whisk together all of the ingredients in a small bowl.

3 Combine the pork, salad greens, capsicum, coriander, mint and ginger, if using, in a large bowl. Add the vermicelli and the dressing, and toss to combine. Divide the salad among four serving bowls and serve immediately.

Purchase Chinese barbecued pork from an Asian barbecue store, or substitute it with cooked boneless, skinless chicken breast or pork loin.

Seared tuna and bean salad

olive oil, for brushing

400 g (14 oz) piece tuna steak, about 5 cm (2 inches) thick

freshly ground black pepper

$^{1}/_{3}$ cup (80 ml) extra virgin olive oil

1 tablespoon lemon juice, or to taste

1 clove garlic, crushed

1 tablespoon dijon mustard

pinch of salt

400 g (14 oz) can cannellini beans, rinsed and drained

2 red capsicums (bell peppers), thinly sliced

$^{1}/_{2}$ telegraph (long) cucumber, quartered lengthwise and sliced

1 small red onion, thinly sliced

100 g (3$^{1}/_{2}$ oz) watercress, trimmed

lemon wedges, to serve

1 Brush a chargrill pan or cast-iron frying pan with a little olive oil and heat over medium heat. Season the tuna on both sides with freshly ground black pepper.

2 Sear the tuna in the hot pan over medium-high heat for 4 minutes on each side, until browned and marked with grill lines on the outside and light pink in the centre. Take care not to overcook the tuna or it will become tough and dry. Transfer the tuna to a plate to rest while you prepare the rest of the salad.

3 Combine the extra virgin olive oil, lemon juice, garlic and mustard in a salad bowl. Season with salt and freshly ground black pepper. Taste and add more lemon juice, if needed. Add the cannellini beans, capsicums, cucumber, onion and watercress to the bowl. Gently toss the salad to coat with the dressing.

4 Slice the tuna and arrange on top of the salad, then spoon a little of the dressing over the tuna. Serve the salad with lemon wedges.

Canned beans are a useful source of iron, and the vitamin C found in the watercress and capsicums will help enhance its absorption.

Tomato pasta salad with pancetta and basil

Serves 4

Preparation
15 minutes

Cooking
10 minutes

Per serving
1935 kJ, 462 kcal,
13 g protein, 22 g fat
(4 g saturated fat),
52 g carbohydrate
(<1 g sugars), 3 g fibre,
466 mg sodium

300 g (10 oz) small pasta shells

90 g (3 oz) pancetta, cut into thin strips

2 tablespoons red wine vinegar

2 teaspoons balsamic vinegar

pinch of salt

freshly ground black pepper

⅓ cup (80 ml) olive oil

100 g (3½ oz) tomatoes, finely chopped

1 tablespoon shredded fresh basil

1 Cook the pasta in a large saucepan of boiling water for 10 minutes, until al dente. Drain in a colander, briefly rinse with cold water, then drain again before transferring the pasta to a bowl.

2 While the pasta is cooking, gently cook the pancetta in a non-stick frying pan over low heat. Be careful not to brown the pancetta.

3 Blend the red wine vinegar with the balsamic vinegar and season well with salt and plenty of freshly ground black pepper. Whisk in the oil and toss the warm pasta with the dressing.

4 Fold the warm pancetta, tomatoes and basil through the pasta. Serve the salad immediately or set aside for 1 hour for the flavours to develop, if possible.

This recipe is ideal for using left-over pasta. Briefly warm the cold pasta in the microwave before tossing it with the balsamic dressing to ensure that the pasta absorbs the dressing well.

If you like, add some shaved parmesan to the salad just before serving.

Pancetta is a salt-cured, seasoned Italian bacon, similar to streaky bacon.

Chicken and vegetable burghul salad with mint butter

200 g (7 oz) burghul (bulgur)

600 ml (21 fl oz) hot salt-reduced vegetable stock (page 15)

1 eggplant (aubergine), thickly sliced

2 zucchini (courgettes), thickly sliced

1 large yellow capsicum (bell pepper), thickly sliced

¼ cup (60 ml) olive oil

3 teaspoons red wine vinegar

200 g (7 oz) barbecued chicken pieces (quartered if breast), skin removed

400 g (14 oz) can salt-reduced black-eyed peas, rinsed and drained

2 tablespoons chopped fresh flat-leaf (Italian) parsley

pinch of salt

freshly ground black pepper

30 g (1 oz) butter

2 tablespoons chopped fresh mint, plus extra leaves, to garnish

Serves 4

Preparation
20 minutes

Cooking
25 minutes

Per serving
2171 kJ, 519 kcal,
24 g protein, 26 g fat
(7 g saturated fat),
45 g carbohydrate
(7 g sugars), 10 g fibre,
889 mg sodium

1 Put the burghul in a large bowl, pour in the stock and stir well. Cover and leave to soak for 20–25 minutes, until the burghul is tender and most of the stock is absorbed.

2 Meanwhile, heat the grill (broiler) to medium-high and line the grill pan with foil. Arrange the eggplant, zucchini and capsicum on the grill rack and brush with 1 tablespoon of the oil. Cook for 15–20 minutes, until the vegetables are tender and beginning to char, turning halfway through and brushing the other side with 1 tablespoon of the oil.

3 Drain the burghul in a colander. Whisk the remaining oil and 1 teaspoon of the vinegar in the bowl, then add the chicken, black-eyed peas and parsley, and return the burghul to the bowl. Cut the eggplant slices in half and add to the bowl with the zucchini and capsicum. Mix well. Season with salt and freshly ground black pepper, and spoon onto individual serving plates.

4 Heat the butter and remaining vinegar in a small saucepan. Stir in the chopped mint, then drizzle over the salad. Garnish with mint leaves.

For a spicy dressing, stir a finely chopped, seeded red chilli into the melted butter in step 4, or whisk in ¼ teaspoon chilli paste from a jar.

You can reheat the barbecued chicken pieces in a chargrill pan or under the grill while the vegetables are cooking.

Sensational salad dressings

Brilliantly simple to toss together, the humble salad offers endless scope for creativity. Then there's the salad dressing – drizzled over or tossed through the fresh ingredients, it melds the flavours and textures together to lift your salad out of the ordinary.

Building salad dressings

Salad dressings are so versatile, but generally they contain an oil, an acidic element and any number of flavourings. Experiment with your own substitutions and additions – you can't really go wrong.

❧ **Oil** Use a fruity extra virgin olive oil, or try an aromatic oil such as walnut, hazelnut, avocado or sesame, or a mild peanut (groundnut) or canola oil. The oil gives a salad its characteristic aroma and flavour. It also complements or accentuates the taste of the individual ingredients. For best results, always buy the best-quality oil that you can afford.

❧ **Acid** Choose from a vinegar such as balsamic, cider, white or red wine vinegar, rice wine or sushi vinegar; citrus juice, such as lemon, lime or orange juice; or verjuice (juice of unripe grapes).

❧ **Flavours** Add a pinch of salt or a splash of soy or fish sauce; sweeten the dressing with sugar, honey or palm sugar or jaggery; add spices such as garlic, ginger, chillies, mustard or wasabi; and herbs such as thyme, sage, tarragon, lemongrass or finely shredded makrut (kaffir lime) leaves.

Dressing with herbs

Herb-flavoured dressings go well with green or vegetable salads, and also with pasta or rice, fish or meat salads. To maximise their flavour, make them in advance and store them in the refrigerator for a day or two. Making your own herb vinegars or oils will give even better results.

Classic herb vinaigrette

¼ cup (60 ml) white wine, sherry or herb vinegar, or lemon juice

1 teaspoon dijon or herb mustard

pinch of salt

freshly ground white pepper

⅓ cup (80 ml) good-quality olive oil

5 small sprigs each fresh parsley and dill

small handful of fresh chives

2 sprigs each fresh marjoram and basil

pinch of sugar

Whisk the vinegar or lemon juice, mustard, salt and freshly ground white pepper in a bowl until the salt has dissolved.

Add the olive oil, whisking until the vinaigrette is slightly creamy.

Finely chop the herb leaves, then stir into the vinaigrette.

Add the sugar and more salt and white pepper, to taste.

Marvellous ways with mayo

Mayonnaise-style sauces that form a coating over salad ingredients are perfect for potato or pasta salads (thin with a little yogurt for delicate green or vegetable salads). Stir the following ingredients into 1 cup (250 g) good-quality mayonnaise for a simple dressing.

❧ Herb $\frac{1}{2}$ cup (30 g) chopped mixed fresh herbs, such as chives, parsley, basil and thyme

❧ Mustard 1 tablespoon dijon mustard

❧ Lime or lemon 2 teaspoons grated zest and 1 tablespoon juice

❧ Curry 1 tablespoon curry powder

❧ Horseradish 2 tablespoons grated horseradish, from a jar, and 2 tablespoons snipped fresh chives

❧ *If you prefer, you can use $\frac{1}{2}$ cup (125 g) mayonnaise mixed with $\frac{1}{2}$ cup (125 g) natural (plain) yogurt, sour cream or crème fraîche.*

Classic mayonnaise

2 very fresh egg yolks	Whisk the egg yolks, mustard and vinegar or lemon juice in a bowl.
1 teaspoon dijon mustard	Using an electric whisk, add the oil, one drop at a time at first, then in a slow, steady stream. (If the mixture curdles or splits, add a little hot water and beat vigorously.)
2 tablespoons white wine vinegar or lemon juice	
1 cup (250 ml) olive oil	Season with salt and freshly ground white pepper.
pinch of salt	
freshly ground white pepper	Refrigerate for 1 to 2 days.

7 super salad dressings

Classic vinaigrette

Combine $\frac{1}{4}$ cup (60 ml) olive oil and 2 tablespoons lemon juice or balsamic vinegar. Season with a pinch of salt and freshly ground black pepper.

Variation Add $\frac{1}{2}$ teaspoon caster (superfine) sugar and some fresh or dried herbs.

French dressing

Combine $\frac{1}{4}$ cup (60 ml) extra virgin olive oil with 1 tablespoon red wine vinegar, 1 teaspoon dijon mustard, 1 teaspoon caster (superfine) sugar and a pinch of salt.

Asian dressing

Combine 2 tablespoons lemon juice, 2 tablespoons soy sauce, 2 teaspoons sesame oil and 2 teaspoons grated fresh ginger.

Variation Add 1 teaspoon fish sauce.

Mustard dressing

Combine 2 tablespoons olive oil, 2 tablespoons white wine vinegar and 1 tablespoon wholegrain mustard. Season with a pinch of salt and freshly ground black pepper.

Oil-free dressing

Combine 2 tablespoons rice vinegar, 1 tablespoon caster (superfine) sugar and a pinch of salt.

Thousand island dressing

Combine $\frac{1}{2}$ cup (125 g) mayonnaise, 2 tablespoons tomato paste (concentrated purée), 2 tablespoons tomato sauce (ketchup), 2 teaspoons worcestershire sauce and $\frac{1}{4}$ teaspoon Tabasco sauce.

Hummus dressing

Dilute some hummus with orange juice, lemon juice or water to the preferred consistency.

Gnocchi salad with pesto dressing

Serves 4

Preparation
20 minutes

Cooking
10 minutes

Per serving
*1781 kJ, 425 kcal,
13 g protein, 24 g fat
(7 g saturated fat),
38 g carbohydrate
(6 g sugars), 3 g fibre,
607 mg sodium*

400 g (14 oz) fresh small gnocchi

¼ cup (60 ml) olive oil

1 yellow capsicum (bell pepper), chopped

2 teaspoons soft brown sugar

1½ tablespoons white balsamic vinegar

200 g (7 oz) red cherry tomatoes

200 g (7 oz) marinated button mushrooms in oil

1 tablespoon pesto

pinch of salt

freshly ground black pepper

⅓ cup (50 g) pitted black olives

150 g (5 oz) bocconcini (fresh baby mozzarella balls)

The gnocchi can be replaced with any cooked small pasta shapes, such as shells or macaroni.

1 Cook the gnocchi according to the packet instructions. Drain, briefly rinse under cold water and drain again.

2 While the gnocchi is cooking, heat half the oil in a frying pan over high heat. Cook the capsicum for 2 minutes, until starting to soften. Sprinkle with 1 teaspoon of the sugar and briefly cook until caramelised. Remove the pan from the heat and drizzle the capsicum with half the vinegar. Pour the capsicum and juices into a large salad bowl.

3 Add 3 teaspoons of the oil to the pan and cook the whole tomatoes for 2 minutes, until they burst and release some of their juices. Sprinkle with the remaining sugar, briefly cook until caramelised and then drizzle with the remaining vinegar.

4 Add the tomatoes and juices to the capsicum, then add the mushrooms, pesto and remaining oil. Toss to combine. Season with salt and freshly ground black pepper.

5 Fold the gnocchi, olives and bocconcini through the capsicum mixture. Season again with salt and pepper. Set aside for at least 15 minutes for the flavours to develop, if possible.

Greek salad with chickpeas

Salads don't get much healthier than this Greek salad that is low in fat, high in fibre and full of anti-oxidants. This dish conjures visions of lazy days in the sun, and delivers on taste with every mouthful.

400 g (14 oz) can salt-reduced chickpeas, rinsed and drained

1 green capsicum (bell pepper), chopped

1 small onion, thinly sliced

$1/4$ cucumber, chopped

1 clove garlic, crushed

20 pitted black olives

2 tablespoons olive oil

200 g (7 oz) red cherry tomatoes, halved

$1/3$ cup (10 g) chopped fresh parsley

$1^1/3$ cups (200 g) crumbled reduced-fat fetta

250 g (8 oz) mixed salad leaves

lemon wedges, to serve

1 Combine the chickpeas, capsicum, onion, cucumber, garlic, olives and oil in a large bowl. Stir in the tomatoes and parsley, then gently stir in the fetta.

2 Divide the mixed salad leaves among four plates or bowls. Spoon the salad over the leaves and serve with lemon wedges.

Serves 4

Preparation
15 minutes

Cooking
Nil

Per serving
1327 kJ, 317 kcal,
18 g protein, 20 g fat
(6 g saturated fat),
16 g carbohydrate
(3 g sugars), 4 g fibre,
802 mg sodium

If you find the taste of raw garlic too strong, rub a cut clove around the bowl before adding the salad. This will give the salad a mild garlic flavour.

Summer beef salad

Serves 4

Preparation
20 minutes

Cooking
5 minutes

Per serving
*1048 kJ, 250 kcal,
20 g protein, 17 g fat
(3 g saturated fat),
3 g carbohydrate
(2 g sugars), 2 g fibre,
393 mg sodium*

$\frac{1}{2}$ teaspoon salt

1 small red onion, halved
and thinly sliced

100 g (3$\frac{1}{2}$ oz) radishes,
thinly sliced

1 thick-cut lean rump (round)
steak, about 350 g (12 oz)

1 tablespoon olive oil

$\frac{1}{4}$ teaspoon mixed dried
herbs

freshly ground black pepper

2 tablespoons walnut oil

1 tablespoon balsamic vinegar

4 celery stalks, diagonally
sliced

125 g (4 oz) rocket (arugula)
or mixed salad leaves

1 Dissolve the salt in a bowl of cold water. Add the onion and radishes, and leave to soak while the steak is cooking.

2 Heat a chargrill pan or non-stick frying pan over high heat. Trim the steak of fat and pat dry with paper towel. Rub the steak on both sides with 2 teaspoons of the olive oil, then season with the dried herbs and freshly ground black pepper. Cook the steak for 2$\frac{1}{2}$ minutes on each side for medium-rare or 3$\frac{1}{2}$ minutes on each side for medium. Transfer to a chopping board to rest for a few minutes.

3 Whisk the remaining olive oil, walnut oil and vinegar in a large bowl.

4 Cut the steak into very thin slices. Pour any meat juices into the dressing.

5 Drain the onion and radishes, and add to the dressing, along with the celery and beef slices. Gently toss together. Divide the rocket or salad leaves among four plates, then spoon the beef mixture on top and serve immediately.

To make a horseradish dressing for the salad, whisk together $\frac{1}{3}$ cup (80 ml) olive oil, the juice of 1 small lemon and 2 teaspoons grated horseradish from a jar.

Soaking the onion and radishes takes away some of the heat and sharpness, and prevents the radishes from discolouring.

Spicy three-bean salad

1 Cook the green beans in a saucepan of boiling salted water for 3-5 minutes, then drain and rinse under cold running water. Drain again and tip into a large bowl.

2 To make the curry dressing, put the olive oil, vinegar, curry powder or paprika, garlic, salt and some freshly ground black pepper in a screw-top jar. Shake well to blend.

3 Add the kidney beans, cannellini beans or black-eyed peas, spring onions and mozzarella to the bowl with the green beans. Pour in the dressing and toss well to combine.

4 Lay the tomato slices on a large serving plate. Spoon the bean mixture over the tomatoes and sprinkle with the chopped parsley or coriander. Chill the salad before serving, if possible.

Serves 4

Preparation
20 minutes

Cooking
5 minutes

Per serving
*1346 kJ, 321 kcal,
20 g protein, 18 g fat
(7 g saturated fat),
19 g carbohydrate
(6 g sugars), 11 g fibre,
809 mg sodium*

Instead of the mozzarella, try using fetta, stilton or a full-flavoured cheddar. Add a chopped avocado.

125 g (4 oz) green beans, halved

420 g (15 oz) can red kidney beans, rinsed and drained

400 g (14 oz) can cannellini beans or black-eyed peas, rinsed and drained

6 spring onions (scallions), chopped

150 g (5 oz) firm mozzarella, chopped

2 large or 4 medium ripe tomatoes, thinly sliced

4 tablespoons chopped fresh flat-leaf (Italian) parsley or coriander (cilantro) leaves

Curry dressing

2 tablespoons olive oil

2 tablespoons white wine vinegar

1 teaspoon mild curry powder or smoked paprika

1 clove garlic, crushed

$1/2$ teaspoon sea salt

freshly ground black pepper

Quinoa salad with asparagus

Serves 4

Preparation
20 minutes

Cooking
15 minutes

Per serving
1587 kJ, 379 kcal,
15 g protein, 21 g fat
(7 g saturated fat),
34 g carbohydrate
(9 g sugars), 6 g fibre,
731 mg sodium

350 ml (12 fl oz) salt-reduced vegetable stock (page 15)

¾ cup (150 g) quinoa

300 g (10 oz) asparagus spears, diagonally sliced

150 g (5 oz) snow peas (mangetout), diagonally sliced

4 small vine-ripened tomatoes, cut into thin wedges

1-2 tablespoons finely chopped fresh dill, plus extra sprigs, to garnish

50 g (1¾ oz) parmesan

Citrus dressing

2 tablespoons orange juice

2 tablespoons lemon juice

1 teaspoon dijon mustard

1 teaspoon honey

¼ cup (60 ml) olive oil

pinch of salt

freshly ground black pepper

1 Bring the stock to a boil in a saucepan. Put the quinoa in a sieve and rinse under running water. Add to the boiling stock, then cover, reduce the heat to low and cook for about 15 minutes.

2 Meanwhile, cook the asparagus in a saucepan of boiling water for 5 minutes, until cooked but still firm. Add the snow peas about 2 minutes before the end of the cooking time. Drain the cooked vegetables and refresh them under cold water to stop the cooking process. Drain well.

3 Drain the cooked quinoa into a sieve and set aside to cool.

4 To make the citrus dressing, combine the orange juice, lemon juice, mustard and honey in a large bowl. Whisk in the olive oil, then season with salt and freshly ground black pepper.

5 Add the quinoa, asparagus, snow peas, tomatoes and chopped dill to the bowl and toss with the dressing. Shave the parmesan over the salad using a vegetable peeler or a sharp knife. Garnish with dill sprigs and serve immediately.

Amaranth can be used instead of the quinoa as another protein-rich salad cereal. Note that amaranth takes about 5 minutes longer to cook than quinoa.

Quinoa salad with fried button mushrooms

Cook the quinoa in boiling vegetable stock as in step 1 of the main recipe. Heat **1 tablespoon olive oil** in a frying pan. Thinly slice **250 g (8 oz) button mushrooms**, cut **1 red capsicum (bell pepper)** into strips and crush **1 clove garlic.** Add to the frying pan and cook over medium heat for 2 minutes. Remove from the heat. Whisk **2 tablespoons balsamic vinegar** with **¼ cup (60 ml) olive oil,** a **pinch of salt** and **freshly ground black pepper.** Toss the quinoa, vegetables and **5 sliced spring onions (scallions)** with the dressing.

Broad bean and artichoke salad

Serves 4

Preparation
15 minutes

Cooking
5 minutes

Per serving
1376 kJ, 329 kcal,
15 g protein, 26 g fat
(6 g saturated fat),
6 g carbohydrate
(2 g sugars), 9 g fibre,
388 mg sodium

*For extra flavour,
thinly slice 100 g
($3^1\!/_2$ oz) rindless
bacon. Fry in
1 tablespoon oil
over medium heat
until crisp. Toss
with the dressing,
together with
the remaining
ingredients.*

*This hearty bean
salad goes well
with fresh ciabatta
or pitas.*

$2^1\!/_2$ cups (400 g) frozen
broad (fava) beans

1 baby cos (romaine) lettuce

1 radicchio

2 tablespoons cider vinegar

pinch of salt

freshly ground black pepper

$1^1\!/_2$ tablespoons olive oil

$^1\!/_4$ cup (60 ml) walnut oil

250 g (8 oz) bottled artichoke
hearts, drained and cut into
quarters

150 g (5 oz) bocconcini
(fresh baby mozzarella balls)

2 tablespoons chopped fresh
flat-leaf (Italian) parsley

1 Add the frozen broad beans to a saucepan of boiling
salted water. Return to a boil, cover and simmer over
low heat for about 5 minutes. Drain in a colander, refresh
under cold water and leave to drain again.

2 Trim and wash the lettuce and radicchio and tear the
leaves into bite-sized pieces.

3 Combine the cider vinegar with salt and freshly ground
black pepper in a large bowl, then whisk in the olive oil and
walnut oil.

4 Add the broad beans, lettuce, radicchio, artichokes,
bocconcini and parsley to the bowl and toss with the
dressing. Season with extra salt and freshly ground black
pepper if necessary.

Fattoush

2 large white or sesame
seed pitas

1/3 cup (80 ml) olive oil

juice of 1 lemon

pinch of salt

freshly ground black pepper

2 tablespoons chopped fresh
coriander (cilantro) leaves

2 tablespoons chopped
fresh mint, plus extra leaves,
to garnish

1/2 Lebanese or other small
cucumber, diced

4 large tomatoes, chopped

4 spring onions (scallions),
diagonally sliced

400 g (14 oz) can chickpeas
or black-eyed peas, rinsed
and drained

1 Warm the pitas in the toaster to make them easier
to open up, then split each in half using a knife. Toast the
four halves for 1 minute, until crisp and lightly browned.
Tear or cut the pitas into bite-sized pieces.

2 Whisk the oil and lemon juice in a small bowl. Season
with salt and freshly ground black pepper, and stir in the
coriander and chopped mint.

3 Combine the cucumber, tomatoes, spring onions
and chickpeas or black-eyed peas in a large salad bowl.
Drizzle with the dressing, then toss until well mixed.
Just before serving, toss the pita pieces through the
salad and garnish with mint leaves.

Serves 4

Preparation
15 minutes

Cooking
5 minutes

Per serving
*1637 kJ, 391 kcal,
11 g protein, 20 g fat
(3 g saturated fat),
41 g carbohydrate
(6 g sugars), 7 g fibre,
587 mg sodium*

*There are countless
variations of this
Middle Eastern
salad of mixed
vegetables and
pieces of toasted
flat bread.*

*Instead of spring
onions, use 1 finely
chopped small red
onion. Replace the
chickpeas with a
200 g (7 oz) can
French-style green
(puy) lentils.*

Tuna and olive salad

Serves 4

Preparation
20 minutes

Cooking
15 minutes

Per serving
*1479 kJ, 353 kcal,
16 g protein, 30 g fat
(5 g saturated fat),
5 g carbohydrate
(2 g sugars), 3 g fibre,
849 mg sodium*

2 sashimi-quality tuna steaks,
about 150 g (5 oz)

1 tablespoon olive oil

3 eggs

1/2 iceberg lettuce, shredded

100 g (3 1/2 oz) red cherry
tomatoes

1 Lebanese or other small
cucumber, quartered
lengthwise and sliced

1 yellow capsicum (bell
pepper), cut into strips

2/3 cup (100 g) pitted mixed
olives

3 teaspoons black
peppercorns

1 teaspoon coriander seeds

1/2 teaspoon sea salt flakes

Dressing

75 ml (2 1/2 fl oz) olive oil

1/4 cup (60 ml) white wine
vinegar

1-2 teaspoons dijon mustard

pinch of salt

freshly ground black pepper

1 Rinse the tuna steaks under cold water. Pat dry with paper towels, brush with the oil, cover and set aside.

2 Place the eggs in a small saucepan and cover with cold water. Bring to a boil, then reduce the heat and cook for 8-10 minutes, until the eggs are hard-boiled. Remove from the saucepan and place in cold water until ready to use.

3 To make the dressing, add the oil, vinegar, mustard, salt and freshly ground black pepper to a screw-top jar. Shake until the ingredients are thoroughly blended.

4 Combine the lettuce, tomatoes, cucumber, capsicum and olives in a large bowl. Fold in the dressing, then divide the salad among four serving plates. Peel and quarter the eggs and arrange on top of the salad.

5 Coarsely pound the peppercorns, coriander seeds and sea salt in a mortar and pestle.

6 Heat a non-stick frying pan over medium heat and sear the tuna steaks for 2-3 minutes on each side, making sure they are still rare.

7 Remove the tuna steaks from the pan, cut into cubes and roll in the ground spices. Arrange the tuna cubes on top of the salad and serve immediately.

This autumn salad goes perfectly with some buttered hazelnut or walnut bread.

Fig and prosciutto salad

1 large oakleaf lettuce, leaves separated

4 ripe figs

100 g (3½ oz) thinly sliced prosciutto, cut into wide strips

16 fresh basil leaves, shredded

40 g (1½ oz) parmesan

Orange vinaigrette

2 tablespoons orange juice

1 teaspoon balsamic vinegar

1 teaspoon wholegrain mustard

½ teaspoon finely grated orange zest

2 pinches of salt

⅓ cup (80 ml) olive oil

1 To make the orange vinaigrette, combine the orange juice, vinegar, mustard, orange zest and salt in a large bowl. Whisk in the oil until well blended.

2 Add the lettuce leaves to the bowl and gently toss to coat with the vinaigrette. Divide the lettuce among four serving plates.

3 Cut the figs lengthwise into quarters. If desired, use a sharp knife to make small incisions just underneath the skin to make it easier to remove the flesh when eating.

4 Arrange the prosciutto and basil on top of the lettuce. Place the figs on the side. Shave the parmesan over the top of the salad as a garnish.

Serves 4

Preparation
20 minutes

Cooking
Nil

Per serving
1255 kJ, 300 kcal, 12 g protein, 26 g fat (7 g saturated fat), 6 g carbohydrate (6 g sugars), 2 g fibre, 777 mg sodium

Asparagus salad with prosciutto

Prepare the asparagus as directed in the main recipe and arrange it on a platter with **200 g (7 oz) red cherry tomatoes, 1 handful mixed salad leaves** and **85 g (3 oz) sliced prosciutto.** Drizzle with the balsamic vinaigrette. Add some **small fresh basil leaves** and **grated parmesan,** if desired.

Asparagus and snow pea salad with balsamic vinaigrette

Asparagus and snow pea salad with balsamic vinaigrette

200 g (7 oz) snow peas (mangetout)

500 g (1 lb) asparagus spears, cut into short lengths

2 small avocados, sliced crosswise

chervil or flat-leaf (Italian) parsley, to garnish

Balsamic vinaigrette

1 tablespoon raspberry vinegar

2 teaspoons balsamic vinegar

2 pinches of salt

pinch of sugar

freshly ground black pepper

1/4 cup (60 ml) olive oil

1 Cook the snow peas in a large saucepan of boiling water for 2 minutes. Remove with a slotted spoon, reserving the cooking water. Rinse the snow peas with cold water, then drain and set aside.

2 Boil the asparagus in the cooking water for 3 minutes. Drain in a large colander, rinse with cold water, then drain well and set aside.

3 To make the balsamic vinaigrette, whisk the raspberry vinegar with the balsamic vinegar. Add the salt, sugar and some freshly ground black pepper. Whisk in the oil until well combined.

4 Arrange the asparagus, snow peas and avocado slices on a platter. Drizzle with the balsamic vinaigrette and garnish with chervil or parsley.

Serves 4

Preparation
20 minutes

Cooking
5 minutes

Per serving
1295 kJ, 309 kcal,
6 g protein, 30 g fat
(5 g saturated fat),
5 g carbohydrate
(4 g sugars), 4 g fibre,
308 mg sodium

A lemon-flavoured vinaigrette is also lovely with this salad: substitute a lemon-infused olive oil and season with salt and black pepper.

Falafel pita pockets, page 114

Light meals

These fuss-free dishes are perfect for when you only feel like a bite to eat. Sandwiches, wraps, pizzas, tacos and omelettes are filled with healthy ingredients, and have much less fat and salt than the store-bought versions.

Individual tomato clafoutis

Mushroom clafoutis

Heat **2 tablespoons (40 g) butter** in a frying pan and sauté **250 g (8 oz) thinly sliced button mushrooms** and **1 crushed garlic clove** until the liquid from the mushrooms has evaporated. Season with a **pinch of salt** and **freshly ground black pepper.** Transfer the mixture to a buttered 25 cm (10 inch) quiche dish. Prepare the clafoutis mixture as directed in the main recipe, omitting the chopped parsley, and spread over the mushrooms. Bake for 35 minutes, until set. Sprinkle with **black pepper** and serve immediately.

Individual tomato clafoutis

butter, for greasing

2 eggs

2 tablespoons cream

100 g (3^1/$_2$ oz) light herb cream cheese

3–4 fresh flat-leaf (Italian) parsley leaves, finely chopped

pinch of salt

freshly ground black pepper

1 tablespoon semolina

^{1}/$_2$ cup (50 g) grated Swiss-style cheese

10–15 red cherry tomatoes, halved

olive oil, for drizzling

1 Preheat the oven to 200°C (400°F/Gas 6). Generously butter four ^{1}/$_2$ cup (125 ml) baking dishes or ramekins.

2 Combine the eggs, cream, cream cheese, parsley, salt and freshly ground black pepper in a bowl. Whisk using an electric mixer. Stir in the semolina and grated cheese.

3 Divide the mixture among the prepared dishes. Top with the tomato halves, cut side up, and drizzle with a little olive oil.

4 Bake the clafoutis for about 30 minutes, until set. Remove from the oven, grind some black pepper on top and serve immediately.

Serves 4

Preparation
15 minutes

Cooking
30 minutes

Per serving
618 kJ, 148 kcal,
10 g protein, 10 g fat
(5 g saturated fat),
5 g carbohydrate
(2 g sugars), 1 g fibre,
309 mg sodium

Use three ripe roma (plum) tomatoes instead of the cherry tomatoes. Slice them crosswise and arrange on top of the egg and cheese mixture.

For extra flavour, spread each of the buttered baking dishes with 1 tablespoon pesto before adding the egg and cheese mixture.

Eggs in ramekins with mushrooms and roasted capsicums

Serves 4

Preparation
15 minutes

Cooking
20 minutes

Per serving
554 kJ, 132 kcal,
8 g protein, 11 g fat
(5 g saturated fat),
2 g carbohydrate
(1 g sugars), 1 g fibre,
266 mg sodium

1 tablespoon (20 g) butter, chopped, plus extra, for greasing

50 g (1¾ oz) roasted red capsicums (bell peppers) in oil

1 small onion, finely diced

10 small button mushrooms, finely diced

pinch of salt

freshly ground black pepper

4 eggs

1 Preheat the oven to 190°C (375°F/Gas 5). Generously grease four 150 ml (5 fl oz) ramekins with butter.

2 Drain the capsicum pieces, reserving 2 tablespoons of the oil from the jar. Finely dice the capsicum pieces.

3 Heat the reserved capsicum oil in a frying pan over medium heat. Cook the onion, mushrooms and capsicum for 5 minutes, until the liquid has evaporated. Season with salt and freshly ground black pepper.

4 Divide the mushroom mixture among the ramekins. Crack an egg on top of the mixture in each ramekin and dot with the chopped butter.

5 Place the ramekins in a deep roasting pan (baking dish) and loosely cover with a sheet of foil. Pour in enough hot water to come one-third of the way up the sides of the ramekins. Slide the pan into the oven and cook for 15 minutes, until the eggwhites are set but the yolks are still soft. Serve the eggs immediately.

To make this small dish more hearty, add 50 g (1¾ oz) cubed ham or finely diced smoked pork loin to step 3 to cook with the mushroom mixture.

For extra flavour, add 1 finely chopped clove garlic and 2 tablespoons finely chopped fresh sage to the mushroom mixture. Serve garnished with sage leaves.

Variations

Make the basic omelettes, but instead try the following fillings:

❧ Sautéed **baby spinach leaves,** crumbled **fetta** and some chopped fresh **dill**

❧ Sliced **ham,** chopped **tomato** and grated **cheddar**

❧ Cooked **small prawns (shrimp)** and/or **crabmeat**

❧ **Smoked salmon,** creamy **goat's cheese** and some chopped fresh **parsley.**

Mushroom omelettes

Mushroom omelettes

1 tablespoon vegetable oil

3 spring onions (scallions), thinly sliced

100 g (3½ oz) mixed mushrooms, thinly sliced

4 eggs

2 teaspoons kecap manis

1 tablespoon chopped fresh coriander (cilantro)

1 Heat 2 teaspoons of the oil in a non-stick frying pan measuring 18 cm (7 inches) across the base. Cook the spring onions and mushrooms over medium heat for 5 minutes, until just softened. Transfer to a plate.

2 Wipe the frying pan clean with paper towels, then heat 1 teaspoon oil over medium heat. In a bowl, whisk the eggs with a fork, then pour half the mixture into the frying pan, swirling to coat the base. Draw the egg from the side of the pan into the centre as the omelette cooks, letting the uncooked egg run to the side. Cook for 1 minute, until set underneath but still runny on top.

3 Sprinkle half the mushroom mixture across the centre of the omelette. Fold one-third of the omelette towards the centre, then over again to enclose the filling. Slide onto a plate, drizzle with half the kecap manis and sprinkle with half the coriander. Keep warm.

4 Repeat with the remaining ingredients to make another omelette. Serve hot.

Serves 2

Preparation
10 minutes

Cooking
10 minutes

Per serving
1054 kJ, 252 kcal, 15 g protein, 20 g fat (4 g saturated fat), 5 g carbohydrate (4 g sugars), 2 g fibre, 365 mg sodium

Kecap manis is a thick and sweet Indonesian-style soy sauce. You can use oyster sauce if you prefer.

Loosely cover the first omelette with a sheet of foil to keep it warm while you cook the second omelette.

Chickpea and vegetable eggah

Serves 4

Preparation
10 minutes

Cooking
25 minutes

Per serving
*1456 kJ, 348 kcal,
16 g protein, 23 g fat
(4 g saturated fat),
20 g carbohydrate
(4 g sugars), 6 g fibre,
408 mg sodium*

¼ cup (60 ml) extra virgin olive oil

1 small onion, chopped

1 clove garlic, crushed

1 teaspoon ground cumin

1 teaspoon ground coriander

pinch of cayenne pepper

250 g (8 oz) small new potatoes, scrubbed and chopped

1 small red capsicum (bell pepper), chopped

1 small eggplant (aubergine), chopped

400 g (14 oz) can chickpeas, rinsed and drained

6 eggs

2 tablespoons chopped fresh coriander (cilantro) leaves

pinch of salt

freshly ground black pepper

1 Heat 1 tablespoon of the olive oil in a 25 cm (10 inch) non-stick ovenproof frying pan and cook the onion for 2–3 minutes, until just starting to soften. Stir in the garlic, cumin, ground coriander and cayenne pepper, and cook, stirring constantly, for 1 minute.

2 Add another 1 tablespoon of the oil to the pan, then add the potatoes, capsicum and eggplant. Cook, stirring often, for 5 minutes, until the vegetables are lightly browned.

3 Pour in ⅓ cup (80 ml) water, then cover and steam for 5 minutes. Remove the lid and cook until the excess liquid has evaporated, then stir in the chickpeas.

4 Lightly beat the eggs in a large bowl. Add the fresh coriander and season with salt and freshly ground black pepper. Stir in the vegetable and chickpea mixture from the pan.

5 Preheat the grill (broiler) to high. Heat the remaining oil in the pan over medium heat. Pour in the egg and vegetable mixture, spreading the vegetables out evenly. Cook the eggah, shaking the pan from time to time, for 3–4 minutes, until it is almost set (there will be some uncooked egg mixture on the top).

6 Place the pan under the grill and cook the eggah for 2 minutes, until the top is set. Remove from the heat and allow the eggah to rest in the pan for 2 minutes, then slide it onto a serving plate. Serve hot, cut into wedges.

Popular throughout the Middle East, this chunky omelette is served flat, not rolled or folded. It is packed with vegetables and chickpeas, and can be served hot or cold.

Quesadillas

Serves 4

Preparation
15 minutes

Cooking
15 minutes

Per serving
1403 kJ, 335 kcal,
24 g protein, 13 g fat
(7 g saturated fat),
31 g carbohydrate
(4 g sugars), 5 g fibre,
735 mg sodium

2 cups (250 g) reduced-fat
grated cheddar

3 spring onions (scallions),
thinly sliced

$\frac{1}{3}$ cup (20 g) chopped fresh
coriander (cilantro)

8 flour tortillas, about 20 cm
(8 inches) in diameter

vegetable oil, for brushing

$\frac{2}{3}$ cup (160 g) Mexican-style
tomato salsa

1 Combine the cheese, spring onions and coriander in
a bowl. Lay four tortillas on a clean surface and divide the
cheese mixture among them. Place another tortilla on top
of each base.

2 Heat a frying pan over medium heat, then lightly brush
with oil. Carefully place a quesadilla in the pan and cook
for about 1$\frac{1}{2}$ minutes, until the tortilla is lightly golden
underneath and the cheese has started to melt.

3 Turn the quesadilla over and cook the other side for
about 1$\frac{1}{2}$ minutes, then transfer to a chopping board.
Cook the remaining quesadillas in the same way.

4 Cut the quesadillas into wedges and serve drizzled
with a little salsa.

*Experiment with
other fillings, but
don't be tempted
to overfill the
quesadillas – they
need to be thin so
they don't fall apart.*

*To speed things up,
use two frying pans
so you can cook two
quesadillas at once.*

Mini spinach and quail egg pizzas

The quail eggs add the final, nutritious touch to these delicious mini pizzas. They supply a rich variety of essential amino acids and can even be enjoyed by people allergic to chicken eggs. The recipe partners them perfectly with health-promoting fresh English spinach.

Serves 4

Preparation
20 minutes,
plus 30 minutes
resting

Cooking
25 minutes

Per serving
*1250 kJ, 299 kcal,
15 g protein, 18 g fat
(8 g saturated fat),
20 g carbohydrate
(1 g sugars), 3 g fibre,
549 mg sodium*

Pizza bases

70 g (2 oz) low-fat quark or light sour cream

1 tablespoon olive oil

1 egg

100 g (3½ oz) spelt flour or plain (all-purpose) flour

1 teaspoon baking powder

pinch of salt

Topping

300 g (10 oz) English spinach

1 tablespoon (20 g) butter

1 small onion, finely diced

1 clove garlic, crushed

pinch of salt

freshly ground black pepper

freshly grated nutmeg

125 g (4 oz) bocconcini (fresh baby mozzarella balls), diced

4 quail eggs

If you can't find quail eggs, substitute a large chicken egg. Whisk with a fork and divide among the wells in the pizzas.

1 To make the pizza bases, combine the quark, oil, egg, flour, baking powder and salt to make a smooth dough. Cover and set aside to rest for 30 minutes.

2 Preheat the oven to 180°C (350°F/Gas 4) and line a baking tray with baking (parchment) paper.

3 Pick through the spinach leaves and wash. Heat a saucepan over medium heat, add the wet spinach, cover and cook until wilted. Transfer to a colander, squeeze out the excess liquid and chop the spinach.

4 Heat the butter in a frying pan and sauté the onion until translucent. Add the garlic and spinach, and season with salt, freshly ground black pepper and a little nutmeg. Sauté the spinach for a few minutes, then remove from the heat and set aside to cool.

5 Knead the dough on a surface dusted with flour, then divide into quarters. Using a rolling pin, roll the dough into round pizza bases. Transfer the bases onto the baking tray and roll up the edges to form rims.

6 Divide the spinach mixture and diced bocconcini among the bases. Make a well in the middle of each pizza, crack a quail egg into each well and season with a little salt. Bake for about 20 minutes, until the egg is set and the cheese has melted. Serve immediately.

Quick yeast-free pizza bases

To make an easy base in about 5 minutes, put **1½ cups (225 g) self-raising flour**, **½ teaspoon baking powder** and **¼ teaspoon salt** in a bowl. Stir, then make a well in the centre and pour in **150 ml (5 fl oz) low-fat milk** and **1 tablespoon olive oil.** Mix to a soft dough and roll out. Top as directed in the main recipe, but bake for 12–15 minutes.

Sun-dried tomato and fetta pizza

1 teaspoon balsamic vinegar

1/3 cup (50 g) sun-dried tomatoes in oil, thinly sliced, plus 2 tablespoons oil from the jar

1 small red onion, thinly sliced

1 large, thin ready-made pizza base, about 250 g (8 oz), or 2 x 150 g (5 oz) pizza bases

1/4 cup (60 g) sun-dried tomato paste

8 red cherry tomatoes, halved

12 pitted black or green olives

3 spring onions (scallions), thinly sliced

3/4 cup (110 g) crumbled salt-reduced fetta

freshly ground black pepper

1 Preheat the oven to 220°C (425°F/Gas 7). Whisk the balsamic vinegar with 1 tablespoon of the oil from the jar of sun-dried tomatoes in a bowl, add the onion rings and toss to coat. Set aside.

2 Spread the pizza base with the sun-dried tomato paste. Arrange the onion rings and cherry tomatoes on top, then scatter with the sun-dried tomatoes, olives, spring onions and fetta. Drizzle the remaining 1 tablespoon of sun-dried tomato oil over the pizza.

3 Put the pizza directly on the top shelf of the oven, with a baking tray on the shelf below to catch any drips. Bake for 10 minutes, until the base is crisp and the topping is lightly browned. Season with freshly ground black pepper. Cut into wedges and serve.

Serves 4

Preparation
10 minutes

Cooking
10 minutes

Per serving
1796 kJ, 429 kcal, 13 g protein, 23 g fat (8 g saturated fat), 41 g carbohydrate (10 g sugars), 6 g fibre, 658 mg sodium

For extra crispness, heat extra baking trays in the oven and put the pizza (on a tray) on top of these. This will cook the pizza base quickly and evenly.

Quick ideas for pizza

Takeaway pizza is often high in saturated fat and salt. Fresh, homemade pizza is often far healthier. With some ready-made bases, basic pantry staples and a few fresh ingredients, you can whip up a tasty pizza in no time at all.

Base

Keep a few pizza bases in the freezer (you can make these yourself or buy them at the supermarket). You can also use thin pitas, or pide (Turkish flat bread), split horizontally. Tightly wrap in plastic wrap and freeze for up to 2 months.

Cheese

Mozzarella is the cheese most widely used on pizza, but you can also use cheddar where mozzarella is called for, and vice versa. You can buy pre-grated cheese, packaged in a zip-lock bag for convenience. This cheese freezes well for up to 3 months, and can be used straight from the freezer without thawing.

You can wrap any unrolled dough in plastic wrap and freeze it in a zip-lock bag. When you are ready to use the dough, thaw it overnight in the fridge, then return to room temperature, punch down again and roll out.

Homemade pizza bases

Serves 4   **Time** 1¼ hours

2 teaspoons dry (powdered) yeast
1 teaspoon caster (superfine) sugar
1 teaspoon salt
¾ cup (180 ml) lukewarm water
2 cups (300 g) plain (all-purpose) flour
2 tablespoons olive oil

Sprinkle the yeast, sugar and salt into the water. Stir, then stand for 5–10 minutes, until frothy.

Put the flour in a bowl and make a well in the centre. Add the yeast mixture and oil. Mix with a wooden spoon, then gather the dough together, turn out onto a lightly floured surface and knead for 5 minutes, until smooth.

Place the dough in a clean, lightly oiled bowl, cover and stand for 45 minutes, until doubled in size.

Punch down the dough, then divide it into two or four portions. Roll the dough out into two 22 cm (9 inch) rounds, or four smaller rounds. Place on a pizza tray or trays and top as desired.

Per serving
1459 kJ, 349 kcal, 9 g protein, 10 g fat (1 g saturated fat), 55 g carbohydrate (1 g sugars), 3 g fibre, 610 mg sodium

Sauce

Many types of tomato-based pizza and pasta sauces are now available, in jars or small tubs. Any left-over sauce will keep in the fridge for up to 3 days; you can also freeze it in ice-cube trays, then pop the cubes in a zip-lock bag for easy access (expel the air from the bag each time to keep it airtight).

Toppings

These toppings are enough for a 22 cm (9 inch) pizza base; simply double the ingredients if you are making two pizzas. Bake the pizzas in a preheated 210°C (415°F/Gas 6) oven for 18 minutes, until the crust is golden brown.

Prosciutto and tomato

Spread the pizza base with **1 tablespoon tomato pizza sauce**. Top with **4 torn fresh basil leaves, 2 chopped prosciutto slices, 3 thickly sliced red cherry tomatoes** and **1 sliced bocconcini (fresh baby mozzarella ball)**. Serve scattered with **small fresh basil leaves**.

Satay chicken

Spread the pizza base with **1 tablespoon satay sauce** and sprinkle with **2 tablespoons grated cheddar**. Top with **$\frac{1}{2}$ cup (80 g) shredded cooked chicken, 1 sliced spring onion (scallion)** and another **2 tablespoons grated cheddar**. Serve with a dollop of **natural (plain) yogurt**, with a few **snow pea (mangetout) sprouts** scattered over the top.

Spicy salami

Spread the pizza base with **1 tablespoon tomato pizza sauce**. Top with **50 g ($1\frac{3}{4}$ oz) shredded salami, 40 g ($1\frac{1}{2}$ oz) sliced roasted red capsicums (bell peppers), 5 halved red cherry tomatoes** and **$\frac{1}{4}$ cup (10 g) shredded baby spinach leaves**. Sprinkle **2 tablespoons grated mozzarella** over the top.

Rosemary and garlic potato

Combine **1 tablespoon olive oil, $\frac{1}{2}$ small crushed garlic clove** and **$\frac{1}{2}$ teaspoon chopped fresh rosemary** in a bowl, and season with a **pinch of salt** and **freshly ground black pepper**. Brush half the mixture over the pizza base. Thinly slice **1 small desiree potato** and then arrange on top, overlapping slightly. Brush with the remaining rosemary and garlic mixture.

Asparagus and salmon

Spread the pizza base with **1 tablespoon softened cream cheese**. Thinly slice **3 asparagus spears** on the diagonal, and place on top of the pizza with **$\frac{1}{2}$ teaspoon rinsed capers**. Serve topped with **25 g (1 oz) smoked salmon slices**, a drizzle of **olive oil** and **lemon wedges**.

Pumpkin and pesto

Spread the pizza base with **1 tablespoon pesto**. Top with **90 g (3 oz) cooked diced pumpkin (winter squash), 25 g (1 oz) crumbled blue cheese** and **$1\frac{1}{2}$ tablespoons walnut pieces**. Serve with **rocket (arugula)** scattered over the top.

Gourmet vegetarian

Spread the pizza base with **1 tablespoon tomato pizza sauce**. Top with **$\frac{1}{2}$ small thinly sliced red onion, $\frac{1}{2}$ small sliced red capsicum (bell pepper), 30 g (1 oz) sliced button mushrooms** and **2 quartered artichoke hearts**. Crumble **50 g ($1\frac{3}{4}$ oz) fetta** over the top.

Chicken and pinto bean tacos

Serves 4

Preparation
25 minutes

Cooking
10 minutes

Per serving
*2146 kJ, 513 kcal,
29 g protein, 31 g fat
(7 g saturated fat),
31 g carbohydrate
(8 g sugars), 9 g fibre,
528 mg sodium*

350 g (12 oz) boneless,
skinless chicken breast,
cut into strips

3 cloves garlic, chopped

juice of 1 lime

$\frac{1}{2}$–1 teaspoon Mexican
seasoning mix

pinch of salt

freshly ground black pepper

1 tablespoon extra virgin
olive oil

2 red, green or yellow
capsicums (bell peppers),
thinly sliced

400 g (14 oz) can pinto or
borlotti (cranberry) beans,
rinsed and drained

8 taco shells

1 avocado, diced

100 g (3$\frac{1}{2}$ oz) crisp lettuce
leaves, shredded

3 spring onions (scallions),
thinly sliced

1 tomato, diced

$\frac{1}{4}$ cup (7 g) fresh coriander
(cilantro) leaves

Tabasco sauce, to taste

$\frac{1}{3}$ cup (90 g) fromage frais
or yogurt

1 Preheat the oven to 180°C (350°F/Gas 4).

2 Combine the chicken, garlic, lime juice and Mexican seasoning mix in a bowl. Season with salt and freshly ground black pepper. Mix well.

3 Heat the olive oil in a non-stick frying pan or wok. Cook the chicken mixture, without stirring, for 1 minute. Add the capsicums and stir-fry over high heat for 3–5 minutes, until the chicken is lightly browned. Add the beans and cook, stirring occasionally, until heated through.

4 Meanwhile, arrange the taco shells, open end down, on a baking tray and warm in the oven for 2–3 minutes.

5 Divide the chicken mixture among the taco shells. Add the avocado, lettuce, spring onions, tomato, coriander and Tabasco sauce, to taste. Serve immediately, with the fromage frais or yogurt to be spooned over the top.

Herbs, spices and mixtures such as the Mexican seasoning used in this recipe are a good way of adding flavour to food rather than using lots of salt.

Potato and zucchini tortilla

Tortilla, one of Spain's most famous tapas dishes, is made from the simplest of ingredients – eggs, onions and potatoes – cooked like a flat omelette and served warm or cold, cut into wedges. Extra ingredients can be added, depending on what you have in the fridge.

625 g (1¼ lb) boiling (waxy) potatoes, cut into small cubes

2 tablespoons extra virgin olive oil

1 red onion, finely chopped

1 zucchini (courgette), about 150 g (5 oz), diced

2 slices lean rindless back bacon (bacon strips), chopped

6 eggs

2 tablespoons chopped fresh flat-leaf (Italian) parsley

freshly ground black pepper

1 Add the potato cubes to a saucepan of boiling water. Bring back to a boil, then reduce the heat slightly and cook for 3 minutes. Drain and set aside.

2 Heat the oil in a 25 cm (10 inch) heavy-based, non-stick, ovenproof frying pan over medium heat. Cook the potato cubes, onion, zucchini and bacon, stirring occasionally, for 10 minutes, until the potatoes are tender and lightly golden.

3 Preheat the grill (broiler) to high. Crack the eggs into a bowl and beat in 1 tablespoon water. Add the parsley and season with freshly ground black pepper. Pour the egg mixture over the vegetables in the frying pan and cook for 3-4 minutes, until the egg has set on the base, lifting the edges to allow the uncooked egg to run underneath.

4 When there is just a little uncooked egg on the top, place the pan under the hot grill and cook for a further 2 minutes to set the top. Slide the tortilla out onto a plate or board and allow to cool for 2-3 minutes. Cut into wedges and serve warm, or cool before cutting and serving.

Serves 8

Preparation
15 minutes

Cooking
20 minutes

Per serving
706 kJ, 169 kcal,
9 g protein, 9 g fat
(2 g saturated fat),
11 g carbohydrate
(1 g sugars), 2 g fibre,
214 mg sodium

Zucchini are a good source of vitamin B₆ and niacin. The skins contain the greatest concentration of these vitamins.

Eggs provide inexpensive protein. Although they contain cholesterol, this has only a small effect on blood cholesterol levels.

Lentil and rocket rice paper rolls

These savoury vegetarian rolls are full of flavour and are bound to entice. Lentils supply valuable protein and isoflavones, plant hormones that help support healthy liver function.

Serves 2

Preparation
15 minutes

Cooking
15 minutes

Per serving
1318 kJ, 315 kcal, 27 g protein, 8 g fat (5 g saturated fat), 34 g carbohydrate (5 g sugars), 4 g fibre, 723 mg sodium

50 g (1³⁄₄ oz) red lentils

pinch of salt

³⁄₄ cup (30 g) rocket (arugula)

¹⁄₂ small cucumber, finely diced

5 sprigs fresh dill, chopped

1 cup (250 g) cottage cheese

¹⁄₂ teaspoon dijon mustard

4 sheets rice paper, about 22 cm (9 inches) in diameter

1 Wash and thoroughly drain the lentils. Add the lentils, salt and 1 cup (250 ml) water to a saucepan. Cook for 12-15 minutes, until the lentils are soft.

2 Meanwhile, remove any tough stems from the rocket and finely chop the leaves.

3 Combine the rocket, cucumber, dill, cottage cheese and mustard in a bowl. Rinse the lentils under cold water, then drain and add to the rocket mixture. Taste and season with extra salt if necessary.

4 Pour some warm water into a shallow bowl. Dip a rice paper sheet in the water and remove when softened, after about 1 minute. Spread on a cutting board or damp tea towel (dish towel) and place a quarter of the lentil mixture across the centre. Fold in the uncovered sides of the rice paper and roll up tightly to enclose the filling.

5 Make three more rolls from the remaining rice paper sheets and lentil mixture. Halve the rolls diagonally and arrange on a small platter.

Rice paper sheets (usually from Japan, Thailand or Vietnam) are made from rice flour, water and salt, and are therefore gluten-free.

Nutrients such as iron and zinc that are found in lentils strengthen the immune system and provide protection against free radicals.

Turkey and bean tortillas

Beef and bean tortillas

Brown **300 g (10 oz) minced (ground) beef** and **1 diced onion** in a frying pan. Season with **1 teaspoon chilli powder**, **¹⁄₂ teaspoon dried oregano**, **¹⁄₂ teaspoon ground cumin** and **freshly ground black pepper**. Add **2 diced tomatoes** and **1 tablespoon tomato paste (concentrated purée)**. Cover and simmer for 5 minutes. Rinse and drain a **420 g (15 oz) can red kidney beans** and stir into the beef mixture. Divide the mixture among the tortillas and sprinkle with the grated cheese. Fold the tortillas in half and transfer to a greased ovenproof dish with **2¹⁄₂ tablespoons vegetable stock**. Brush the tortillas with **2 tablespoons oil**, top with **125 g (4 oz) sliced bocconcini (fresh baby mozzarella balls)** and bake as directed.

Turkey and bean tortillas

1/4 cup (60 ml) olive oil

400 g (14 oz) boneless, skinless turkey breast, cut into strips

1 onion, diced

1 red capsicum (bell pepper), finely diced

2 tablespoons tomato paste (concentrated purée)

150 ml (5 fl oz) salt-reduced vegetable stock (page 15)

2/3 cup (140 g) corn kernels

420 g (15 oz) can no added salt red kidney beans, rinsed and drained

1 clove garlic, crushed

1 teaspoon chilli powder

1/2 teaspoon dried oregano

pinch of salt

freshly ground black pepper

12 small flour or corn tortillas, about 10 cm (4 inches) in diameter

80 g (3 oz) bocconcini (fresh baby mozzarella balls), drained and cut into strips

1/2 cup (60 g) grated Swiss-style cheese

1 Preheat the oven to 220°C (425°F/Gas 7).

2 Heat half the olive oil in a frying pan over high heat and cook the turkey, turning occasionally, for 1 minute. Add the onion and capsicum, and cook for 2 minutes.

3 Stir in the tomato paste, then add 100 ml (3 1/2 fl oz) of the stock with the corn and kidney beans. Add the garlic, chilli powder and oregano, and season with salt and freshly ground black pepper. Cover and simmer over low heat for 5 minutes.

4 Grease a large, shallow ovenproof dish. Divide the turkey and bean mixture among the tortillas and spread over one half of each tortilla. Top with the bocconcini strips. Fold the tortillas in half and place in the prepared dish, overlapping them to fit. Carefully pour the remaining stock into the side of the dish.

5 Brush the tortillas with the remaining olive oil and sprinkle with the grated cheese. Bake on the middle rack of the oven for 8 minutes, until the cheese is melted and starting to brown. Serve hot.

Serves 4

Preparation
20 minutes

Cooking
20 minutes

Per serving
2284 kJ, 546 kcal, 39 g protein, 27 g fat (8 g saturated fat), 35 g carbohydrate (6 g sugars), 8 g fibre, 736 mg sodium

Serve the tortillas with some thinly sliced spring onions (scallions), diced capsicum (bell pepper) and sour cream for diners to help themselves.

You can substitute the turkey breast strips with chicken breast strips. Buy ready-cut strips to save time.

Spinach and potato frittata

This chunky frittata makes a lovely vegetarian main course, and can be eaten hot or at room temperature. Serve with toasted ciabatta and sliced tomatoes or a mixed green salad.

Serves 4

Preparation
15 minutes

Cooking
25 minutes

Per serving
1079 kJ, 258 kcal,
15 g protein, 13 g fat
(4 g saturated fat),
19 g carbohydrate
(3 g sugars), 4 g fibre,
343 mg sodium

500 g (1 lb) potatoes, scrubbed and chopped

5 cups (225 g) baby spinach leaves, trimmed of any large stalks

1 tablespoon extra virgin olive oil

1 red capsicum (bell pepper), quartered lengthwise and thinly sliced

5-6 spring onions (scallions), thinly sliced

5 eggs

pinch of salt

freshly ground black pepper

$^1/_4$ cup (25 g) grated parmesan

1 Cook the potatoes in a saucepan of boiling water for 5-6 minutes, until almost tender. Put the spinach leaves in a steamer basket or colander over the potatoes and cook for a further 5 minutes, until the potatoes are tender and the spinach has wilted. Drain the potatoes. Press the spinach with the back of a spoon to extract the moisture, then roughly chop.

2 Heat the oil in a non-stick frying pan that is about 25 cm (10 inches) in diameter. Sauté the capsicum slices over medium heat for 2 minutes. Stir in the potatoes and spring onions, and continue cooking for 2 minutes.

3 Beat the eggs in a large bowl, season with salt and freshly ground black pepper, and mix in the spinach. Using a slotted spoon, scoop about half of the vegetables from the pan into the egg mixture, leaving the oil in the pan. Briefly stir the egg and vegetables to mix, then pour into the pan. Cover and cook, without stirring, for 6 minutes, until the omelette is almost set but still a little soft on top. Meanwhile, preheat the grill (broiler).

4 Sprinkle the parmesan over the top of the frittata and place under the grill. Cook for 3-4 minutes, until browned and puffed around the edges. Cut into wedges and serve.

Frittata is a versatile dish, as you can add almost any ingredient. It's a great way to use left-over roasted meat, chicken or vegetables.

Wrap it up

Tortillas and other flat breads are a versatile base for an endless variety of tasty and healthy fillings and toppings. They make a welcome change from sandwiches for lunchboxes and also make fabulous light meals.

Moroccan wraps

Serves 4   **Time** 20 minutes

½ small cucumber, finely diced

3 ripe tomatoes, finely diced

2 spring onions (scallions), sliced

¼ teaspoon salt

2 tablespoons roughly chopped fresh mint

400 g (14 oz) can chickpeas, rinsed and drained

½ teaspoon ground cumin

1 clove garlic, crushed

2 tablespoons extra virgin olive oil

1 tablespoon lemon juice

1 tablespoon tahini

freshly ground black pepper

4 large soft flour tortillas

Put the cucumber, tomatoes and spring onions in a sieve, sprinkle with the salt and leave to drain for 5 minutes. Transfer to a bowl and mix in the mint.

Roughly mash the chickpeas with a fork. Add the cumin, garlic, oil, lemon juice and tahini, and mash until fairly smooth. Season with freshly ground black pepper.

Spread the chickpea mixture over the tortillas, leaving a small border. Spoon the cucumber mixture down the centre of each tortilla, then roll up to enclose the filling.

Per serving
1285 kJ, 307 kcal, 9 g protein, 17 g fat (3 g saturated fat), 30 g carbohydrate (4 g sugars), 7 g fibre, 562 mg sodium

Californian wraps

Serves 4   **Time** 10 minutes

150 g (5 oz) natural (plain) yogurt

1 tablespoon chopped fresh dill

freshly ground black pepper

4 large soft flour tortillas

200 g (7 oz) firm goat's cheese, thinly sliced

¼ cos (romaine) lettuce, finely shredded

1½ cups (50 g) rocket (arugula)

1 tablespoon sunflower seeds or toasted mixed seeds

Put the yogurt, dill and some freshly ground black pepper in a small bowl and mix well.

Spread about 2 tablespoons of the yogurt mixture over each tortilla. Arrange some of the goat's cheese down the centre of each tortilla. Top with the lettuce and rocket, then scatter with the sunflower seeds or toasted mixed seeds.

Fold in the sides of each tortilla to meet the filling, then roll up and cut in half on the diagonal to serve.

Per serving
1073 kJ, 256 kcal, 13 g protein, 13 g fat (7 g saturated fat), 21 g carbohydrate (4 g sugars), 2 g fibre, 427 mg sodium

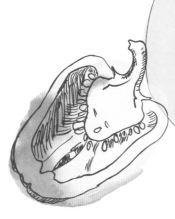

Tortillas are more pliable for folding if warm. The simplest way is to heat one at a time on a plate in the microwave on High for 15 seconds, or cook a stack of four tortillas for 1 minute.

Alternatively, wrap the tortilla stack in foil and warm them in a 180°C (350°F/Gas 4) oven for 10 minutes, or according to the packet instructions.

Tofu and capsicum wraps

Serves 4   **Time** 25 minutes

350 g (12 oz) firm tofu pieces

$\frac{1}{4}$ cup (60 g) sun-dried tomato pesto

1 yellow capsicum (bell pepper), cut into squares

1 green capsicum (bell pepper), cut into squares

4 large soft flour tortillas

250 g (8 oz) tzatziki

Preheat the grill (broiler) to medium-high. Put the tofu in a bowl, add the pesto and toss to coat the tofu.

Thread the tofu and capsicum pieces onto skewers. Cook under the grill, turning several times, for 8-10 minutes, until the capsicums are tender and slightly charred. Remove the tofu and capsicum pieces from the skewers.

Warm the tortillas, then spread them with the tzatziki, leaving a small border. Divide the tofu and capsicum pieces among the tortillas, spooning them onto one half of each. Fold the other half over the filling, then carefully fold again into a fan shape.

Per serving
1372 kJ, 328 kcal, 19 g protein, 18 g fat (4 g saturated fat), 22 g carbohydrate (5 g sugars), 5 g fibre, 460 mg sodium

Tuna and cheese melt flat breads

Serves 4   **Time** 15 minutes

2 x 185 g (6 oz) cans tuna in springwater, drained

$\frac{1}{4}$ cup (60 g) mayonnaise

1 tablespoon lemon juice

2 teaspoons tomato paste (concentrated purée)

1 small red onion, thinly sliced

1 tablespoon French dressing

2 large flat breads or focaccias

6 large slices emmenthal or Swiss cheese, or gruyère

Put the tuna, mayonnaise, lemon juice and tomato paste in a bowl, and mash together.

Put the onion and French dressing in a small bowl and marinate for a few minutes to mellow the flavour.

Warm the flat breads or focaccias under a medium-high grill (broiler) for 1 minute. Spread the tuna mixture over the breads. Scatter with the marinated onion, then divide the cheese slices between them. Cook under a medium-high grill for 3 minutes, until the cheese is lightly browned and bubbling.

Cut each bread into four wedges and serve two to each person.

Per serving
1806 kJ, 431 kcal, 33 g protein, 19 g fat (7 g saturated fat), 32 g carbohydrate (6 g sugars), 2 g fibre, 870 mg sodium

Spicy chicken wraps

Salmon and mustard cream wraps

Combine **100 g (3½ oz) crème fraîche or sour cream** with **1 tablespoon hot mustard** and **2 teaspoons honey,** and season with **freshly ground black pepper.** Heat the tortillas as directed in the main recipe and spread with the mustard cream. Top with **lettuce leaves** and **200 g (7 oz) sliced smoked salmon.** Sprinkle with **finely sliced spring onions (scallions)** and **chopped fresh dill** before rolling up and serving.

Spicy chicken wraps

50 g (1¾ oz) mixed sprouts (e.g. alfalfa, radish, lentils)

1 tablespoon vegetable oil

1 teaspoon sesame oil

400 g (14 oz) boneless, skinless chicken breast, cut into strips

1 thin leek, white part only, cut into thin strips

1½ tablespoons soy sauce

2–3 teaspoons sambal oelek

4 flour tortillas or wraps, about 20 cm (8 inches) in diameter

100 g (3½ oz) peanut butter

1 Rinse the sprouts under cold water and leave to drain.

2 Heat the oils in a frying pan or wok over high heat. Stir-fry the chicken for 5 minutes, then add the leek and cook for a further 3 minutes. Season with the soy sauce and sambal oelek.

3 Meanwhile, warm the tortillas individually in a hot, non-stick frying pan, then place on a cutting board.

4 Spread the tortillas with the peanut butter, leaving a 2 cm (¾ inch) border. Divide the chicken mixture and sprouts among the tortillas.

5 Fold the bottom quarter of each tortilla towards the centre, then fold in the two sides (not too tightly) and serve immediately.

Serves 4

Preparation
15 minutes

Cooking
10 minutes

Per serving
1969 kJ, 470 kcal, 31 g protein, 28 g fat (6 g saturated fat), 23 g carbohydrate (3 g sugars), 2 g fibre, 777 mg sodium

Sambal oelek is a South-East Asian chilli paste. You can substitute some diced fresh red chilli, if you prefer.

You can heat the tortillas in the oven instead of in a frying pan. Heating the tortillas makes them more pliable and less likely to crack.

Puttanesca pizzinis

Serves 6

Preparation
30 minutes, plus
15 minutes rising

Cooking
50 minutes

Per serving
*1949 kJ, 466 kcal,
14 g protein, 19 g fat
(5 g saturated fat),
59 g carbohydrate
(4 g sugars), 6 g fibre,
996 mg sodium*

1 tablespoon extra virgin olive oil

1 red onion, finely chopped

4 cloves garlic, crushed

500 g (1 lb) ripe tomatoes, diced

1 red chilli, seeded and finely chopped

¼ cup (40 g) pitted black and green olives, roughly chopped

2 teaspoons capers, rinsed and squeezed dry

freshly ground black pepper

1½ quantities of pizza dough (page 92)

400 g (14 oz) can artichoke hearts, drained and cut into quarters

100 g (3½ oz) gorgonzola cheese, crumbled

1 Heat the oil in a heavy-based saucepan over low heat and cook the onion and garlic, stirring occasionally, for 10 minutes, until softened. Stir in the tomatoes and chilli, and cook over medium heat, stirring occasionally, for 25 minutes, until very thick.

2 Remove the pan from the heat. Stir in the olives and capers, and season with freshly ground black pepper. Set aside to cool.

3 Turn the risen dough onto a lightly floured surface and knock it back. Knead it very lightly, then divide into six portions. Shape each portion into a ball, then pat or roll into a disc 12.5 cm (5 inches) in diameter. Arrange the discs on two lightly greased baking trays.

4 Spread the topping evenly over the discs of dough, leaving a 5 mm (¼ inch) border. Top with the quartered artichokes, then the crumbled gorgonzola. Leave to rise in a warm place for 15 minutes.

5 Preheat the oven to 230°C (450°F/Gas 8). Bake the pizzinis for 15 minutes, until the crusts are golden and the cheese has melted. Serve hot.

Steak sandwich

Serves 4

Preparation
15 minutes

Cooking
5 minutes

Per serving
*2133 kJ, 509 kcal,
33 g protein, 11 g fat
(4 g saturated fat),
69 g carbohydrate
(5 g sugars), 6 g fibre,
875 mg sodium*

2 thin slices round or minute steak, about 350 g (12 oz) in total

freshly ground black pepper

2 teaspoons extra virgin olive oil

4 small ciabatta or other rolls, about 150 g (5 oz) each

1½ tablespoons tapenade (olive paste)

4 tomatoes, sliced

1½ cups (50 g) rocket (arugula)

juice of ½ lemon

1 Heat a chargrill pan or non-stick frying pan over high heat. Season the steak with freshly ground black pepper. Brush the pan with the oil, then add the steak, in batches if necessary, and cook for 30 seconds on each side for rare, or 1 minute on each side for medium to well-done.

2 Quickly split each roll in half lengthwise. Top the bases with the tapenade and tomatoes. Cut the steak to fit the loaves and place on top of the tomatoes.

3 Toss the rocket with the lemon juice, then pile on top of the steak and drizzle with the pan juices. Top with the remaining bread halves and serve immediately.

Chicken and ham roll

The pride of New Orleans, the muffaletta is a family-sized sandwich made from a big round crusty loaf, filled with generous portions of ham, salami, provolone and pickled garden vegetables. Our version uses chicken breast and lean ham for a meal that is lower in sodium and saturated fat.

Serves 8

Preparation
30 minutes,
plus chilling

Cooking
Nil

Per serving
*1880 kJ, 449 kcal,
33 g protein, 17 g fat
(5 g saturated fat),
37 g carbohydrate
(5 g sugars), 3 g fibre,
894 mg sodium*

1 ciabatta or round crusty loaf, about 20 cm (8 inches) in diameter

1 clove garlic, halved

2 tablespoons olive oil

$^1/_2$ cup (80 g) pimiento-stuffed green olives, chopped

1 celery stalk, quartered lengthwise and thinly sliced

1 red capsicum (bell pepper), finely chopped

2 cooked boneless, skinless chicken breast halves, thinly sliced crosswise

80 g (3 oz) thinly sliced provolone cheese

175 g (6 oz) thinly sliced skinless smoked chicken or turkey

125 g (4 oz) thinly sliced, good-quality lean ham

150 g (5 oz) jar pickled garden vegetables, drained and chopped

1 Slice the loaf in half horizontally. Using your fingers, remove and discard 2.5 cm (1 inch) of bread from the bottom half of the loaf, leaving a 1 cm ($^1/_2$ inch) shell. Rub the garlic clove over the inside of the bottom half of the loaf. Brush the oil over the inside of the loaf.

2 Combine the olives, celery and capsicum in a bowl, then spoon into the bottom of the loaf. Layer the chicken breast, provolone, smoked chicken and ham on top. Spoon the pickled vegetables on top of the meats, then replace the top of the loaf.

3 Wrap the loaf in foil. Place on a large plate and set a heavy weight on top. Refrigerate the loaf overnight, or for at least 6 hours.

4 To serve, unwrap the roll and cut it into eight wedges.

Poach a boneless, skinless chicken breast and allow it to cool before slicing, or slice some left-over roasted chicken for the roll.

Mushroom and thyme toasts

The rich flavour of Swiss brown mushrooms is enhanced by cooking them with garlic, herbs and a dollop of tangy crème fraîche or light sour cream, and they taste wonderful piled on top of toast spread with ricotta.

Serves 4

Preparation
25 minutes

Cooking
5 minutes

Per serving
1491 kJ, 356 kcal, 18 g protein, 13 g fat (6 g saturated fat), 42 g carbohydrate (4 g sugars), 11 g fibre, 689 mg sodium

½ cup (125 g) ricotta

2 celery stalks, chopped

¼ cup (15 g) finely chopped fresh parsley

large pinch of cayenne pepper

500 g (1 lb) Swiss brown or porcini mushrooms

1 clove garlic, crushed

2 tablespoons chopped fresh thyme

2 tablespoons crème fraîche or light sour cream

1 teaspoon lemon juice

pinch of salt

freshly ground black pepper

8 thick slices cut from a small loaf of mixed seed bread, about 400 g (14 oz) in total

1 Put the ricotta, celery, parsley and cayenne pepper in a bowl and mix well. Set aside in a cool place until needed.

2 Preheat the grill (broiler) to high.

3 Leave any small mushrooms whole and halve the larger ones. Put the mushrooms, garlic, thyme, crème fraîche and 1 teaspoon water in a large non-stick frying pan. Cook over low heat, covered, for 3-4 minutes, until the mushrooms are just tender and have released their juices. Stir in the lemon juice and season the mixture with salt and freshly ground black pepper.

4 While the mushrooms are cooking, toast the bread on both sides under the grill. While still warm, spread one side of each toast with the ricotta mixture, then cut it in half.

5 Arrange the toasts on individual plates. Top with the hot mushroom mixture and serve immediately.

Like other cheeses, ricotta is a good source of protein and calcium. Due to its high moisture content, it is lower in fat than many other soft cheeses.

Spicy tuna and corn rolls

Corn is a useful source of dietary fibre, which helps to keep the digestive system healthy and working efficiently. For a light lunch that is satisfying and well balanced, serve these rolls with a mixed tomato and leaf salad.

4 large, rounded, crusty white bread rolls, about 10 cm (4 inches) in diameter

2 tablespoons low-fat sour cream

2 tablespoons low-fat mayonnaise

1 teaspoon hot or medium chilli sauce

2 teaspoons lime juice

200 g (7 oz) can tuna in springwater, drained

200 g (7 oz) can corn kernels, drained

200 g (7 oz) can red kidney beans, rinsed and drained

1/2 green capsicum (bell pepper), diced

2 tablespoons chopped fresh coriander (cilantro)

pinch of salt

freshly ground black pepper

Serves 4

Preparation
20 minutes

Cooking
20 minutes

Per serving
1322 kJ, 316 kcal, 19 g protein, 5 g fat (2 g saturated fat), 49 g carbohydrate (6 g sugars), 5 g fibre, 874 mg sodium

1 Preheat the oven to 180°C (350°F/Gas 4).

2 Slice the tops off the bread rolls and set aside. Scoop out most of the soft interior, leaving a shell about 1 cm (1/2 inch) thick. Make the scooped-out bread into crumbs, either by crumbling with your fingers or using a food processor. Spread 1 cup (80 g) of the breadcrumbs on a baking tray and toast in the oven for 10 minutes, until dry and crisp. Remove from the oven and set aside, leaving the oven on.

3 Combine the sour cream, mayonnaise, chilli sauce and lime juice. Add the tuna, corn, kidney beans, diced capsicum, coriander and dried breadcrumbs. Season with salt and freshly ground black pepper. Mix together, taking care not to break up the chunks of tuna too much.

4 Spoon the tuna and corn mixture into the hollowed-out rolls and replace the lids. Place on the baking tray and loosely cover with foil. Bake for 5 minutes, then remove the foil and bake for a further 5 minutes, until the crust is crisp. The filling should be warm, but not bubbling. Serve immediately.

Green capsicums are a good source of vitamin C. This vitamin aids in the absorption of iron, particularly from non-meat sources such as the red kidney beans included in this sandwich filling.

Falafel pita pockets

Lamb yeeros pitas

Season **400 g (14 oz) lamb fillet strips** with **1 tablespoon lemon juice** and **1 tablespoon yeeros seasoning or sumac**. Heat $1/4$ **cup (60 ml) olive oil** in a frying pan and cook the lamb strips with **1 sliced onion** for 5 minutes, stirring frequently. Season with **freshly ground black pepper**. Quarter **1 large pita (400 g)** and slice open, without cutting all the way through. Fill with some **cos (romaine) lettuce leaves, tomato slices** and the lamb strips. Divide **150 g (5 oz) thick (Greek-style) yogurt** among the pitas and dust with **hot paprika** before serving.

Falafel pita pockets

2 x 400 g (14 oz) cans chickpeas, rinsed and drained

2 spring onions (scallions), thinly sliced

1 egg

1-2 tablespoons dry packaged breadcrumbs

1 teaspoon ground cumin, plus extra, to serve

1 teaspoon harissa paste

pinch of salt

freshly ground black pepper

$1/4$ cup (60 ml) olive oil

6 pitas

1 baby cos (romaine) lettuce, shredded

1 small red onion, halved and thinly sliced

100 g ($3^{1}/_{2}$ oz) red cherry tomatoes, cut into quarters

$3/4$ cup (200 g) thick (Greek-style) yogurt

1 Combine the chickpeas and spring onions in a food processor and blend until smooth, gradually adding the egg, 1 tablespoon breadcrumbs, cumin and harissa paste with salt and freshly ground black pepper.

2 Wet your hands and shape 12 small balls from the chickpea mixture, adding more breadcrumbs if necessary. Flatten the balls a little with the ball of your hand.

3 Heat the oil in a non-stick frying pan and cook the falafels over medium heat for about 8-10 minutes, until golden brown.

4 Toast the pitas and slice them open, then fill with the lettuce, onion, tomatoes and two falafels each. Serve with the yogurt, sprinkled with a little cumin.

Serves 6

Preparation
25 minutes

Cooking
10 minutes

Per serving
1834 kJ, 438 kcal, 15 g protein, 16 g fat (4 g saturated fat), 58 g carbohydrate (5 g sugars), 6 g fibre, 760 mg sodium

You can warm up the pitas in a preheated 200°C (400°F/Gas 6) oven for 5 minutes instead of toasting them individually.

Add 2 tablespoons chopped fresh parsley and 1 tablespoon chopped fresh mint to the pitas with the falafels and salad.

Cheese and watercress soufflé

Serves 4

Preparation
15 minutes

Cooking
40 minutes

Per serving
*1154 kJ, 276 kcal,
20 g protein, 15 g fat
(7 g saturated fat),
15 g carbohydrate
(6 g sugars), 1 g fibre,
442 mg sodium*

butter, for greasing

2 tablespoons grated parmesan

2 tablespoons dry packaged breadcrumbs

¼ cup (30 g) cornflour (cornstarch)

300 ml (10 fl oz) low-fat milk

4 eggs, separated

3 cups (90 g) watercress, trimmed and finely chopped

1 tablespoon wholegrain mustard

⅔ cup (90 g) grated gruyère

pinch of salt

freshly ground black pepper

1 Preheat the oven to 200°C (400°F/Gas 6). Lightly butter a 6 cup (1.5 litre) soufflé dish. Sprinkle half the combined parmesan and breadcrumbs over the bottom and side of the dish, turning and tilting the dish to coat evenly. Set aside.

2 Put the cornflour in a heatproof bowl and whisk in a little of the milk to make a smooth paste. Heat the rest of the milk in a saucepan until almost boiling, then pour the hot milk onto the cornflour mixture, stirring constantly. Return the mixture to the pan and stir over medium heat until the sauce is smooth and thickened.

3 Remove the pan from the heat. Thoroughly beat the egg yolks into the sauce. Stir in the chopped watercress, mustard and gruyère, and season with salt and freshly ground black pepper.

4 Using electric beaters, whisk the eggwhites in a clean, dry bowl until they hold soft peaks. Fold a quarter of the eggwhites into the watercress mixture to loosen it, then gently fold in the rest of the eggwhites.

5 Spoon the mixture into the prepared soufflé dish and sprinkle with the remaining parmesan and breadcrumbs. Bake the soufflé for 30–35 minutes, until well risen and golden brown. Serve immediately.

Smoked turkey baguettes

4 mini baguettes

2 heads witlof (Belgian endive), about 250 g (8 oz) in total

2 handfuls mustard cress

350 g (12 oz) smoked turkey breast slices

1 large yellow capsicum (bell pepper), thinly sliced

2 celery stalks, diagonally sliced

Chive dressing

¼ cup (60 ml) extra virgin olive oil

1 tablespoon lemon juice

1 teaspoon dijon mustard

1 tablespoon snipped fresh chives

pinch of salt

freshly ground black pepper

Serves 4

Preparation
15 minutes

Cooking
Nil

Per serving
2059 kJ, 492 kcal, 35 g protein, 20 g fat (3 g saturated fat), 42 g carbohydrate (5 g sugars), 4 g fibre, 832 mg sodium

If you have time, it's always better to make your own dressing rather than using a bottled one. Not only will it taste better, you can control the amount and type of oil you use. Also, being fresh and flavoured with fresh herbs, mustard, black pepper and so on, the dressing won't need any flavour enhancers or preservatives.

1 Using a bread knife, split the baguettes open along the top. Cut the witlof into diagonal slices about 1 cm (½ inch) thick. Snip the mustard cress using kitchen scissors.

2 To make the chive dressing, whisk the oil, lemon juice, mustard and chives, and season with salt and freshly ground black pepper.

3 To assemble the baguettes, arrange the slices of witlof and mustard cress in the base of each baguette, then add the turkey slices. Arrange the capsicum and celery slices on top of the turkey. Drizzle the dressing over the filling, and serve within 1 hour.

Brilliant burgers

Homemade with healthy ingredients, burgers are ideal for barbecues, quick and easy weekday meals or casual entertaining. They take so little time to prepare and you can dress them up with many different flavour combinations.

Mediterranean burgers

Serves 4   **Time** 30 minutes

250 g (8 oz) lean minced (ground) pork

250 g (8 oz) lean minced (ground) beef

2 cloves garlic, crushed

8 semi-dried (sun-blushed) tomatoes, chopped

2 tablespoons finely chopped pine nuts

2 tablespoons chopped fresh basil

freshly ground black pepper

1 tablespoon vegetable oil

4 hamburger buns

rocket (arugula), to serve

red cherry tomatoes, sliced, to serve

Combine the pork, beef, garlic, semi-dried tomatoes, pine nuts, basil and some freshly ground black pepper in a bowl. Divide the mixture into four portions and shape each into a burger.

Brush the burgers with the oil. Cook on a hot chargrill pan or plate, or under a hot grill (broiler), turning once, for 10–12 minutes, until golden brown.

Serve the burgers in the hamburger buns with the rocket and sliced cherry tomatoes.

Per serving
1891 kJ, 452 kcal, 33 g protein, 21 g fat (5 g saturated fat), 31 g carbohydrate (4 g sugars), 5 g fibre, 436 mg sodium

Blue cheese beef burgers

Serves 4   **Time** 25 minutes

500 g (1 lb) lean minced (ground) beef

1 onion, finely chopped

2 teaspoons dried thyme

2 teaspoons dijon mustard

pinch of salt

freshly ground black pepper

1 tablespoon crumbled roquefort or stilton cheese

1 tablespoon vegetable oil

4 hamburger buns

You can substitute the roquefort or stilton with chopped cheddar, Swiss-style or gouda cheese.

Combine the beef, onion, thyme and mustard in a bowl. Season with salt and freshly ground black pepper, and mix well. Divide the mixture into eight portions, shape each portion into a round and flatten it slightly.

Top four of the beef rounds with the crumbled cheese. Put the remaining beef rounds on top, pressing firmly around the edges to completely seal in the cheese.

Brush the burgers with the oil and cook in a hot frying pan or chargrill pan, or under a hot grill (broiler), turning once, for 10–12 minutes, until golden brown.

Serve the burgers in the hamburger buns.

Per serving
1767 kJ, 422 kcal, 34 g protein, 17 g fat (6 g saturated fat), 31 g carbohydrate (3 g sugars), 4 g fibre, 741 mg sodium

Shape the burger mixture into patties that are an equal size and thickness so they will take the same time to cook. The beef or lamb burgers can be cooked until slightly pink inside, if you like, but the pork must be cooked through.

Always buy good-quality lean minced (ground) meat when making your own burgers at home, to give the best flavour with the least fat.

Pork, sage and onion burgers

Serves 4   **Time** 25 minutes

350 g (12 oz) lean minced (ground) pork

150 g (5 oz) sausage mince (meat)

1 onion, finely chopped

1 tablespoon worcestershire sauce

2 tablespoons chopped fresh sage

pinch of salt

freshly ground black pepper

¼ cup (35 g) plain (all-purpose) flour

1-2 tablespoons vegetable oil

4 hamburger buns

Combine the pork, sausage mince, onion, worcestershire sauce and sage in a bowl. Season with salt and freshly ground black pepper, then mix well. Divide the mixture into four portions and shape each into a burger. Lightly dust the burgers with a little flour.

Heat the oil in a heavy-based frying pan and cook the burgers over medium-high heat, turning once, for 10-12 minutes, until golden brown. Remove from the pan and drain on paper towels.

Serve the burgers in the hamburger buns.

Per serving
2010 kJ, 480 kcal, 30 g protein, 22 g fat (8 g saturated fat), 38 g carbohydrate (4 g sugars), 5 g fibre, 888 mg sodium

Greek lamb burgers

Serves 4   **Time** 25 minutes

500 g (1 lb) lean minced (ground) lamb

⅓ cup (25 g) fresh white breadcrumbs

1 clove garlic, crushed

1 tablespoon chopped fresh oregano, or 1 teaspoon dried oregano

60 g (2 oz) fetta, roughly mashed

freshly ground black pepper

1 tablespoon olive oil

4 large pitas

1 small red onion, sliced into rings

1 cucumber, thickly sliced

low-fat thick (Greek-style) yogurt or tzatziki, to serve

Combine the lamb, breadcrumbs, garlic, oregano and fetta in a bowl. Season with freshly ground black pepper, and mix well. Divide the mixture into four portions and shape each into an oval about 8 x 12 cm (3 x 5 inches).

Brush the burgers with the oil and cook under a hot grill (broiler) or on a barbecue, turning once, for 10-12 minutes, until golden brown.

Serve the burgers in the pitas with the red onion rings, cucumber and yogurt or tzatziki.

Per serving
2373 kJ, 567 kcal, 39 g protein, 18 g fat (7 g saturated fat), 61 g carbohydrate (2 g sugars), 3 g fibre, 837 mg sodium

Smoked salmon bagels

Serves 4

Preparation
15 minutes

Cooking
Nil

Per serving
*1089 kJ, 260 kcal,
17 g protein, 7 g fat
(4 g saturated fat),
32 g carbohydrate
(7 g sugars), 2 g fibre,
898 mg sodium*

150 g (5 oz) light cream cheese

2 tablespoons sour cream

2 teaspoons grated horseradish, from a jar

freshly ground black pepper

4 sesame bagels

1 Lebanese or other small cucumber, thinly sliced

120 g (4 oz) thinly sliced smoked salmon

4 sprigs fresh dill, coarsely chopped

1 Whisk the cream cheese, sour cream and horseradish until creamy. Season with freshly ground black pepper. Halve the bagels and spread each half with the cream cheese mixture.

2 Divide the cucumber slices among the bottom bagel halves. Cut the smoked salmon into pieces and arrange on top of the cucumber.

3 Divide the chopped dill among the bagels. Replace the bagel tops and serve.

Tightly wrap the filled bagels with plastic wrap and refrigerate until serving, for a maximum of 10 hours.

Substitute thinly sliced gravlax for smoked salmon.

Trout is an oily fish with a high content of essential omega-3 fatty acids. These can help to protect the body against strokes and heart disease. Trout also contains high levels of vitamin E, which helps to protect cells from damage by free radicals.

Smoked trout wraps

8 large flour tortillas, about 350 g (12 oz) in total

175 g (6 oz) taramasalata

3 cups (90 g) watercress, trimmed

$\frac{1}{2}$ telegraph (long) cucumber, thinly sliced

4 skinless smoked trout fillets, about 75 g (2$\frac{1}{2}$ oz) each, flaked

1 Preheat the oven to 180°C (350°F/Gas 4). Wrap the stack of tortillas in foil and warm them in the oven for 10 minutes, or according to the packet instructions.

2 Spread a little taramasalata in the centre of each warm tortilla, then top with the watercress, cucumber slices and smoked trout. Tightly roll up to enclose the filling. Cut each rolled tortilla in half on the diagonal and serve immediately.

Serves 8

Preparation
5 minutes

Cooking
10 minutes

Per serving
1078 kJ, 257 kcal, 15 g protein, 10 g fat (3 g saturated fat), 26 g carbohydrate (<1 g sugars), 2 g fibre, 488 mg sodium

Tuna salad baguettes

185 g (6 oz) can tuna
in springwater

4 small vine-ripened
tomatoes

1 orange capsicum (bell
pepper), cut into thin strips

1 small onion, halved
and sliced

6 lettuce leaves, shredded

4 sprigs fresh basil, shredded

6 pitted black olives, sliced

2 baguettes, about 250 g
(8 oz) each

Mustard vinaigrette

$^1/_2$ clove garlic

1 tablespoon white wine
vinegar

1 teaspoon dijon mustard

freshly ground black pepper

$^1/_4$ cup (60 ml) olive oil

1 Drain the tuna and flake it into chunks. Cut each tomato into eight wedges.

2 To make the mustard vinaigrette, rub a salad bowl with the halved garlic clove. Combine the vinegar and mustard with some freshly ground black pepper in the bowl. Whisk in the olive oil until well combined.

3 Add the tuna, tomatoes, capsicum, onion, lettuce, basil and olives to the bowl, and toss with the dressing.

4 Using a sharp bread knife, slice the baguettes in half horizontally. Divide the salad mixture among the bottom halves and replace the top halves. Cut each filled baguette in half and serve.

Serves 4

Preparation
20 minutes

Cooking
Nil

Per serving
*2326 kJ, 556 kcal,
22 g protein, 20 g fat
(3 g saturated fat),
71 g carbohydrate
(9 g sugars), 7 g fibre,
849 mg sodium*

*Add four drained,
chopped anchovies
to the salad for a
stronger flavour.*

*If you have time, set the
filled baguettes aside at
room temperature for
30 minutes to allow the
flavours to mingle.*

Lettuce, herb and tomato smoothie

Enjoy your greens very differently for a change: this smoothie combines delicate lettuce leaves, herbs and fruit to make a refreshing beverage.

Serves 2

Preparation
10 minutes

Cooking
Nil

Per serving
1304 kJ, 311 kcal,
4 g protein, 28 g fat
(6 g saturated fat),
12 g carbohydrate
(11 g sugars), 6 g fibre,
623 mg sodium

½ butter (Boston) or oakleaf lettuce

5 sprigs each fresh parsley, basil and lemon balm

1 apple

1 clove garlic

1 avocado, diced

1 tomato, diced

pinch of chilli powder

½ teaspoon salt

1 Trim and wash the lettuce and spin dry. Tear the leaves into pieces. Wash the herbs, shake off the excess water and pick off the leaves.

2 Wash or peel the apple, then dice, removing the core.

3 Crush the garlic using the flat side of a large knife.

4 Put the lettuce leaves, herbs, avocado, tomato, apple and garlic in a blender. Add 150 ml (5 fl oz) warm water, the chilli powder and salt, and blend well.

5 Divide the smoothie between two glasses and serve immediately. Transfer any leftovers to a sealable jar and store in the refrigerator for up to a day.

Lettuce has a very high water content (90 per cent) and is very low in calories, which makes it an ideal dieting food.

As a rich source of potassium, the tomato in this smoothie can help to regulate blood pressure, which helps reduce the risk of stroke.

Rigatoni with pork and fennel, page 142

Rice, pasta and grains

Rice, pasta and grains are nutritious and convenient – you'll always have one of these staples in the pantry. With them, you can create an amazing range of flavoursome grain-based dishes, which make great comfort food.

Mexican fried rice

Spicy fried rice

Cook the rice as described in step 1 of the main recipe, then set aside to cool. Fry **200 g (7 oz) thinly sliced cabanossi** in **1 tablespoon vegetable oil,** remove from the frying pan and set aside. Fry the **rice, 2 finely diced chillies** and **8 thinly sliced spring onions (scallions)** for 5 minutes in the pan. Add the **red kidney beans, corn kernels** and fried **cabanossi.** Stir in **1/3 cup (80 ml) salt-reduced vegetable stock (page 15)** and **2 tablespoons ajvar (spicy capsicum relish).** Season with some **freshly ground black pepper** and **lime juice,** and serve garnished with **chopped fresh parsley.**

Mexican fried rice

1 cup (200 g) long-grain rice

2 tablespoons olive oil

250 g (8 oz) lean minced (ground) beef

pinch of salt

freshly ground black pepper

1 teaspoon sweet paprika

1 leek, white part only, thinly sliced

420 g (15 oz) can red kidney beans, rinsed and drained

270 g (9 oz) can corn kernels, rinsed and drained

2 tablespoons hot taco sauce or salsa

⅓ cup (80 ml) salt-reduced beef stock (page 14)

fresh coriander (cilantro) leaves, to garnish

1 Combine the rice and 400 ml (14 fl oz) water in a saucepan. Bring to a boil, then reduce the heat, cover and simmer for 10 minutes. Drain and set aside to cool a little.

2 Heat 1 tablespoon of the oil in a large non-stick frying pan. Cook the beef over medium heat for 5–6 minutes, until crumbly. Season the beef with salt, freshly ground black pepper and the paprika. Remove the mixture from the pan and set aside.

3 Heat the remaining 1 tablespoon of oil in the frying pan. Cook the rice and leek, stirring often, for 5 minutes, until the rice has browned.

4 Add the kidney beans, corn and beef to the pan. Cook for 3 minutes, then stir in the taco sauce or salsa and stock.

5 Season the rice with salt and black pepper, and cook for a further 2–3 minutes, until well combined and heated through. Garnish with the coriander leaves and serve.

Serves 4

Preparation
15 minutes

Cooking
30 minutes

Per serving
1900 kJ, 454 kcal, 22 g protein, 15 g fat (3 g saturated fat), 58 g carbohydrate (4 g sugars), 7 g fibre, 634 mg sodium

The quick-cooking long-grain rice in this recipe can be easily replaced with burghul (bulgur), parboiled spelt or wheat.

This Mexican fried rice goes perfectly with some low-fat sour cream, seasoned with sweet or hot paprika, and with grated cheddar.

Lentil risotto

Lentils add flavour and texture to this mushroom risotto, and also make it more nutritious. You could serve the risotto with chargrilled Italian vegetables or a mixed salad.

Serves 4

Preparation
20 minutes

Cooking
45 minutes

Per serving
1842 kJ, 440 kcal, 22 g protein, 11 g fat (4 g saturated fat), 57 g carbohydrate (6 g sugars), 9 g fibre, 893 mg sodium

Lentils are the seeds of a variety of leguminous plants. They are a good source of protein, starchy carbohydrate, dietary fibre and B vitamins.

1 cup (185 g) green lentils

2 cups (500 ml) salt-reduced vegetable stock (page 15)

1 tablespoon extra virgin olive oil

1 onion, finely chopped

1 clove garlic, crushed

3 celery stalks, chopped

1 red capsicum (bell pepper), diced

1 teaspoon ground coriander

1 teaspoon ground cumin

200 g (7 oz) mushrooms, sliced

³/₄ cup (165 g) risotto rice

200 ml (7 fl oz) dry white wine

¹/₄ cup (15 g) coarsely chopped fresh coriander (cilantro), plus extra, to garnish

pinch of salt

freshly ground black pepper

¹/₂ cup (50 g) shaved parmesan

1 Cook the lentils in a saucepan of boiling water for 20 minutes, then drain and set aside. Pour the stock into the pan and bring to simmering point over medium heat. Reduce the heat so the stock is gently simmering.

2 Heat the oil in another large saucepan. Cook the onion, garlic and celery, stirring occasionally, for 5 minutes, until softened. Add the capsicum and the ground coriander and cumin, and cook, stirring, for 1 minute.

3 Stir in the mushrooms, rice and lentils. Pour in the wine and a ladleful of the hot stock. Bring to a gentle boil and cook, stirring frequently, until most of the liquid has been absorbed. Add another ladleful of stock and cook, stirring frequently, until absorbed. Continue adding the remaining stock until it has all been used. The rice should be creamy and tender but still with some bite, and the lentils cooked.

4 Stir in the fresh coriander and season with salt and freshly ground black pepper. Serve hot, sprinkled with the parmesan and extra chopped coriander.

Asparagus risotto with truffle oil

Risotto is a great vehicle for whatever fresh vegetables are in season. A little truffle oil is a luxurious finishing touch for this risotto with fresh asparagus and chives.

2 tablespoons extra virgin olive oil

1 red onion, chopped

3 cloves garlic, chopped

1²⁄₃ cups (360 g) risotto rice

1 cup (250 ml) dry white wine

550 ml (18 fl oz) boiling salt-reduced vegetable stock (page 15)

200 ml (7 fl oz) boiling water

300 g (10 oz) asparagus spears, cut into short lengths

pinch of salt

freshly ground black pepper

1 teaspoon truffle oil

¹⁄₃ cup (35 g) grated parmesan

4 teaspoons butter

2-3 tablespoons snipped fresh chives

1 Heat the olive oil in a heavy-based saucepan. Lightly sauté the onion and garlic for 2-3 minutes, until softened. Add the rice and cook over medium-high heat, stirring, for 1-2 minutes, until the rice is lightly toasted.

2 Pour in the wine and stir until it has been absorbed. Combine the stock with the boiling water. Add a ladleful of the stock mixture and stir until absorbed. Continue adding the stock, allowing each ladleful to be absorbed before adding the next, and stirring frequently.

3 After about 15 minutes, when the rice is almost al dente, stir in the asparagus. Cook for a further 5 minutes, until the asparagus is tender and the rice is completely cooked. Continue adding stock during this time. The finished risotto should have a slightly soupy, almost creamy texture.

4 Remove the pan from the heat. Season the risotto with salt and freshly ground black pepper, then stir in the truffle oil and parmesan. Spoon into warmed serving bowls, top each portion with 1 teaspoon of the butter and a sprinkling of chives, and serve.

Serves 4

Preparation
15 minutes

Cooking
30 minutes

Per serving
2350 kJ, 561 kcal,
13 g protein, 18 g fat
(6 g saturated fat),
76 g carbohydrate
(5 g sugars), 2 g fibre,
895 mg sodium

Asparagus has been cultivated for over 2000 years and has been used medicinally since the 16th century. It is a rich source of many of the B vitamins, folate in particular. A good intake of folate is important during the early stages of pregnancy to prevent birth defects such as spina bifida.

Chicken, almond and brown rice pilaf

Serves 4

Preparation
20 minutes

Cooking
1 hour 5 minutes

Per serving
*2199 kJ, 525 kcal,
32 g protein, 23 g fat
(4 g saturated fat),
48 g carbohydrate
(3 g sugars), 4 g fibre,
467 mg sodium*

1 bay leaf

4–5 black peppercorns

1–2 star anise, crushed
(optional)

2 boneless, skinless chicken
breasts, about 200 g (7 oz)
each

2 tablespoons extra virgin
olive oil

1 small onion, finely chopped

2 cloves garlic, crushed

2 teaspoons ground coriander

2 teaspoons ground cumin

1 cup (210 g) medium-grain
brown rice

2½ cups (625 ml) salt-
reduced chicken stock
(page 14)

½ cup (45 g) flaked almonds,
toasted

2 tablespoons currants

1 cup (30 g) fresh coriander
(cilantro) leaves or flat-leaf
(Italian) parsley

1 Half fill a saucepan with water and add the bay leaf, peppercorns and star anise. Cover and simmer over low heat for 5 minutes. Add the chicken, cover and simmer for 10 minutes, until just cooked. Drain the chicken, cool slightly, then finely shred. Refrigerate until needed.

2 Heat the oil in a frying pan over medium-low heat. Cook the onion and garlic, stirring, for 1–2 minutes. Add the ground coriander, cumin and rice. Cook, stirring, for about 2 minutes, until the grains just begin to colour to a light golden brown.

3 Add the chicken stock and bring to a boil, stirring occasionally. Reduce the heat to low and cook, covered, for 40–45 minutes, until the rice is tender. Remove from the heat and leave to stand, covered, for 5 minutes.

4 Separate and fluff up the rice with a fork or spatula. Stir in the almonds, currants, fresh coriander or parsley and shredded chicken, and serve.

The chicken can be poached and shredded 2–3 hours ahead. This tasty rice dish makes a great lunch for the office or for a picnic.

Shredded chicken, toasted almonds and brown rice, together with anti-oxidant-rich spices, combine to make a simple dish that provides whole grains and complete protein.

Seafood paella

No trip to Spain would be complete without sampling the country's famous rice dish, paella. The ingredients vary from region to region, but we've used fish, squid and mussels for this version.

large pinch of saffron threads

4 cups (1 litre) salt-reduced fish stock (page 15)

400 g (14 oz) squid

12 mussels

2 tablespoons extra virgin olive oil

200 g (7 oz) firm white fish fillets, cut into bite-sized pieces

2 large cloves garlic, crushed

1 large onion, finely chopped

$1/2$ teaspoon paprika, or to taste

2 large red capsicums (bell peppers), chopped

$1^1/_4$ cups (250 g) long-grain rice

1 cup (250 g) chopped canned tomatoes

1 cup (150 g) frozen peas

pinch of salt

freshly ground black pepper

$1/_4$ cup (7 g) finely chopped fresh flat-leaf (Italian) parsley

1 Put the saffron threads in a large, wide, heavy-based pan over medium heat. Cook, stirring, until they begin to release their aroma. Pour in the stock and bring to a boil. Remove from the heat, cover and set aside to infuse.

2 Pull the head, tentacles and insides from the squid. Discard the head and the hard beak from the base of the tentacles. Pull out the clear quill from the bodies. Use your fingers to rub the thin grey skin from the bodies, holding them under running water. Slice the bodies into thin strips and chop the tentacles. Set aside. Scrub the mussels and pull out the hairy beards. Discard any broken mussels, or open ones that don't close when tapped. Rinse well.

3 Heat 1 tablespoon of the oil in a frying pan. Briefly cook the fish until lightly browned all over. Remove and set aside. Add the remaining oil to the pan and cook the garlic, onion and paprika over medium heat, stirring occasionally, for 2 minutes. Stir in the capsicums and cook for 3 minutes, until the vegetables are softened but not brown.

4 Add the rice and stir to coat with the oil. Bring the stock to a simmer and add half of it to the rice. Stir, then bring to a boil. Reduce the heat to low and simmer for 5 minutes. Add the rice mixture to the stock in the large pan.

5 Gently stir in the tomatoes, peas and fish. Arrange the mussels on the top. Simmer for 5 minutes, then very gently stir in the squid and simmer for a further 15 minutes, until the rice is tender and the liquid has been absorbed. Season with salt and freshly ground black pepper.

6 Remove the pan from the heat, cover and stand for 5 minutes. Discard any mussels that have not opened. Serve the paella sprinkled with the parsley.

Serves 4

Preparation
15 minutes

Cooking
45 minutes

Per serving
2331 kJ, 557 kcal, 44 g protein, 12 g fat (2 g saturated fat), 63 g carbohydrate (8 g sugars), 6 g fibre, 743 mg sodium

Spanish chicken rice with capsicum and olives

Serves 4

Preparation
15 minutes

Cooking
25 minutes

Per serving
2217 kJ, 530 kcal,
36 g protein, 18 g fat
(4 g saturated fat),
56 g carbohydrate
(9 g sugars), 3 g fibre,
845 mg sodium

4 boneless, skinless chicken breasts, about 125 g (4 oz) each

2 tablespoons olive oil

1 large onion, chopped

2 red capsicums (bell peppers), diced

1 green capsicum (bell pepper), diced

2 large cloves garlic, crushed

225 g (8 oz) long-grain rice

600 ml (21 fl oz) hot salt-reduced chicken stock (page 14)

410 g (15 oz) can chopped tomatoes

$^1/_2$ cup (60 g) pitted black olives, roughly chopped

1 tablespoon chopped fresh flat-leaf (Italian) parsley

pinch of salt

freshly ground black pepper

1 Cut each piece of chicken lengthwise into three thick strips. Heat the oil in a large frying pan with a lid and cook the chicken over medium heat for 3 minutes, until browned but not cooked through. Transfer the chicken to a plate.

2 Add the onion, capsicums and garlic to the pan. Cook, stirring, for 5 minutes, until slightly softened. Return the chicken and any juices to the pan and sprinkle in the rice. Add the hot stock, then pour in the tomatoes and bring to a boil over high heat. Stir, then reduce the heat, cover and simmer for 15 minutes, until the rice is tender. Stir once to prevent the rice from sticking to the base of the pan.

3 Sprinkle the olives and parsley over the rice. Remove from the heat and season with salt and freshly ground black pepper. Leave to stand, covered, for 1–2 minutes before serving.

Lean chicken is a good source of the amino acid tyrosine, which can help to promote mental alertness. It also contains niacin, the B vitamin that can help to boost energy levels, especially when you eat chicken with starchy foods such as rice.

Easy asparagus and broccoli risotto

Serves 4

Preparation
15 minutes

Cooking
20 minutes

Per serving
*1758 kJ, 420 kcal,
16 g protein, 10 g fat
(4 g saturated fat),
66 g carbohydrate
(1 g sugars), 5 g fibre,
505 mg sodium*

1½ cups (330 g) arborio rice

2 vegetable stock (bouillon) cubes

1 large head of broccoli, about 400 g (14 oz)

12 thin asparagus spears

freshly ground black pepper

½ cup (50 g) grated parmesan or Grana Padano, plus extra, to serve

1 tablespoon extra virgin olive oil

1 Bring 4 cups (1 litre) water to a boil in a large saucepan. Add the rice and crumbled stock cubes, cover and bring to a boil over high heat. Remove the lid and briefly stir, then reduce the heat to medium-low. Put the lid back on, tilted slightly, and cook, stirring occasionally, for 10 minutes.

2 Meanwhile, trim the stalk from the broccoli, then cut the head into small florets. Trim the asparagus spears and cut diagonally into 3 cm (1¼ inch) lengths.

3 Stir the broccoli and asparagus through the rice. Increase the heat to medium and cook, tightly covered, for 4-5 minutes – the rice should be a soft consistency.

4 Remove the risotto from the heat. Season with freshly ground black pepper and stir in the parmesan and olive oil. Cover and leave to stand for 5 minutes before serving, sprinkled with a little extra parmesan.

Use good Italian arborio rice for this recipe. The short, plump, starchy grains hold their shape and absorb flavours well.

You can use blue cheese instead of parmesan. Before serving, stir some hot barbecued chicken through the risotto.

Beluga lentil bolognese

Serves 4

Preparation
20 minutes

Cooking
30 minutes

Per serving
*2572 kJ, 615 kcal,
23 g protein, 12 g fat
(2 g saturated fat),
99 g carbohydrate
(10 g sugars), 7 g fibre,
692 mg sodium*

150 g (5 oz) dried black beluga lentils

1½ cups (375 ml) salt-reduced vegetable stock (page 15)

2 tablespoons olive oil

2 carrots, finely diced

2 celery stalks, finely diced

1 onion, finely diced

1 clove garlic, crushed

pinch of sugar

pinch of salt

freshly ground black pepper

1½ tablespoons tomato paste (concentrated purée)

1 teaspoon dried oregano

1 teaspoon dried thyme

½ cup (125 ml) red wine

410 g (15 oz) can chopped tomatoes

400 g (14 oz) spaghetti, linguine or fettuccine

chopped fresh parsley, to serve

1 Combine the lentils and stock in a saucepan, and bring to a boil. Reduce the heat to medium, cover and simmer, stirring occasionally, for 15 minutes.

2 Heat the oil in a saucepan and sauté the carrots, celery, onion and garlic, stirring often, for 2–3 minutes. Season with the sugar, salt and freshly ground black pepper. Stir in the tomato paste and cook for 1 minute.

3 Stir in the oregano, thyme and red wine, and cook until slightly reduced. Add the chopped tomatoes, lentils and stock. Simmer over medium heat for 10 minutes.

4 Meanwhile, cook the pasta in a large saucepan of boiling water for 10 minutes, or according to the packet instructions, until al dente. Drain and toss with the sauce.

5 Serve the lentil bolognese and pasta garnished with chopped parsley.

Substitute the dried beluga lentils with 260 g (9 oz) drained, canned brown lentils. Stir into the tomato and vegetable mixture, and heat through for about 5 minutes.

Beluga lentil bolognese

Beluga lentil and cheese pasta sauce

Heat **1 tablespoon (20 g) butter** in a saucepan and fry **1 finely diced onion** and **1 crushed clove garlic** until translucent. Stir in **125 g (4 oz) dried black beluga lentils**. Pour in **200 ml (7 fl oz) tomato passata (puréed tomatoes)** and **400 ml (14 fl oz) salt-reduced vegetable stock (page 15)**. Bring to a boil, stirring; cover and simmer over low heat for 20 minutes. Add **100 g (3½ oz) diced gorgonzola cheese** and stir until melted. Season with **freshly ground black pepper** and **freshly grated nutmeg**. Fold in **250 g (8 oz) halved red cherry tomatoes**. Serve with **penne or macaroni**.

Soy mince, pumpkin and bok choy lasagne

This lasagne is most likely different from any other you have tasted, but it is well worth trying: it combines colourful, vitamin-rich vegetables with soy mince (textured soy protein) for valuable protein, lecithin and omega-3 fatty acids. Look for it in health food stores and large supermarkets.

1 pumpkin (winter squash), about 600 g (1¼ lb)

2 tablespoons olive oil

pinch of salt

freshly ground black pepper

300 g (10 oz) bok choy

400 ml (14 fl oz) salt-reduced vegetable stock (page 15)

2 tablespoons (40 g) butter

2 tablespoons plain (all-purpose) flour

⅓ cup (35 g) grated parmesan

ground paprika

freshly grated nutmeg

150 g (5 oz) instant lasagne sheets (no-cook lasagne noodles)

2 tablespoons chopped pepitas (pumpkin seeds)

Tomato sauce

1 tablespoon olive oil

1 clove garlic, crushed

50 g (1¾ oz) soy mince (textured soy protein)

200 g (7 oz) canned diced tomatoes

1 teaspoon fresh thyme

pinch of salt

freshly ground black pepper

1 Preheat the oven to 180°C (350°F/Gas 4). Peel the pumpkin, scoop out the seeds and dice the flesh. Spread the diced pumpkin on a baking tray in a single layer, drizzle with 1 tablespoon of the oil and season with salt and freshly ground black pepper. Bake for about 30 minutes, until the pumpkin is soft and begins to caramelise.

2 Meanwhile, to make the tomato sauce, heat the oil in a saucepan and briefly cook the garlic. Add the soy mince and cook for 2 minutes. Stir in the tomatoes, thyme and ⅓ cup (80 ml) water, and simmer, stirring occasionally, for 20 minutes. Season with salt and freshly ground black pepper. Remove from the heat and set aside.

3 Slice the bok choy into fine strips. Heat the remaining oil in a saucepan. Sauté the bok choy for 2 minutes, then add the stock and simmer for 15 minutes. Strain the bok choy through a sieve, reserving 300 ml (10 fl oz) of the cooking liquid.

4 Melt the butter in a saucepan, stir in the flour and cook for 1 minute. Gradually whisk in the bok choy cooking liquid and bring to a boil over medium heat, stirring. Stir in half the grated parmesan and simmer until the sauce thickens. Season with salt, pepper, paprika and nutmeg.

5 Lightly grease a lasagne dish and spread with a layer of pumpkin, followed by a layer of lasagne sheets, bok choy, tomato sauce and cheese sauce. Repeat the layers, finishing with a layer of lasagne sheets and cheese sauce. Sprinkle with the pepitas and remaining parmesan. Bake for 30 minutes, until golden.

Serves 6-8

Preparation
40 minutes

Cooking
1 hour

Per serving
1485 kJ, 355 kcal, 11 g protein, 21 g fat (7 g saturated fat), 30 g carbohydrate (6 g sugars), 4 g fibre, 636 mg sodium

Rigatoni with pork and fennel

Ridged, tubular rigatoni is the perfect pasta base for a full-bodied sauce made with pork and beef, plus aromatic fresh fennel and its dried seeds. You could also use large conchiglie (pasta shells) or ridged penne.

Serves 4

Preparation
15 minutes

Cooking
25 minutes

Per serving
2781 kJ, 664 kcal, 41 g protein, 18 g fat (4 g saturated fat), 84 g carbohydrate (12 g sugars), 10 g fibre, 564 mg sodium

2 small bulbs fennel, trimmed, quartered lengthwise, green fronds chopped

2 tablespoons olive oil

1 onion, finely chopped

1 clove garlic, crushed

350 g (12 oz) lean minced (ground) pork

150 g (5 oz) lean minced (ground) beef

2 teaspoons fennel seeds

150 g (5 oz) carrots, diced

1 cup (250 ml) salt-reduced vegetable stock (page 15)

400 ml (14 fl oz) no added salt tomato passata (puréed tomatoes)

pinch of salt

freshly ground black pepper

400 g (14 oz) rigatoni

1 Cut out the hard core from the fennel quarters. Thinly slice the fennel.

2 Heat the oil in a large frying pan over medium heat and sauté the onion for 3-5 minutes, until translucent. Add the garlic and sauté briefly. Add the pork and beef, and cook for 5 minutes, breaking up any lumps with a spatula or two forks, until well browned and crumbly.

3 Crush the fennel seeds with a mortar and pestle, then add to the pork mixture, along with the carrots and fennel. Briefly fry to allow the fennel seeds to release their flavour.

4 Pour in the stock and tomato passata, and bring to a boil. Season with salt and freshly ground black pepper, then reduce the heat, cover and simmer for 10 minutes.

5 Meanwhile, cook the rigatoni in a large saucepan of boiling water for 10-12 minutes, or according to the packet instructions, until al dente.

6 Season the pork and fennel sauce to taste. Drain the pasta and combine with the sauce. Top with the chopped fennel fronds and serve.

This nourishing meat sauce would also work well in a pasta bake, topped with some breadcrumbs and grated parmesan.

Top 10 pasta sauces

Pasta meals are always a big hit. While ready-made pasta sauces are convenient, it's quick and easy to cook up luscious versions of your favourite sauces at home – just make our basic tomato or cream sauce and add any variation that takes your fancy.

Super-easy tomato sauce

Serves 4   **Time** 20 minutes

1 tablespoon olive oil

1 onion, finely chopped

2 cloves garlic

2 x 410 g (15 oz) cans chopped tomatoes

pinch of sugar

pinch of salt

freshly ground black pepper

Heat the oil in a saucepan over medium-low heat. Add the onion and cook for 4 minutes, until soft.

Crush the garlic into the pan and cook, stirring, for 1 minute.

Stir in the tomatoes and sugar, and bring to a boil. Reduce the heat to low and simmer for 5 minutes.

Season with salt and freshly ground black pepper, and serve over any type of pasta.

Per serving
367 kJ, 88 kcal, 2 g protein, 5 g fat (<1 g saturated fat), 8 g carbohydrate (8 g sugars), 3 g fibre, 282 mg sodium

Seafood marinara

When the tomato sauce has come to a boil, add **500 g (1 lb) mixed seafood (marinara mix),** or any prepared raw seafood such as prawns (shrimp), scallops, mussels, baby octopus and fish pieces. Simmer for 5 minutes, until the seafood is cooked through. Stir in **1 tablespoon chopped fresh parsley,** season and serve.

Arrabiata

Add 1½ **teaspoons dried red chilli flakes** with the canned tomatoes. Stir in **1 tablespoon chopped fresh parsley,** season and serve.

Puttanesca

Add **4 chopped, canned anchovy fillets** with the garlic; before seasoning, add **2 tablespoons chopped pitted black olives.**

Amatriciana

Add **100 g (3½ oz) chopped bacon or pancetta** with the onion. Serve sprinkled with **finely grated pecorino or parmesan cheese.**

Bolognese

Add **400 g (14 oz) minced (ground) beef** with the onion and cook over medium-high heat, breaking up any lumps with a wooden spoon. Add **2 tablespoons tomato paste (concentrated purée)** with the canned tomatoes, if desired, to help thicken the sauce.

Simple creamy sauce

Serves 6   **Time** 10 minutes

1 tablespoon (20 g) butter

300 ml (10 fl oz) cream

²/₃ cup (70 g) finely grated parmesan

pinch of salt

freshly ground black pepper

Drain hot, cooked pasta into a large colander and set aside.

Combine the butter, cream and parmesan in the hot pasta pot. Stir over medium heat until the cream is hot and the cheese has almost melted.

Add the drained pasta and toss to coat in the sauce. Season with salt and freshly ground black pepper, then serve.

Per serving
1152 kJ, 275 kcal, 5 g protein, 28 g fat (18 g saturated fat), 1 g carbohydrate (1 g sugars), 0 g fibre, 302 mg sodium

Quick tricks to speed things up

✼ To cook pasta quickly, fill an electric kettle with water and bring to a boil. Pour the water into a large saucepan, cover and return to a boil over high heat. Stir a little salt into the water, and add 400 g (14 oz) dried pasta (to serve 4).

✼ Cover and return to a boil again. As soon as the water boils, remove the lid and cook the pasta over high heat according to the packet instructions, or until al dente. While the pasta is cooking, prepare the sauce.

✼ Fresh pasta takes about 3 minutes to cook. In this case, get the water boiling but don't cook the pasta until the sauce is almost ready.

Boscaiola

Before you make the creamy sauce, and while the pasta is cooking, chop **4 slices rindless bacon (bacon strips).** Melt the butter in a frying pan over medium heat and cook the bacon for 4 minutes, until lightly browned. Add **200 g (7 oz) sliced button mushrooms** and cook for a further 2 minutes, until soft. Drain the pasta, then scrape the bacon mixture into the hot pasta pot. Stir in the cream and grated parmesan, add the hot pasta and toss to coat.

Mornay

Add **2 teaspoons finely grated lemon zest** to the cream mixture. Drain a **425 g (15 oz) can tuna in oil,** and flake with a fork. Add to the hot sauce with the pasta, and toss to combine.

Primavera

While the pasta is cooking, cut **175 g (6 oz) asparagus spears** into 4 cm (1½ inch) lengths (cut the spears in half lengthwise if thick). Put the asparagus and **1 cup (150 g) frozen peas** in a heatproof bowl, cover with boiling water and stand for 2 minutes. Meanwhile, drain the pasta and make the creamy sauce. Drain the vegetables and add to the sauce with the pasta.

Herb

Stir **4 tablespoons chopped fresh parsley** and **4 tablespoons snipped fresh chives** into the creamy sauce with the hot pasta. Also try other fresh herbs such as dill and basil.

Carbonara

While the pasta is cooking, chop **4 slices rindless bacon (bacon strips).** Melt the butter in a frying pan over medium heat and cook the bacon for 4 minutes, until lightly browned. Using a fork, whisk the cream and cheese with **3 eggs.** Drain the pasta, then scrape the bacon mixture into the hot pasta pot. Add the hot pasta, then pour in the cream mixture. Toss over medium heat for 2-3 minutes, until the sauce thickens slightly as the egg sets.

Spaghetti vongole

Serves 4

Preparation
10 minutes

Cooking
10 minutes

Per serving
*2627 kJ, 627 kcal,
45 g protein, 13 g fat
(2 g saturated fat),
82 g carbohydrate
(<1 g sugars), <1 g fibre,
141 mg sodium*

400 g (14 oz) spaghetti

1 kg (2 lb) small purged clams (vongole)

2 tablespoons olive oil

2 cloves garlic

2 teaspoons dried red chilli flakes

⅓ cup (10 g) chopped fresh flat-leaf (Italian) parsley

lemon wedges, to serve

Purged clams, with the grit removed from their shells, are available from selected fishmongers, but it's also easy to clean them at home. Simply cover the clams with salted water until ready to use. Drain and rinse under running water, rubbing the clam shells against each other to remove any grit.

1 Cook the spaghetti in a large saucepan of boiling water for 10 minutes, or according to the packet instructions, until al dente.

2 Meanwhile, rinse the clams and set aside. Heat the oil in a large deep frying pan. Crush the garlic into the oil, add the chilli flakes and cook over medium heat for 30 seconds. Add the clams, then cover and cook for 5 minutes. Discard any clams that haven't opened in this time.

3 Drain the spaghetti and add it to the pan with the clams. Sprinkle with the parsley and toss to combine. Serve the spaghetti immediately, with lemon wedges for squeezing.

Pappardelle with chicken and cherry tomatoes

2 tablespoons olive oil

1 red onion, halved and thinly sliced

2 cloves garlic, crushed

500 g (1 lb) boneless, skinless chicken breast, cubed

400 g (14 oz) cherry tomatoes, halved

400 g (14 oz) pappardelle

150 g (5 oz) rocket (arugula)

pinch of salt

freshly ground black pepper

1 Heat the oil in a frying pan with a lid. Gently cook the onion and garlic for 2 minutes. Add the chicken and stir-fry over medium heat until lightly coloured. Slightly reduce the heat and stir in the tomatoes. Cover and simmer, stirring occasionally, for 8-10 minutes, until the tomatoes are very soft and the chicken is cooked through.

2 Meanwhile, cook the pappardelle in a large saucepan of boiling water for 10-12 minutes, or according to the packet instructions, until al dente; drain.

3 Stir the rocket into the sauce and season with salt and freshly ground black pepper. Transfer the pappardelle to a large warmed serving bowl. Spoon over the sauce and gently toss to combine thoroughly. Serve immediately.

Serves 4

Preparation
15 minutes

Cooking
15 minutes

Per serving
2564 kJ, 613 kcal, 40 g protein, 18 g fat (4 g saturated fat), 73 g carbohydrate (4 g sugars), 6 g fibre, 253 mg sodium

Meatballs and spaghetti

This is a great dish to prepare on the weekend, freeze and reheat for a quick midweek dinner. It can be refrigerated for up to three days, or frozen for up to six weeks and thawed in the refrigerator overnight.

500 g (1 lb) minced (ground) veal

500 g (1 lb) minced (ground) pork

2 onions, finely chopped

2 cloves garlic, crushed

zest and juice of 1 lemon

1 tablespoon fennel seeds

1/2 cup (50 g) dry packaged breadcrumbs

1 teaspoon salt

1 tablespoon olive oil

1 teaspoon soft brown sugar

2 x 410 g (15 oz) cans diced tomatoes

1 cup (250 ml) salt-reduced chicken stock (page 14)

1/4 cup (60 g) tomato paste (concentrated purée)

1 tablespoon sweet paprika

400 g (14 oz) spaghetti

freshly ground black pepper

1 handful fresh flat-leaf (Italian) parsley, chopped

1 Put the veal, pork, half of the onion and garlic, lemon zest, fennel seeds, breadcrumbs and salt in a large bowl, and mix well. Take heaped teaspoons of the mixture and roll it into balls. Place the meatballs on a tray lined with baking (parchment) paper. Cover and refrigerate until firm, about 15 minutes.

2 Heat the oil in a large frying pan over medium heat. Cook the remaining onion until softened, then add the remaining garlic and cook for 1 minute, until fragrant. Stir in the sugar. Add the lemon juice, tomatoes, chicken stock, tomato paste and paprika, and bring to a simmer. Cook over medium-low heat for 5 minutes.

3 Drop the meatballs into the tomato mixture and cook for 25-30 minutes, until the meatballs are cooked through and the sauce has thickened. Shake the pan occasionally while the meatballs are cooking.

4 Meanwhile, cook the spaghetti in a large saucepan of boiling water for 10 minutes, or according to the packet instructions, until al dente. Drain well.

5 Season the sauce with freshly ground black pepper. Spoon the meatballs into serving bowls with the spaghetti and sprinkle with the parsley.

Serves 6

Preparation
20 minutes, plus 15 minutes chilling

Cooking
40 minutes

Per serving
2445 kJ, 584 kcal, 47 g protein, 17 g fat (5 g saturated fat), 61 g carbohydrate (8 g sugars), 5 g fibre, 853 mg sodium

For added richness, stir a little pouring cream through the finished tomato sauce before seasoning with salt and black pepper.

Fiery Italian vegetable pasta

Serves 4

Preparation
10 minutes

Cooking
20 minutes

Per serving
*2002 kJ, 478 kcal,
16 g protein, 20 g fat
(5 g saturated fat),
58 g carbohydrate
(6 g sugars), 6 g fibre,
479 mg sodium*

300 g (10 oz) pasta shapes, such as shells, bows, spirals or tubes

¼ cup (60 ml) olive oil

2 celery stalks, diced

1 onion, finely chopped

1 red chilli, finely chopped

2 cloves garlic, finely chopped

600 g (1¼ lb) ripe tomatoes, chopped

6 sun-dried tomato halves, sliced

⅓ cup (40 g) pitted black olives, halved

pinch of salt

freshly ground black pepper

¾ cup (25 g) chopped fresh flat-leaf (Italian) parsley

finely grated zest of 1 lemon

½ cup (50 g) shaved parmesan

1 Add the pasta to a large saucepan of boiling water. Return to a boil and stir once. Reduce the heat and partly cover the pan. Boil for 12 minutes, or according to the packet instructions, until al dente. Drain in a colander.

2 Heat the oil in the saucepan over high heat. Cook the celery, onion, chilli and half the garlic, stirring frequently, for 5 minutes.

3 Stir in the fresh tomatoes, sun-dried tomatoes and olives. Cook the sauce for 3 minutes, then add the pasta and stir to combine and warm through. Season with salt and freshly ground black pepper.

4 Combine the remaining chopped garlic with the parsley and lemon zest.

5 Divide the pasta among four bowls and serve topped with the parsley mixture and shaved parmesan.

Roma (plum) tomatoes are ideal for this recipe because they have firm flesh with fewer seeds than other varieties.

Mixed seafood (marinara mix) usually contains a combination of prawns (shrimp), mussels, calamari or squid, scallops and fish.

Garlic seafood pasta

400 g (14 oz) linguine

2 tablespoons olive oil

3 cloves garlic, crushed

$\frac{1}{3}$ cup (80 ml) dry white wine or vermouth

250 g (8 oz) red cherry tomatoes, cut into quarters

475 g (1 lb) mixed seafood (marinara mix)

$\frac{1}{4}$ cup (60 g) crème fraîche or light sour cream

pinch of salt

freshly ground black pepper

$\frac{3}{4}$ cup (25 g) chopped fresh flat-leaf (Italian) parsley

1 Cook the linguine in a large saucepan of boiling water for 10 minutes, or according to the packet instructions, until al dente.

2 While the pasta is cooking, heat the oil in a frying pan. Add the garlic and stir in the wine or vermouth. Gently simmer for 1 minute, then stir in the tomatoes.

3 Add the seafood and return to a simmer. Cook, stirring occasionally, for 4 minutes, until the fish flakes easily, the prawns (shrimp) have turned pink and the tomatoes have started to soften. Stir in the crème fraîche or sour cream and gently heat through. Season with salt and freshly ground black pepper.

4 Drain the pasta and transfer to a large warmed serving bowl. Spoon the sauce over the pasta. Add the parsley and gently toss to combine. Serve immediately.

Serves 4

Preparation
15 minutes

Cooking
10 minutes

Per serving
2619 kJ, 626 kcal, 35 g protein, 19 g fat (7 g saturated fat), 76 g carbohydrate (3 g sugars), 5 g fibre, 892 mg sodium

Pearl barley pilaf with green vegetables

A member of the grain family, pearl barley contains many nutrients, including B vitamins and folate, which help to produce healthy red blood cells. Pearl barley also contains some soluble dietary fibre that is effective in lowering cholesterol.

Serves 4

Preparation
10 minutes

Cooking
30 minutes

Per serving
*1969 kJ, 470 kcal,
10 g protein, 24 g fat
(3 g saturated fat),
53 g carbohydrate
(12 g sugars), 13 g fibre,
217 mg sodium*

1 cup (220 g) pearl barley

1 bay leaf

600 ml (21 fl oz) boiling water

¼ cup (60 ml) olive oil

300 g (10 oz) leeks, white part only, thinly sliced

3 stalks celery, thinly sliced

pinch of salt

freshly ground black pepper

250 g (8 oz) English spinach leaves

1 clove garlic, crushed

⅓ cup (50 g) pine nuts

¾ cup (70 g) dried blueberries

1 Place the barley and bay leaf in a large saucepan. Pour in the boiling water and bring to a boil. Stir once, reduce the heat, partially cover the pan and cook for 25 minutes, until the water has been absorbed and the barley is tender.

2 While the barley is cooking, heat 2 tablespoons of the olive oil in a frying pan over high heat. Cook the leeks and celery, stirring often, for 5 minutes, until the vegetables are tender. Stir the vegetables into the cooked barley and season with salt and freshly ground black pepper. Cover the pan and keep warm.

3 Pour the remaining oil into the pan. Add the spinach and cook over medium heat for 3 minutes, until wilted. Add the garlic, pine nuts and blueberries, and cook for 1 minute.

4 Discard the bay leaf and divide the barley among four serving plates. Serve topped with the spinach, blueberries and pine nuts.

You can also use a mixture of brown rice and pearl barley. Try raisins or currants instead of blueberries, and sunflower seeds instead of pine nuts.

The way raw garlic is prepared – crushed, sliced or chopped – influences the flavour of the finished dish. Crushed garlic gives the most intense result.

Chicken and sausage jambalaya

A typical Cajun recipe, this dish is full of spicy, complex flavours. With lots of rice and vegetables, it is a great way to make a small amount of meat go a long way, and offers a healthy balance of protein and carbohydrate.

Serves 6

Preparation
20 minutes

Cooking
35 minutes

Per serving
1910 kJ, 456 kcal,
23 g protein, 13 g fat
(3 g saturated fat),
60 g carbohydrate
(6 g sugars), 2 g fibre,
898 mg sodium

Even when used in moderation, sunflower oil provides good amounts of vitamin E, an anti-oxidant that protects cell membranes from damage by free radicals. Other good sources of vitamin E include sunflower seeds and other oils that are derived from vegetables and nuts.

300 g (10 oz) boneless, skinless chicken breast, cut into cubes

2 teaspoons Cajun seasoning

1 teaspoon dried sage or marjoram

2 tablespoons sunflower or vegetable oil

1 onion, sliced

1 green capsicum (bell pepper), sliced

2 stalks celery, sliced

2 cloves garlic, crushed

2 cups (400 g) long-grain rice

700 ml (24 fl oz) salt-reduced chicken stock (page 14)

100 g (3½ oz) cooked smoked ham, cut into cubes

100 g (3½ oz) chorizo or other spicy sausage, sliced

410 g (15 oz) can Italian cherry tomatoes or chopped tomatoes

Tabasco sauce, to taste

pinch of salt

freshly ground black pepper

4-6 spring onions (scallions), sliced, to serve

chopped fresh parsley, to serve

1 Sprinkle the chicken with the Cajun seasoning and the sage or marjoram, making sure the chicken is coated all over. Heat 1 tablespoon of the oil in a large flameproof casserole dish or pan over medium-high heat. Cook the chicken, stirring frequently, for 5 minutes, until browned all over. Remove from the pan with a slotted spoon.

2 Add the remaining oil to the pan along with the onion, capsicum and celery, and cook, stirring, for 2 minutes. Add the garlic and rice, and cook, stirring, for 1 minute.

3 Pour in the stock and 300 ml (10 fl oz) water, and stir well. Return the chicken to the pan and bring to a boil, then reduce the heat, cover and simmer for 15 minutes. Add the ham, chorizo or sausage and canned tomatoes with their juice. Cook, covered, for 5-10 minutes, until the rice has absorbed all the liquid.

4 Season to taste with the Tabasco sauce, salt and freshly ground black pepper. Serve hot, sprinkled with the spring onions and parsley.

Lamb, mint and eggplant couscous

The lamb in this Middle Eastern-style dish supplies B vitamins for the nerves, iron for the blood, zinc for wound healing and the immune system, and copper for blood cell production.

1 Lebanese eggplant (aubergine), thinly sliced

pinch of herb salt

²⁄₃ cup (125 g) couscous

150 ml (5 fl oz) hot salt-reduced vegetable stock (page 15)

¹⁄₃ cup (40 g) raisins

2 teaspoons chopped, toasted hazelnuts

1 tablespoon chopped pistachios

¹⁄₄ cup (15 g) finely chopped fresh mint, plus extra leaves, to garnish

¹⁄₂ teaspoon ras el hanout (Moroccan spice mix)

freshly ground black pepper

150 g (5 oz) natural (plain) yogurt

1 tablespoon lemon juice

1¹⁄₂ tablespoons olive oil

1 lamb loin fillet, about 250 g (8 oz), thinly sliced

Serves 2

Preparation
20 minutes, plus standing

Cooking
15 minutes

Per serving
3008 kJ, 719 kcal, 42 g protein, 30 g fat (8 g saturated fat), 70 g carbohydrate (21 g sugars), 3 g fibre, 777 mg sodium

1 Lay the eggplant slices in a single layer on paper towel. Sprinkle with herb salt and set aside for about 20 minutes.

2 Cook the couscous in the stock according to the packet instructions. Fold the raisins, nuts and 2 tablespoons of the mint into the couscous. Add the ras el hanout and season with freshly ground black pepper. Cover and keep warm.

3 Combine the yogurt, lemon juice and the remaining chopped mint. Season with freshly ground black pepper.

4 Heat 1 tablespoon of the oil in a frying pan. Pat the eggplant slices dry and cook in the hot oil until tender. Season the lamb with herb salt and freshly ground black pepper. Heat the remaining oil in the pan and cook the lamb for 3–5 minutes, until just cooked through.

5 Combine the couscous, eggplant and lamb in a bowl. Garnish with mint leaves and serve with the yogurt.

Lebanese or lady finger eggplant are small and cylindrical in shape. Larger eggplant can be substituted.

Quinoa with summer vegetables

Pronounced 'keen-wah', quinoa is a whole grain with a low glycaemic index (GI). It is also a source of magnesium, needed for healthy bones, muscle and nerve functions, and high in protein – good news for vegetarians.

1 cup (200 g) quinoa

400 ml (14 fl oz) hot salt-reduced chicken stock (page 14)

1⅓ cups (200 g) baby broad (fava) beans, thawed if frozen

2 tablespoons olive oil

4 spring onions (scallions), thinly sliced

400 g (14 oz) red cherry tomatoes, halved

6 sprigs fresh basil, shredded

pinch of salt

freshly ground black pepper

60 g (2 oz) gouda cheese, grated or pared

1 Put the quinoa in a large saucepan and pour in the hot stock. Cover the pan and bring to a boil, then reduce the heat to medium and simmer for 10 minutes. Add the baby broad beans, cover and return to a boil, then reduce the heat and simmer for a further 5 minutes.

2 Increase the heat and boil the mixture, uncovered, for 1 minute to evaporate any excess stock. If any remains in the pan after this time, drain the quinoa through a fine-meshed sieve.

3 Pour the oil into a serving bowl and add the spring onions, tomatoes and basil. Add the cooked quinoa and broad beans to the bowl and stir to combine. Season with salt and freshly ground black pepper, divide among four bowls and top with the gouda cheese.

Serves 4

Preparation
15 minutes

Cooking
20 minutes

Per serving
1578 kJ, 377 kcal, 17 g protein, 17 g fat (8 g saturated fat), 37 g carbohydrate (4 g sugars), 9 g fibre, 531 mg sodium

Quinoa is cooked when the grains burst open and the germ (inside the grain) has formed into an opaque curl. Quinoa is gluten-free and therefore suitable for coeliacs.

Baby broad beans can be eaten in their skins, but you may prefer to pop them out to reveal the delicate bright green legumes inside.

Minted barley and beans

Barley is believed to be the world's oldest cultivated grain. It is low in fat and rich in starchy carbohydrate, and, like other cereals, it is a good source of B vitamins.

Serves 4

Preparation
20 minutes

Cooking
45 minutes

Per serving
*1664 kJ, 397 kcal,
14 g protein, 14 g fat
(2 g saturated fat),
56 g carbohydrate
(13 g sugars), 15 g fibre,
835 mg sodium*

3 cups (750 ml) salt-reduced vegetable stock (page 15)

1 strip lemon zest

1 bay leaf

250 g (8 oz) baby leeks, trimmed

1 teaspoon sunflower or vegetable oil

1 cup (220 g) pearl barley

400 g (14 oz) can salt-reduced black-eyed peas, rinsed and drained

6 firm, ripe roma (plum) tomatoes, cut into thin wedges

3 cups (140 g) baby spinach leaves, shredded

85 g (3 oz) spring onions (scallions), halved lengthwise and shredded

Dressing

2 sun-dried tomatoes in oil, drained and finely chopped

2 tablespoons oil from the sun-dried tomatoes

1 tablespoon red wine vinegar

1 clove garlic, crushed

2 tablespoons chopped fresh mint

1 tablespoon chopped fresh chervil

freshly ground black pepper

1 Put the stock and 3 cups (750 ml) water in a saucepan with the lemon zest and bay leaf. Bring to a rapid boil, then add the leeks and cook for 2–3 minutes, until just tender. Remove with a slotted spoon and briefly refresh in cold water. Cut the leeks on the diagonal into 2.5 cm (1 inch) lengths. Set aside.

2 Add the sunflower oil to the stock in the pan and bring back to a boil. Add the barley, then cover and simmer for 30–40 minutes, until tender.

3 Spoon out 2 tablespoons of the stock and reserve, then drain the barley. Discard the lemon zest and bay leaf. Tip the barley into a bowl and leave to cool.

4 Add the leeks, black-eyed peas, tomatoes, spinach and spring onions to the barley and gently combine.

5 To make the dressing, combine the sun-dried tomatoes, oil, vinegar, garlic, mint, chervil, 2 tablespoons reserved stock, and some freshly ground black pepper in a screw-top jar. Shake until well blended.

6 Drizzle the dressing over the barley and vegetables, and toss until well coated. Serve at room temperature.

Lamb and ginger stir-fry, page 172

Stir-fries and pan-fries

When you want fast food that is tasty and healthy, get out the wok or deep-sided frying pan. Quick cooking retains many of the ingredients' nutritional benefits, while aromatics, sauces and spices add great flavour.

Veal escalopes with sage and lemon

1 tablespoon olive oil

$1/2$ small onion, chopped

1 zucchini (courgette), diced

1 clove garlic, crushed

250 g (8 oz) red cherry tomatoes, halved

2 cups (90 g) baby spinach leaves

pinch of salt

freshly ground black pepper

2 veal escalopes, about 150 g (5 oz) each, cut in half

4 large fresh sage leaves, shredded

2 tablespoons lemon juice

crusty bread, to serve

1 Heat half the oil in a non-stick frying pan over medium heat. Sauté the onion for 3-4 minutes, until soft. Add the zucchini and garlic. Cook, stirring often, for 3-4 minutes, until the vegetables are tender.

2 Add the tomatoes and spinach. Cook, stirring often, for 5 minutes, until the tomatoes have softened slightly and the spinach has wilted. Season with salt and freshly ground black pepper, then transfer to serving plates and set aside in a warm place.

3 Wipe out the pan and heat the remaining oil over high heat. Cook the veal for 1 minute on each side, until browned and cooked through. Transfer to the serving plates with the vegetables.

4 Reduce the heat to medium and add the sage to the pan. Cook, stirring, for 30 seconds, then stir the lemon juice into the pan juices. Pour the juices over the veal and serve with crusty bread.

Serves 2

Preparation
10 minutes

Cooking
20 minutes

Per serving
1177 kJ, 281 kcal, 37 g protein, 12 g fat (2 g saturated fat), 6 g carbohydrate (5 g sugars), 4 g fibre, 404 mg sodium

If your veal escalopes are thicker than 5 mm ($1/4$ inch), or they are of an uneven thickness, beat them with a meat mallet or rolling pin to make them thinner.

Nick the edges of the veal escalopes with a sharp knife to prevent them from curling during cooking.

Veal steaks with creamy grape sauce

Serves 4

Preparation
10 minutes

Cooking
20 minutes

Per serving
1554 kJ, 371 kcal,
38 g protein, 13 g fat
(3 g saturated fat),
25 g carbohydrate
(19 g sugars), <1 g fibre,
207 mg sodium

2 tablespoons plain (all-purpose) flour

4 veal leg steaks, about 125 g (4 oz) each

2 tablespoons olive oil

1 clove garlic, crushed

375 ml (13 fl oz) can light evaporated milk

1 tablespoon cornflour (cornstarch)

⅓ cup (80 ml) salt-reduced chicken stock (page 14)

1 cup (180 g) purple or red grapes, halved

1 tablespoon snipped fresh chives, plus extra, to serve

freshly ground black pepper

mixed salad leaves, to serve

1 Put the flour on a plate. Dip the veal steaks in the flour to coat on both sides, shaking off the excess.

2 Heat the oil in a large frying pan over medium-high heat. Add two of the veal steaks and cook for 2 minutes on each side, until golden and just cooked through. Transfer to a warmed plate and keep warm. Cook the remaining veal steaks, transfer to the plate and set aside.

3 Reduce the heat to medium and return the pan to the heat. Cook the garlic, stirring constantly, for 10 seconds, until just starting to colour. Combine the evaporated milk, cornflour and stock in a small bowl, then add to the pan and stir. Reduce the heat to low and simmer, stirring occasionally, for 3-4 minutes, until slightly thickened.

4 Stir in the grapes, then return the veal steaks to the pan. Turn the steaks to coat with the sauce and cook for 1-2 minutes, until the steaks and grapes are heated through. Stir in the chives.

5 Place the steaks on warmed serving plates with a spoonful of the grape sauce. Serve sprinkled with chives and some freshly ground black pepper, accompanied by some mixed salad leaves.

Prepare this dish just before serving so that the grapes retain their texture. Use seedless purple or red grapes.

Grape and chicken salad

Toss ½ cup (90 g) red grapes, 2 chopped red apples and ¼ cup (25 g) walnut halves in a dressing of extra virgin olive oil, lemon juice and 1 teaspoon wholegrain mustard. Shred 2 grilled (broiled) boneless, skinless chicken breasts and toss with the salad, then served piled on top of mixed leaves.

Veal steaks with creamy grape sauce

Pan-fried haloumi

For a vegetarian version, serve the sauce with grilled (broiled) slices of **haloumi cheese** instead of the steak. Serve 2 slices haloumi per person; brush with **olive oil** before cooking under a hot grill (broiler) or in a chargrill pan until golden.

Pan-fried steaks with Italian sauce

Pan-fried steaks with Italian sauce

4 thin rump (round) or sirloin steaks, about 125 g (4 oz) each, trimmed of fat

2 tablespoons olive oil

freshly ground black pepper

1 onion, finely chopped

2 cloves garlic, crushed

410 g (15 oz) can chopped tomatoes

100 ml (3½ fl oz) dry white or red wine

300 g (10 oz) tagliatelle

1 tablespoon capers, rinsed and squeezed dry

12 pitted green or black olives, halved

2 tablespoons chopped fresh basil, plus extra leaves, to garnish

freshly ground black pepper

1 Rub the steaks on both sides with 1 tablespoon of the olive oil and a little freshly ground black pepper. Heat a large frying pan and cook the steaks, in batches if needed, for 2½ minutes on each side for rare, 4 minutes each side for medium, or 7 minutes each side for well-done. Transfer to a plate using a slotted spoon and keep warm.

2 Heat the remaining oil in the pan and cook the onion and garlic over low heat for 5 minutes, until softened. Stir in the tomatoes and wine. Gently cook for 5-10 minutes, stirring occasionally to break down the tomatoes.

3 While the sauce is cooking, cook the pasta in a large saucepan of boiling water for 8 minutes, or according to the packet instructions, until al dente; drain.

4 Stir the capers, olives and chopped basil into the sauce, and season with freshly ground black pepper. Return the steaks to the frying pan to heat through, spooning the sauce over the meat.

5 Divide the pasta among four plates and garnish with basil leaves. Serve with the steak and sauce over the top.

Serves 4

Preparation
15 minutes

Cooking
30 minutes

Per serving
2485 kJ, 594 kcal, 41 g protein, 20 g fat (6 g saturated fat), 57 g carbohydrate (5 g sugars), 4 g fibre, 308 mg sodium

The sauce goes well with barbecued pork or lamb steaks and chops, and with barbecued fish, so it's worth preparing a double batch and freezing half.

Cool the sauce quickly after cooking, pack into a freezer container and freeze for up to 1 month. To use, thaw, reheat and simmer for 3 minutes.

Pan-fried lamb with green beans

Freshly made croutons add crunch and a garlicky kick to tender morsels of lamb. Choose summer savory, an annual herb with a delicate flavour, over perennial winter savory, which tends to be slightly bitter. Alternatively, readily available thyme is a good substitute.

Serves 4

Preparation
20 minutes

Cooking
15 minutes

Per serving
2246 kJ, 536 kcal,
33 g protein, 28 g fat
(5 g saturated fat),
39 g carbohydrate
(5 g sugars), 7 g fibre,
587 mg sodium

350 g (12 oz) green beans, halved diagonally

2 sprigs fresh savory or thyme

450 g (1 lb) lamb fillet

⅓ cup (80 ml) olive oil

1 baguette, about 250 g (8 oz), cut into cubes

2 cloves garlic, crushed

pinch of salt

freshly ground black pepper

300 g (10 oz) red cherry tomatoes or small vine tomatoes, halved

1 tablespoon chopped fresh rosemary

1 Add the green beans and savory or thyme to a large saucepan of boiling water. Cook for 3–5 minutes, until just tender. Drain and rinse with cold water, then drain again.

2 While the beans are cooking, pat the lamb fillet dry with paper towels. Slice on the diagonal into bite-sized pieces.

3 Heat 2 tablespoons of the olive oil in a large non-stick frying pan. Toast the bread cubes, turning frequently, for 5 minutes, until golden brown. Add the garlic and briefly fry. Remove the garlic croutons from the pan and drain on paper towels.

4 Heat the remaining oil in the pan over high heat and sear the lamb for 2 minutes, stirring so that it browns all over. Season with salt and freshly ground black pepper.

5 Add the green beans, tomatoes, rosemary and garlic croutons to the pan and fry with the meat for 2–3 minutes, until the lamb is cooked through. Adjust the seasonings and serve on warmed plates.

4 ways with fried rice

Cook up a batch of fried rice at home and enjoy it fresh and sizzling hot, without the added fat and salt you will find in restaurant dishes.

Creole fried rice

Serves 4   **Time** 25 minutes

2 tablespoons vegetable oil

125 g (4 oz) diced chorizo sausage

3 cloves garlic, crushed

1 green capsicum (bell pepper), diced

6 spring onions (scallions), sliced

3 cups (450 g) shredded cooked chicken

3 cups (550 g) cooked white rice

¼ teaspoon salt

2 teaspoons ground turmeric

2 teaspoons Tabasco sauce

3 tablespoons chopped fresh parsley

Heat the oil over medium-high heat in a wok or large non-stick frying pan. Fry the chorizo for 5 minutes, until slightly crisp. Add the garlic and stir-fry for 30 seconds. Add the capsicum and spring onions, and stir-fry for 5 minutes, until tender but still crisp.

Stir in the chicken and rice until well combined. Add the salt, turmeric and Tabasco sauce, and stir-fry for 7 minutes, until the rice is piping hot and slightly crusty.

Stir in the parsley and serve hot.

Per serving
2333 kJ, 557 kcal, 39 g protein, 25 g fat (7 g saturated fat), 43 g carbohydrate (2 g sugars), 2 g fibre, 637 mg sodium

Fried rice with chicken

Serves 4   **Time** 25 minutes

2 large eggs

½ small red capsicum (bell pepper), diced

¼ cup (60 ml) salt-reduced soy sauce

1½ teaspoons sugar

2 teaspoons sesame oil

2 tablespoons vegetable oil

2 tablespoons grated fresh ginger

2 cloves garlic, crushed

500 g (1 lb) asparagus spears, sliced

6 spring onions (scallions), sliced

3 cups (450 g) shredded cooked chicken

3 cups (550 g) cooked white rice

¼ cup (60 ml) rice vinegar

1½ cups (230 g) peas

In a small bowl, whisk the eggs, capsicum, 1 tablespoon of the soy sauce and ½ teaspoon of the sugar. Heat the sesame oil in a small frying pan over medium-high heat. Add the egg mixture and cook, without stirring, until set. Remove and cut into strips.

Heat the vegetable oil in a wok or large non-stick frying pan over medium-high heat. Cook the ginger and garlic for 30 seconds. Add the asparagus and spring onions, and stir-fry for 3 minutes. Stir in the chicken and rice.

In a small bowl, whisk together the vinegar and remaining soy sauce and sugar. Pour over the rice and stir-fry for 7 minutes, until the rice is piping hot and slightly crusty.

Stir in the peas and egg strips, and cook for 1 minute, until the peas are heated through. Serve hot.

Per serving
2575 kJ, 615 kcal, 47 g protein, 24 g fat (5 g saturated fat), 49 g carbohydrate (7 g sugars), 6 g fibre, 702 mg sodium

Pork nasi goreng

Serves 6   **Time** 30 minutes

5 cups (1.25 litres) salt-reduced chicken stock (page 14)

2½ cups (500 g) long-grain white rice

2 tablespoons vegetable oil

1 onion, finely chopped

2 cloves garlic, crushed

3 carrots, finely diced

2 lean boneless pork leg steaks, about 350 g (12 oz) in total, trimmed and diced

150 g (5 oz) button mushrooms, sliced

1 teaspoon mild chilli powder

½ teaspoon ground turmeric

1 cup (150 g) frozen peas

¼ cup (60 g) no added salt tomato sauce (ketchup)

1½ tablespoons light soy sauce

4 spring onions (scallions), shredded

100 g (3½ oz) peeled cooked prawns (shrimp)

Omelette

1 large egg

½ teaspoon soy sauce

1 teaspoon vegetable oil

Bring the stock to a boil in a large saucepan, add the rice and cook for 10–12 minutes, until the rice is just tender and most of the stock has been absorbed. Remove from the heat, cover and set aside.

Heat a wok or large heavy-based frying pan until hot, add the oil and swirl to coat the wok. Add the onion, garlic and carrots, and stir-fry for 5 minutes, until the onion has softened.

Toss the pork into the wok and stir-fry for 3 minutes, then add the mushrooms and cook for 2 minutes. Add the chilli powder and turmeric. Cook, stirring, for 1–2 minutes, then add the peas, tomato sauce and soy sauce.

Gradually add the cooked rice to the wok, tossing to mix, and stir-fry until the ingredients are well blended and heated through. Toss in the spring onions and then the prawns. Remove from the heat and keep hot.

To make the omelette, beat the egg in a small bowl with the soy sauce and 1 tablespoon water. Heat the oil in a small non-stick frying pan, pour in the egg mixture and cook until just set. Roll up and cut into strips.

Spoon the pork and rice mixture into a warm serving dish, top with the omelette strips and serve hot.

Per serving
2184 kJ, 522 kcal, 30 g protein, 10 g fat (2 g saturated fat), 76 g carbohydrate (8 g sugars), 4 g fibre, 886 mg sodium

Indonesian fried rice with egg and vegetables

Serves 4   **Time** 30 minutes

1 cup (200 g) brown rice

600 ml (21 fl oz) hot salt-reduced vegetable stock (page 15)

¼ cup (60 ml) olive oil

2 onions, sliced

1 teaspoon sesame oil

3 cloves garlic, crushed

2 small carrots, thinly diagonally sliced

225 g (8 oz) can water chestnuts, rinsed and drained, sliced

225 g (8 oz) can sliced bamboo shoots, rinsed and drained

100 g (3½ oz) frozen green beans, thawed

2 teaspoons medium curry powder

100 g (3½ oz) bean sprouts, trimmed

pinch of salt

freshly ground black pepper

3 eggs

1 spring onion (scallion), sliced

¼ cup (15 g) chopped fresh coriander (cilantro)

Place the rice in a large saucepan with the hot stock. Cover, bring to a boil and stir once. Reduce the heat to a simmer and cook for 25 minutes, or according to the packet instructions, until the rice is tender and all the stock has been absorbed.

Halfway through cooking the rice, heat 1 tablespoon of the olive oil in a frying pan over high heat. Add the onions and reduce the heat to medium, then cook for 7 minutes, until browned. Set the onions aside and keep warm.

When the rice is almost cooked, heat 1 tablespoon of the olive oil in the frying pan. Add the sesame oil, garlic, carrots, water chestnuts, bamboo shoots, beans and curry powder. Stir-fry for 2 minutes, until the vegetables are tender. Add the bean sprouts and stir-fry for 1 minute. Mix the vegetables into the rice and season with salt and freshly ground black pepper.

Beat the eggs, spring onion and coriander together. Heat the remaining oil in the frying pan over high heat. Pour in the egg mixture and cook for 1 minute on each side, until set. Cut into thin strips.

Divide the rice among four bowls and top with the fried onions and omelette strips.

Per serving
1862 kJ, 445 kcal, 14 g protein, 21 g fat (4 g saturated fat), 50 g carbohydrate (9 g sugars), 7 g fibre, 619 mg sodium

Lamb and ginger stir-fry

2 teaspoons vegetable oil

200 g (7 oz) lamb backstraps or loin fillets, thinly sliced

1 clove garlic, crushed

1 teaspoon finely grated fresh ginger

1 small red capsicum (bell pepper), thinly sliced

4 spring onions (scallions), diagonally sliced

10 snow peas (mangetout), trimmed and cut in half diagonally

1 tablespoon salt-reduced soy sauce

2 teaspoons honey

few drops of sesame oil

1 teaspoon toasted sesame seeds

steamed rice, to serve

1 Heat the oil in a wok or non-stick frying pan over high heat. Add the lamb and stir-fry for 2-3 minutes, until sealed on both sides.

2 Add the garlic, ginger, capsicum, spring onions and snow peas. Cook, tossing so the vegetables cook evenly, for about 2 minutes.

3 Add the soy sauce, honey and sesame oil, tossing well to coat the meat and vegetables.

4 Serve the lamb and vegetables sprinkled with the sesame seeds, on a bed of steamed rice.

Serves 2

Preparation
10 minutes

Cooking
10 minutes

Per serving
1127 kJ, 269 kcal, 24 g protein, 15 g fat (5 g saturated fat), 11 g carbohydrate (10 g sugars), 2 g fibre, 448 mg sodium

Instead of lamb, try using thinly sliced beef, pork or boneless, skinless chicken breast, or peeled and deveined raw prawns (uncooked shrimp).

Any left-over uncooked lamb can be wrapped tightly and frozen for up to a month. Thaw the lamb before using in another recipe.

Hoisin beef stir-fry

The beef in this colourful stir-fry is an excellent source of zinc and a good source of iron. As a result of modern breeding techniques, beef is much leaner than it used to be – lean cuts can contain less than 3 per cent fat.

Serves 2

Preparation
15 minutes

Cooking
10 minutes

Per serving
*2327 kJ, 556 kcal,
35 g protein, 18 g fat
(4 g saturated fat),
62 g carbohydrate
(15 g sugars), 9 g fibre,
855 mg sodium*

*Hoisin sauce,
a sweet Chinese
barbecue sauce
made from both
soybeans and red
beans, gives the
stir-fry a rich
flavour.*

170 g (6 oz) wok-ready Chinese egg noodles

1 tablespoon sunflower or vegetable oil

2 large cloves garlic, thinly sliced

1 teaspoon grated fresh ginger

1 large red capsicum (bell pepper), thinly sliced

125 g (4 oz) baby button mushrooms, halved

1 sirloin steak, about 200 g (7 oz), trimmed of fat and cut into thin strips

85 g (3 oz) snow peas (mangetout), halved lengthwise

4 spring onions (scallions), cut into short lengths, plus extra shredded spring onion, to garnish

2½ tablespoons hoisin sauce

1 tablespoon light soy sauce

1 teaspoon sesame oil (optional)

1 Soak the noodles in boiling water according to the packet instructions.

2 Meanwhile, heat the sunflower or vegetable oil in a wok or large frying pan. Add the garlic and ginger, and cook very briefly to release their flavour. Toss in the capsicum and mushrooms, then stir-fry over high heat for 2–3 minutes, until starting to soften.

3 Add the beef strips, snow peas and spring onion lengths, and stir-fry for a further 1–2 minutes, until the meat just turns from pink to brown.

4 Mix in the hoisin and soy sauces, and stir well until bubbling, then drizzle in the sesame oil, if using. Drain the noodles. Serve the stir-fry on the noodles, topped with shredded spring onion.

Pork fillet with bamboo shoots and spinach

This Asian-style tasty trio of pork, bamboo shoots and spinach is flavoured with yellow curry paste, and supplies plenty of B vitamins and minerals to kick-start your metabolism and boost your energy levels.

200 g (7 oz) pork fillet, cut into bite-sized pieces

1 tablespoon oyster sauce

½ teaspoon freshly ground black pepper

2 limes

2 tablespoons vegetable oil

1 teaspoon yellow curry paste

1 cup (250 g) canned bamboo shoots, rinsed and drained, cut into strips

1 cup (50 g) baby spinach leaves

1 teaspoon sugar

steamed rice, to serve

1 Combine the pork with the oyster sauce and pepper. Set aside to marinate for about 15 minutes.

2 Halve and juice one lime. Cut the other into wedges.

3 Heat the wok over high heat, add the oil and sear the pork, stirring, for about 2 minutes.

4 Stir in the curry paste. Add the bamboo shoots and spinach. Season with sugar and lime juice, and continue to stir-fry over high heat for a further 3 minutes.

5 Serve the pork and vegetables on steamed rice, with lime wedges for squeezing.

Serves 2

Preparation
15 minutes, plus marinating

Cooking
5 minutes

Per serving
1408 kJ, 336 kcal, 23 g protein, 22 g fat (4 g saturated fat), 13 g carbohydrate (6 g sugars), 5 g fibre, 629 mg sodium

When stir-frying, the food in the wok needs to be moved continuously over very high heat. This helps the ingredients retain their colours, vitamins, minerals and aroma.

Shredded pork with Thai lime dressing

Serves 4

Preparation
15 minutes

Cooking
15 minutes

Per serving
*1079 kJ, 258 kcal,
30 g protein, 11 g fat
(2 g saturated fat),
9 g carbohydrate
(4 g sugars), 4 g fibre,
732 mg sodium*

500 g (1 lb) pork fillet, thinly sliced

3 teaspoons peanut (groundnut) or vegetable oil

1 large carrot, finely shredded

6 cm (2½ inch) piece fresh ginger, peeled and finely shredded

2 spring onions (scallions), finely shredded

1 red capsicum (bell pepper), thinly sliced

1 cup (90 g) bean sprouts, trimmed

1 cup (30 g) fresh coriander (cilantro) leaves

1 cup (20 g) small fresh mint leaves

1 bunch (125 g/4 oz) rocket (arugula), trimmed

Thai lime dressing

1 tablespoon salt-reduced soy sauce

1 tablespoon fish sauce

1 tablespoon sesame oil

grated zest and juice of 2 limes

1 small red chilli, seeded and finely chopped

1 Put the pork and 2 teaspoons of the olive oil in a bowl, and stir to coat well.

2 Heat a large heavy-based frying pan or wok over high heat. Add the remaining olive oil and heat for 10 seconds. Stir-fry the carrot and ginger for 30 seconds, until just wilted. Transfer to a large bowl.

3 Reheat the pan and stir-fry the pork in three batches, for 3-5 minutes each batch, until well cooked. Transfer each batch to a plate and reheat the pan before cooking the next batch.

4 Add the spring onions, capsicum and bean sprouts to the bowl with the carrot and ginger.

5 To make the dressing, put the soy sauce, fish sauce, sesame oil, lime zest, lime juice and chilli in a small bowl, and whisk until well combined.

6 Pour the dressing over the salad, then add the pork and toss to mix. Add the herbs and rocket just before serving, and toss to combine.

For a variation, omit the carrot and spring onions and stir-fry the ginger with the pork. Add two thinly sliced pears with the herbs at the end of step 6.

Pork and mushroom stir-fry

750 g (1½ lb) piece pork fillet

pinch of salt

freshly ground black pepper

2 tablespoons peanut (groundnut) or vegetable oil

200 g (7 oz) oyster mushrooms, trimmed

250 g (8 oz) snow peas (mangetout), trimmed and cut in half

¼ cup (60 ml) sweet sherry, white wine or salt-reduced chicken stock (page 14)

¼ cup (60 ml) black bean sauce

steamed rice, to serve

1 Cut the pork across the grain into thin strips. Place in a bowl and season with salt and freshly ground black pepper.

2 Heat a wok or large frying pan over high heat. Add 1 tablespoon of the oil and swirl to coat. Working in two batches, stir-fry the pork for 3 minutes, until well browned and just cooked through. Transfer each batch to a plate.

3 Reheat the wok and add the remaining oil. Stir-fry the mushrooms and snow peas for 1-2 minutes, until the snow peas turn bright green but are still crisp. Add the sherry, wine or stock and cook until slightly reduced, then add the black bean sauce and stir until simmering.

4 Return the pork to the wok and toss to warm through. Serve hot with steamed rice.

Serves 4

Preparation
10 minutes

Cooking
10 minutes

Per serving
*1501 kJ, 359 kcal,
44 g protein, 14 g fat
(3 g saturated fat),
9 g carbohydrate
(7 g sugars), 4 g fibre,
901 mg sodium*

Ask your butcher to cut the pork fillet into stir-fry strips for you. You could use pork leg, loin or pork scotch steaks instead of fillet.

Pad Thai with chicken

*Instead of chicken,
use pork stir-fry
strips and cook for
5 minutes. Or use
250 g (8 oz) raw
prawns (uncooked
shrimp), adding
them with the fish
sauce in step 3.
Cook for 3 minutes
if fresh, 4 minutes
if frozen, or until
they turn pink.*

225 g (8 oz) dried rice stick noodles

2 tablespoons vegetable oil

2–4 cloves garlic, crushed

1 small onion, finely chopped

1 red or green chilli, seeded and finely chopped

350 g (12 oz) boneless, skinless chicken breast, thinly sliced

2 eggs, beaten

200 g (7 oz) bean sprouts, trimmed

3 teaspoons salt-reduced soy sauce, or to taste

1 tablespoon fish sauce, or to taste

1 tablespoon lime juice

freshly ground black pepper

dried red chilli flakes, to taste (optional)

1 bunch (20 g/^{3}/$_4$ oz) fresh chives, snipped

30 g (1 oz) chopped roasted peanuts (groundnuts)

lime halves, to serve

1 Soak the rice noodles in hot water for 10 minutes, or according to the packet instructions. Gently stir with a fork or chopsticks to separate the noodles. Drain thoroughly and set aside.

2 Meanwhile, heat the oil in a wok or large frying pan until very hot and stir-fry the garlic, onion and chilli for 1 minute. Add the chicken and stir-fry for 2 minutes, until lightly coloured.

3 Push the chicken to one side of the wok. Pour the eggs into the wok and gently stir until lightly scrambled. Add the noodles and ^{1}/$_4$ cup (60 ml) water. Add the bean sprouts, soy sauce, fish sauce and lime juice, and stir-fry with the noodles, chicken and eggs for 2 minutes.

4 Remove the wok from the heat. Taste, then season with freshly ground black pepper or more fish or soy sauce if necessary. If you like, add some chilli flakes. Transfer to a warmed serving dish. Sprinkle with the chives and peanuts and serve immediately, with the lime halves.

Chicken stir-fry with mushrooms and cashew nuts

2 teaspoons cornflour
(cornstarch)

100 ml (3$\frac{1}{2}$ fl oz) dry sherry

2 tablespoons soy sauce

2 teaspoons sesame oil

180 g (6 oz) snow peas
(mangetout), trimmed

$\frac{2}{3}$ cup (100 g) unsalted
cashew nuts

2 tablespoons olive or
canola oil

300 g (10 oz) chicken
stir-fry strips

1 onion, thinly sliced

4 stalks celery, thinly sliced

2 carrots, cut into strips

1 clove garlic, crushed

100 g (3$\frac{1}{2}$ oz) shiitake
mushrooms, thinly sliced

$\frac{1}{2}$ cup (125 ml) boiling water

200 g (7 oz) bean sprouts,
trimmed

steamed rice or noodles,
to serve

1 In a small bowl, mix the cornflour with 1 tablespoon cold water to form a smooth paste. Stir in the sherry, soy sauce and sesame oil.

2 Put the snow peas in a large saucepan. Add just enough boiling water to cover the snow peas. Bring to a boil, then immediately drain and set aside.

3 Dry-fry the cashews in a large frying pan over medium-high heat for 2 minutes, shaking the pan until they begin to brown. Transfer to a plate.

4 Add the olive or canola oil and chicken strips to the pan, and stir-fry for 1 minute, increasing the heat to high, if necessary, so that the chicken begins to brown. Add the onion, celery, carrots and garlic, and stir-fry for 2 minutes.

5 Return the cashews to the pan, add the mushrooms and stir-fry for 2 minutes. Pour in the boiling water, stir in the cornflour paste and bring to a boil. Add the snow peas and bean sprouts, and simmer, stirring, for 2 minutes, until the sauce thickens and the bean sprouts are thoroughly cooked. Serve immediately, with rice or noodles.

Serves 4

Preparation
20 minutes

Cooking
15 minutes

Per serving
*1862 kJ, 445 kcal,
23 g protein, 30 g fat
(6 g saturated fat),
14 g carbohydrate
(8 g sugars), 6 g fibre,
486 mg sodium*

*There are many
kinds of soy sauce,
but the choice in
supermarkets will
usually be between
dark and light
varieties. Dark soy
sauce is richer and
thicker than light
soy sauce, and has
a lower salt content.
If you are watching
your salt intake,
choose salt-reduced
soy sauce.*

Singapore noodles

For a quick, easy and satisfying dinner, these Singapore noodles are hard to beat. The chicken and prawns are briefly marinated in soy sauce, ginger and Chinese rice wine, then stir-fried with the noodles and vegetables.

Serves 4

Preparation
20 minutes,
plus 30 minutes
marinating

Cooking
10 minutes

Per serving
*2021 kJ, 483 kcal,
31 g protein, 14 g fat
(3 g saturated fat),
55 g carbohydrate
(2 g sugars), 4 g fibre,
823 mg sodium*

250 g (8 oz) boneless, skinless chicken breast, thinly sliced

250 g (8 oz) raw prawns (uncooked shrimp), peeled and deveined

1 tablespoon Chinese rice wine

2 cloves garlic, crushed

1½ tablespoons salt-reduced soy sauce

3 teaspoons grated fresh ginger

250 g (8 oz) dried rice vermicelli

2 tablespoons peanut (groundnut) or vegetable oil

1 tablespoon curry powder

1 red capsicum (bell pepper), halved and thinly sliced

4 spring onions (scallions), thinly sliced

¼ cup (60 ml) salt-reduced chicken or vegetable stock (pages 14–15)

1 teaspoon sugar (optional)

pinch of salt

freshly ground black pepper

sprigs fresh coriander (cilantro), to serve

lime wedges, to serve

1 Put the chicken, prawns, rice wine, garlic, 2 teaspoons of the soy sauce and 2 teaspoons of the ginger in a shallow glass or ceramic bowl, and toss to combine. Cover with plastic wrap and refrigerate for 30 minutes.

2 Soak the noodles according to the packet instructions. Drain well and set aside.

3 Heat 1 tablespoon of the oil in a wok or large non-stick frying pan over high heat. Stir-fry half of the chicken and prawn mixture for 2–3 minutes, until just cooked through. Transfer to a plate and repeat with the remaining chicken and prawn mixture.

4 Heat the remaining oil in the clean wok. Add the curry powder and stir-fry for 30 seconds, until aromatic. Add the capsicum, half the spring onions and the remaining ginger, and stir-fry for 1 minute, until the spring onions have softened.

5 Return all of the chicken mixture to the wok, add the stock and remaining soy sauce, and season with the sugar, if using, salt and freshly ground black pepper. Add the noodles to the wok and toss well until the stock has been absorbed and the noodles are heated through.

6 Transfer the noodles to a warmed serving bowl and garnish with the coriander and remaining spring onions. Serve with lime wedges on the side.

Chicken with black bean sauce

500 g (1 lb) boneless, skinless chicken breasts, thinly sliced

$\frac{1}{4}$ cup (60 ml) salt-reduced soy sauce

1 tablespoon dry sherry

1 tablespoon cornflour (cornstarch)

2 teaspoons sesame oil

2 tablespoons salt-reduced fermented black beans

$\frac{1}{4}$ cup (60 ml) peanut (groundnut) or vegetable oil

1 red capsicum (bell pepper), cut into thin strips

1 mild green chilli, chopped (optional)

2 tablespoons grated fresh ginger

2 cloves garlic, crushed

3 baby bok choy, trimmed, leaves separated

1 Put the chicken in a large bowl and add 2 tablespoons of the soy sauce, the sherry and cornflour. Toss until the chicken is well coated. Add 1 teaspoon of the sesame oil and toss again.

2 Rinse the black beans in several changes of cold water, then drain well. Mash half the black beans with the flat side of a knife.

3 Heat 2 tablespoons of the peanut or vegetable oil in a wok or large non-stick frying pan over medium–high heat. Stir-fry the chicken for 4 minutes, until it is lightly browned and cooked through. Transfer the chicken to a plate.

4 Add the remaining peanut oil to the wok, along with the capsicum strips, green chilli (if using), ginger, garlic and black beans; stir to combine. Add the remaining soy sauce and sesame oil, and $\frac{1}{2}$ cup (125 ml) water. Stir-fry for 2 minutes, add the bok choy and stir-fry for 1 minute, until the leaves are just starting to wilt.

5 Return the chicken to the wok and stir-fry for 1 minute, until heated through. Serve hot.

Serves 4

Preparation
20 minutes

Cooking
10 minutes

Per serving
1490 kJ, 356 kcal, 29 g protein, 23 g fat (5 g saturated fat), 7 g carbohydrate (2 g sugars), 2 g fibre, 633 mg sodium

Chinese fermented black beans are a versatile ingredient sold in many supermarkets. They will keep indefinitely, stored in an airtight jar.

Kung pao chicken

Serves 4

Preparation
15 minutes,
plus 30 minutes
marinating

Cooking
10 minutes

Per serving
*1366 kJ, 326 kcal,
26 g protein, 22 g fat
(5 g saturated fat),
6 g carbohydrate
(3 g sugars), 1 g fibre,
574 mg sodium*

500 g (1 lb) boneless, skinless chicken thighs, chopped

1¹⁄₂ tablespoons peanut (groundnut) or rice bran oil

2 cloves garlic, thinly sliced

8 dried red chillies, seeded and chopped

1 teaspoon crushed sichuan peppercorns

2 spring onions (scallions), sliced

2 tablespoons salt-reduced soy sauce

1 tablespoon Chinese rice wine

1 teaspoon sugar

¹⁄₄ cup (40 g) cashew nuts or peanuts (groundnuts), toasted

steamed rice, to serve

Marinade

2 teaspoons salt-reduced soy sauce

2 teaspoons Chinese rice wine

1 teaspoon sesame oil

1¹⁄₂ teaspoons cornflour (cornstarch)

1 To make the marinade, combine all of the marinade ingredients in a bowl. Add the chicken and toss to coat. Cover with plastic wrap and refrigerate for 30 minutes.

2 Heat 1 tablespoon of the oil in a wok or large non-stick frying pan over high heat. Add the chicken, in two batches if necessary, and stir-fry for 5 minutes, until just golden. Transfer to a plate.

3 Heat the remaining oil in the wok and stir-fry the garlic for 30 seconds. Add the chillies, crushed peppercorns and the white part of the spring onions. Stir-fry for 1 minute, until fragrant.

4 Combine the soy sauce, rice wine and sugar in a small bowl, then add to the wok and stir well. Return the chicken to the wok and stir-fry for about 2 minutes to heat through. Stir in the spring onion greens and cashew nuts. Remove from the heat and serve with steamed rice.

You can add seasonal vegetables, such as red capsicum (bell pepper), green beans or snow peas (mangetout).

Thai chicken stir-fry

4 cloves garlic, roughly chopped

4 spring onions (scallions), cut into short lengths

$\frac{1}{3}$ cup (10 g) fresh coriander (cilantro) leaves

$\frac{1}{4}$ teaspoon salt

$\frac{1}{2}$ teaspoon dried red chilli flakes

$\frac{1}{4}$ cup (60 ml) vegetable oil

500 g (1 lb) boneless, skinless chicken breasts, thinly sliced

$1\frac{1}{3}$ cups (250 g) fresh or canned baby corn

2 roma (plum) tomatoes, diced

$1\frac{1}{2}$ tablespoons salt-reduced soy sauce

3 teaspoons fish sauce

$1\frac{1}{2}$ teaspoons sugar

$\frac{1}{2}$ cup (25 g) firmly packed fresh basil, roughly chopped

steamed rice, to serve

1 In a food processor or blender, combine the garlic, spring onions, coriander, salt, chilli flakes, 1 tablespoon of the oil and 2 teaspoons water. Process to a smooth paste.

2 Heat the remaining oil in a wok or large non-stick frying pan over medium-high heat. Add the herb paste and cook for 1 minute. Add the chicken and stir-fry for 4 minutes, until the chicken is no longer pink.

3 Add the remaining ingredients to the wok and cook, stirring constantly, for 2 minutes, until the chicken is just cooked through. Serve hot with steamed rice.

Serves 4

Preparation
15 minutes

Cooking
10 minutes

Per serving
1415 kJ, 338 kcal, 30 g protein, 21 g fat (4 g saturated fat), 7 g carbohydrate (4 g sugars), 4 g fibre, 854 mg sodium

Crisp coriander fish with lemon beans

The omega-3 oils in oil-rich fish such as sardines and mackerel have many benefits beyond keeping the heart healthy. Evidence is emerging about their role in maintaining mental alertness and helping prevent dementia.

Serves 4

Preparation
10 minutes

Cooking
12 minutes

Per serving
1376 kJ, 329 kcal,
31 g protein, 15 g fat
(4 g saturated fat),
14 g carbohydrate
(3 g sugars), 6 g fibre,
304 mg sodium

1 tablespoon olive oil, plus extra, for brushing

2 sprigs fresh rosemary, finely chopped

1 leek, white part only, sliced

420 g (15 oz) can butterbeans (lima beans), rinsed and drained

finely grated zest of 1 lemon

4 mackerel fillets or 8 sardines, butterflied, about 500 g (1 lb) in total

1 tablespoon crushed coriander seeds

lemon wedges, to serve

1 Preheat the grill (broiler) to the hottest setting and line the grill pan with foil.

2 Heat 1 tablespoon of the olive oil in a large frying pan over high heat. Add the rosemary and leek, reduce the heat and cook for 5 minutes, until the leek is tender. Stir in the butterbeans and lemon zest, and cook until heated through. Set aside and keep warm.

3 Place the fish fillets, skin side down, on the grill pan, then brush each one with a little olive oil. Sprinkle half the crushed coriander seeds over the fish and grill (broil) for 2 minutes, until just firm.

4 Turn the fish over and brush the skin with a little more olive oil. Grill for 1 minute, then sprinkle with the remaining crushed coriander seeds. Cook for a further 2 minutes to crisp the skin.

5 Transfer the butterbean mixture to a serving plate. Top with the fish fillets and pour over the juices from the foil. Serve immediately, with lemon wedges on the side.

Use a mortar and pestle to crush the coriander seeds. Put the mortar in a plastic bag, gather the edges around the pestle to prevent the seeds from escaping, and pound the seeds.

Crisp coriander fish with lemon beans

Coriander fish on silverbeet and lentils

Remove the white stems from **1 bunch (1 kg/2 lb) silverbeet (Swiss chard)** leaves, then wash well and roughly chop. Wilt the silverbeet in a frying pan over medium-low heat for 5 minutes, with **1 crushed clove garlic** and **3 thinly sliced spring onions (scallions)**. Add a **400 g (14 oz) can brown lentils,** shaking the pan to mix in and warm through. Remove from the heat and squeeze over the **juice of** $^{1}/_{2}$ **lemon** and a good drizzle of **extra virgin olive oil.** Season with **salt** and **freshly ground black pepper.** Set aside and keep warm while cooking the fish as directed in the main recipe.

Honey mustard salmon

2 teaspoons vegetable oil

2 teaspoons soy sauce

1 teaspoon honey

1 teaspoon wholegrain mustard

1 tablespoon lemon juice, plus some grated lemon zest

2 x 125 g (4 oz) skinless salmon fillets

420 g (15 oz) can butterbeans (lima beans), rinsed and drained

1 clove garlic, crushed

1 tablespoon extra virgin olive oil

pinch of dried red chilli flakes

2 cups (100 g) baby spinach leaves

pinch of salt

freshly ground black pepper

8 vine-ripened red cherry tomatoes

lemon wedges, to serve

1 In a shallow dish, combine the vegetable oil, soy sauce, honey, mustard and half the lemon juice. Add the salmon fillets and turn to coat all over.

2 Place the butterbeans in a saucepan with the garlic, olive oil, chilli flakes, remaining lemon juice and lemon zest, and gently heat through. Roughly crush the beans using a vegetable masher or fork, then stir in the spinach and season with salt and freshly ground black pepper. Gently heat until the spinach wilts.

3 Meanwhile, heat a non-stick frying pan or chargrill pan over high heat. Cook the salmon for 2–3 minutes on each side, until just firm and pink, adding the tomatoes during the last 1–2 minutes to warm them through.

4 Serve the salmon on the beans, with the tomatoes and extra lemon wedges.

Serves 2

Preparation
10 minutes

Cooking
10 minutes

Per serving
2007 kJ, 480 kcal, 36 g protein, 24 g fat (4 g saturated fat), 25 g carbohydrate (9 g sugars), 10 g fibre, 879 mg sodium

Marinating the salmon fillets in the honey and mustard mixture for a few hours or overnight will help to maximise the flavour.

Cook the salmon in the same way, but serve it on a lightly toasted sourdough roll with low-fat mayonnaise and your favourite salad fillings.

Pan-fried fish with tomatoes and asparagus

Serves 4

Preparation
10 minutes

Cooking
8 minutes

Per serving
752 kJ, 180 kcal,
32 g protein, 4 g fat
(1 g saturated fat),
3 g carbohydrate
(3 g sugars), 3 g fibre,
312 mg sodium

8 asparagus spears

2 lemons

4 x 150 g (5 oz) firm white
fish fillets with skin, such as
john dory, snapper, bream,
trevally or halibut

pinch of salt

freshly ground black pepper

olive oil, for brushing

250 g (8 oz) yellow or red
baby roma (plum) or cherry
tomatoes, halved

1 tablespoon small capers,
rinsed and squeezed dry

1 Trim the ends from the asparagus. If the spears are thick, cut them in half lengthwise, then slice them in half on the diagonal. Juice one lemon and cut the other one into wedges.

2 Make two diagonal slashes through the skin of each fish fillet and pat dry with paper towels. Sprinkle the fish with salt and freshly ground black pepper.

3 Heat a large frying pan over medium-high heat. Lightly oil the pan. When the oil is hot, add the fish, skin side down, and cook for 3–5 minutes, until the skin is crisp and the flesh starts to turn white.

4 Turn the fish and add the asparagus, tomatoes, capers and lemon juice to the pan. Cook for a further 1–2 minutes, until the fish is just cooked through.

5 Arrange the fish on a platter and pile the asparagus and tomato mixture on top. Serve immediately, with the lemon wedges for squeezing.

The fish can be lightly dusted in seasoned plain (all-purpose) flour for a crisper texture; you can add flavourings such as cayenne pepper or garlic powder to the flour.

Serve with steamed brown rice, some steamed English spinach, broccoli or a mixture of green and yellow beans.

Red curry prawns

Instead of using the oils and flavourings in the main recipe, stir-fry **2 tablespoons red curry paste** in **2 tablespoons vegetable oil** for 30 seconds before adding the prawns. Stir-fry for 1½ minutes, then stir in **2 tablespoons coconut milk.** Stir-fry for 30–60 seconds, until the prawns are cooked.

Sesame prawns with noodles

Sesame prawns with noodles

40 peeled raw prawns (uncooked shrimp), about 350 g (12 oz) in total

1 tablespoon sesame oil

1½ tablespoons dark soy sauce

2 tablespoons vegetable oil

100 g (3½ oz) baby corn

1 red capsicum (bell pepper), sliced

2 cloves garlic, crushed

2 cups (500 ml) salt-reduced vegetable stock (page 15)

225 g (8 oz) dried egg noodles

100 g (3½ oz) bok choy, shredded

1 large medium-hot red chilli, seeded and finely chopped

1 lemongrass stem, white part only, finely chopped

2 teaspoons grated fresh ginger

1 teaspoon soft brown sugar

1 tablespoon sesame seeds

2 tablespoons chopped fresh coriander (cilantro) leaves

sweet chilli sauce, to serve

1 Pat the prawns dry with paper towels. Combine the prawns, sesame oil and soy sauce in a bowl, and toss to coat the prawns. Tip the prawns and marinade into a sieve over a bowl to catch any marinade. Reserve the marinade.

2 Heat 1 tablespoon of the vegetable oil in a wok or large non-stick frying pan over medium heat. Stir-fry the corn and capsicum for 2–3 minutes, until lightly coloured. Add half the garlic and stir for a few more seconds, then pour in the stock.

3 Add the noodles, cover and cook for 2 minutes, then stir in the shredded bok choy. Cook for a further 1 minute, until the noodles and vegetables are tender. Remove from the wok, cover and keep warm while you cook the prawns.

4 Reheat the clean wok until very hot, add the remaining vegetable oil and swirl to coat the base. Stir-fry the prawns for 1½ minutes, then add the chilli, lemongrass, ginger and remaining garlic. Stir-fry for a further 30–60 seconds, until the prawns have turned pink and are just cooked through (do not overcook them or they will be tough). Stir in the reserved marinade and the cooked noodles.

5 Remove the wok from the heat and stir in the sugar, sesame seeds and coriander. Serve with sweet chilli sauce.

Serves 4

Preparation 15 minutes

Cooking 10 minutes

Per serving
1970 kJ, 471 kcal, 28 g protein, 18 g fat (3 g saturated fat), 47 g carbohydrate (5 g sugars), 3 g fibre, 840 mg sodium

Lamb, fig and chickpea stew, page 213

Casseroles, curries and stews

Long, slow cooking develops melt-in-the mouth tenderness, great depth of flavour and nutrient-rich sauces. These dishes are the ultimate, adaptable one-dish winter warmers.

Lightly spiced vegetable medley

Serves 4

Preparation
20 minutes

Cooking
25 minutes

Per serving
*1098 kJ, 262 kcal,
11 g protein, 13 g fat
(3 g saturated fat),
27 g carbohydrate
(9 g sugars), 10 g fibre,
96 mg sodium*

*To remove seeds
from cardamom
pods, slit the pods
with the point
of a sharp knife
and scrape out
the small black
or beige seeds
with the blade.*

2 tablespoons olive or canola oil

1 onion, thinly sliced

2 celery stalks, thinly sliced

1 large carrot, halved and thinly sliced

4 cloves garlic, crushed

seeds from 10 green cardamom pods

1 eggplant (aubergine), chopped

2 tablespoons ground coriander

450 g (15 oz) potatoes, diced

200 ml (7 fl oz) boiling water

2 cups (250 g) small cauliflower florets

4 cups (250 g) shredded English spinach

⅓ cup (20 g) roughly chopped fresh coriander (cilantro) leaves

finely grated zest of 1 lemon

1 cup (250 g) natural (plain) yogurt

1 Heat the oil in a large saucepan over medium-high heat. Add the onion, celery, carrot, garlic and cardamom seeds. Stir, then cover and cook for 3 minutes. Stir in the eggplant and sprinkle in the ground coriander without stirring. Cover and cook for 3 minutes.

2 Stir in the potatoes and boiling water, cover and bring back to a boil. Reduce the heat and simmer for 10 minutes. Stir in the cauliflower and cook for 8 minutes, until all the vegetables are tender.

3 Add the spinach and cook, stirring, for 1 minute, until the spinach has wilted. Stir in the chopped coriander and grated lemon zest.

4 Divide the vegetables among four plates or bowls and serve with the yogurt.

White bean stew

1 tablespoon olive oil

1 brown (yellow) onion, finely chopped

1 large carrot, diced

1 celeriac (celery root), about 1 kg (2 lb), peeled and diced

2 teaspoons mixed dried herbs

3 bay leaves

2 x 420 g (15 oz) cans butterbeans (lima beans), rinsed and drained

1/2 cup (15 g) roughly chopped fresh flat-leaf (Italian) parsley

freshly ground black pepper

1 Heat the olive oil in a large heavy-based saucepan over medium-high heat. Cook the onion, carrot and celeriac, stirring occasionally, for 10 minutes, until soft and golden.

2 Stir in 3 cups (750 ml) water and bring to a boil. Add the dried herbs and bay leaves. Stir, reduce the heat and simmer for 25 minutes, until the vegetables are tender.

3 Stir in the butterbeans and cook for 20 minutes, until the beans are soft and the mixture has thickened. Stir in three-quarters of the parsley.

4 Season the stew with freshly ground black pepper and serve sprinkled with the remaining parsley.

Serves 4

Preparation
10 minutes

Cooking
1 hour

Per serving
951 kJ, 227 kcal, 11 g protein, 10 g fat (<1 g saturated fat), 24 g carbohydrate (10 g sugars), 19 g fibre, 568 mg sodium

Celeriac is high in fibre and minerals, and creates a great celery flavour and a creamy texture without the stringy effect that celery can have. You can replace the celeriac with diced celery or parsnip.

Pea curry with Indian paneer

Paneer is an Indian cheese, similar to ricotta but drier in texture. It's often combined with peas in a curry. This version uses homemade paneer, which is simple to make. Serve it with basmati rice for a well-balanced meal.

Serves 4

Preparation
15 minutes,
plus 3 hours
draining and
pressing

Cooking
30 minutes

Per serving
2299 kJ, 549 kcal,
27 g protein, 25 g fat
(7 g saturated fat),
22 g carbohydrate
(10 g sugars), 8 g fibre,
245 mg sodium

¼ cup (60 ml) sunflower or vegetable oil

1 large onion, chopped

2 cloves garlic, finely chopped

5 cm (2 inch) piece fresh ginger, peeled and finely chopped

1 green chilli, seeded and thinly sliced

1 tablespoon coriander seeds, crushed

1 tablespoon cumin seeds, crushed

1 teaspoon ground turmeric

1 tablespoon garam masala

500 g (1 lb) firm tomatoes, cut into quarters

pinch of salt

2¼ cups (350 g) frozen peas

2 cups (90 g) baby spinach leaves

¼ cup (15 g) roughly chopped fresh coriander (cilantro) leaves

steamed rice, to serve

Paneer

9 cups (2.25 litres) full-cream (whole) milk

90 ml (3 fl oz) lemon juice

1 To make the paneer, pour the milk into a large saucepan and bring to a boil. Immediately reduce the heat to low and add the lemon juice. Stir for about 1–2 minutes, until the milk separates into curds and whey. Remove from the heat.

2 Line a large sieve or colander with muslin (cheesecloth) and set it over a large bowl. Pour in the milk mixture, and leave to drain for 15 minutes, until cool.

3 Bring together the corners of the muslin to make a bundle containing the curds. Squeeze, then leave to drain for a further 30 minutes, until all the whey has dripped into the bowl. Reserve 1 cup (250 ml) of the whey. Keeping the curds wrapped, place on a board. Set another board on top and press down to flatten into a block. Place some cans on top and leave in a cool place for about 3 hours, until firm.

4 Carefully peel off the muslin and cut the paneer into 2 cm (¾ inch) cubes. Heat 1 tablespoon of the oil in a large non-stick frying pan and cook the paneer for 1–2 minutes on each side, until golden. Remove from the pan and keep warm.

5 Heat the remaining 2 tablespoons oil in the pan and gently cook the onion for 5 minutes, until softened. Stir in the garlic and ginger, and cook for 1 minute. Stir in the chilli and spices, and cook, stirring constantly, for 1 minute.

6 Add the tomatoes, reserved whey and salt, and stir well. Cover and cook over low heat for 5 minutes. Add the peas and bring to a boil, then reduce the heat, cover and simmer for 5 minutes. Gently stir in the spinach and simmer for 3–4 minutes, until the peas are tender. Stir in the fresh coriander, reserving a little for garnishing.

7 Transfer the curry to a serving dish and top with the paneer. Serve the curry with steamed rice, sprinkled with the reserved coriander.

Pea curry with Indian paneer

Sweet potato curry with paneer

Heat **1 tablespoon vegetable oil** in a large frying pan. Sauté **1 diced onion** and **2 finely chopped cloves garlic** for 4-5 minutes, until softened. Add **500 g (1 lb) orange sweet potato (kumara) chunks** and cook, stirring, for 2 minutes. Stir in **1 tablespoon mild curry powder** and **1 tablespoon finely chopped fresh ginger,** and cook for 30 seconds. Stir in a **410 g (15 oz) can chopped tomatoes** and **100 ml (3½ fl oz) diluted salt-reduced vegetable stock** (page 15). Bring to a boil; reduce the heat, cover and gently cook for 15 minutes, until the sweet potato is tender. Stir in **1 cup (150 g) frozen peas** and simmer for 3 minutes, then add **250 g (8 oz) fresh paneer cubes** (see the main recipe). Cook for 2 minutes, until thoroughly heated. Season with **freshly ground black pepper.** Serve sprinkled with **2 tablespoons chopped fresh mint.**

Vegetarian chilli beans

Serves 2

Preparation
10 minutes

Cooking
15 minutes

Per serving
*1076 kJ, 257 kcal,
13 g protein, 8 g fat
(1 g saturated fat),
34 g carbohydrate
(17 g sugars), 14 g fibre,
820 mg sodium*

2 teaspoons olive oil

1 small onion, chopped

1 clove garlic, crushed

$1/2$ teaspoon paprika

$1/2$ teaspoon ground cumin

$1/2$ teaspoon dried red
chilli flakes

410 g (15 oz) can no added
salt chopped tomatoes

$2/3$ cup (100 g) chopped
roasted red capsicum
(bell pepper)

420 g (15 oz) can red kidney
beans, rinsed and drained

$2/3$ cup (160 g) bottled tomato
salsa

2 spring onions (scallions),
diagonally sliced

1 tablespoon chopped
fresh parsley

steamed rice or crusty bread,
to serve (optional)

1 Heat the oil in a saucepan over medium heat. Cook the onion for 3 minutes, until softened. Stir in the garlic, spices and chilli flakes, and cook for a further 1 minute.

2 Stir in the tomatoes, capsicum, kidney beans and salsa, and bring to a boil. Reduce the heat and simmer, stirring occasionally, for 10 minutes, until the mixture has thickened.

3 Sprinkle the chilli beans with the spring onions and parsley, and serve with some steamed rice or crusty bread, if desired.

Use the chilli beans as a filling for a warmed tortilla, with some shredded lettuce, light sour cream and avocado.

Roasted capsicum can be bought in jars and at the delicatessen counter in supermarkets. Drain off the oil before using.

Goulash-style tofu

1 tablespoon olive oil

1 red onion, finely chopped

2 red capsicums (bell peppers), diced

2 cloves garlic, crushed

2 teaspoons sweet paprika

2 tablespoons salt-reduced tomato paste (concentrated purée)

5 ripe tomatoes, about 750 g (1½ lb) in total, peeled and diced

2 x 300 g (10 oz) packets firm tofu, drained and cut into 2 cm (³⁄₄ inch) pieces

½ cup (15 g) roughly chopped fresh flat-leaf (Italian) parsley

freshly ground black pepper

⅓ cup (90 g) low-fat thick (Greek-style) yogurt

1 Heat the oil in a large non-stick frying pan over medium heat. Cook the onion, capsicums and garlic for 5 minutes, until the onion and capsicums are softened. Sprinkle with the paprika and stir to combine.

2 Stir in the tomato paste and 1⅓ cups (330 ml) water. Stir in the tomatoes, then bring to a boil. Reduce the heat and simmer for 5 minutes, until thickened.

3 Stir in the tofu and cook for 2 minutes, until the tofu is heated through. Stir in half of the parsley.

4 Spoon the goulash onto four serving plates. Serve topped with the remaining parsley and a sprinkle of freshly ground black pepper, with the yogurt on the side.

Serves 4

Preparation
15 minutes

Cooking
15 minutes

Per serving
1139 kJ, 272 kcal, 21 g protein, 15 g fat (3 g saturated fat), 13 g carbohydrate (10 g sugars), 7 g fibre, 67 mg sodium

To peel tomatoes, use a small sharp knife to mark a cross on the base. Put in a large heatproof bowl, cover with boiling water and stand for 2 minutes. Drain, then plunge into icy cold water. Drain again and peel off the skin.

You can use an 800 g (28 oz) can chopped tomatoes in place of fresh tomatoes.

Chickpea, sweet potato and carrot stew

1 bunch (125 g/4 oz) fresh coriander (cilantro)

1 tablespoon olive oil

3 teaspoons cumin seeds

2 teaspoons coriander seeds

3 cm (1¼ inch) piece fresh turmeric, peeled and finely grated, or 3 teaspoons ground turmeric

2 orange sweet potatoes (kumara), about 400 g (14 oz) each, cut into small chunks

2 large carrots, cut into small chunks

2 cloves garlic, crushed

finely grated zest of 1 lemon

¼ cup (60 ml) lemon juice

2 x 400 g (14 oz) cans chickpeas, rinsed and drained

steamed basmati or brown rice, to serve

1 Finely chop the coriander roots and stems. Finely chop 2 tablespoons of the coriander leaves, reserving 4 sprigs for garnishing.

2 Heat the oil in a large, deep heavy-based saucepan over medium-high heat. Add the cumin seeds, coriander seeds, turmeric and fresh coriander roots and stems. Cook for 2 minutes, until aromatic.

3 Add the sweet potatoes, carrots and garlic, and stir until combined. Cook for 10 minutes, until softened. Add the lemon zest, lemon juice and 2½ cups (625 ml) water. Stir, then bring to a boil. Reduce the heat and simmer for 25 minutes, until the vegetables are tender.

4 Add the chickpeas and chopped coriander leaves. Cook for 20 minutes, until the chickpeas are very soft and the mixture has thickened. Serve with steamed rice, garnished with coriander sprigs.

Serves 4

Preparation
15 minutes

Cooking
1 hour

Per serving
1406 kJ, 336 kcal, 13 g protein, 9 g fat (1 g saturated fat), 52 g carbohydrate (15 g sugars), 12 g fibre, 358 mg sodium

This stew is rich in anti-oxidants and also high in fibre. Low-GI foods, such as sweet potato and chickpeas, release their energy slowly to keep your blood glucose level stable.

Sauerkraut, bean and bacon hotpot

Serves 4

Preparation
20 minutes

Cooking
1 hour

Per serving
*1567 kJ, 374 kcal,
18 g protein, 13 g fat
(5 g saturated fat),
40 g carbohydrate
(16 g sugars), 11 g fibre,
878 mg sodium*

1½ tablespoons ghee or olive oil

100 g (3½ oz) slices rindless bacon (bacon strips), roughly chopped

2 onions, halved and thinly sliced

2 cloves garlic, crushed

2 red capsicums (bell peppers), cut into 2 cm (¾ inch) pieces

1½ tablespoons sugar

3 teaspoons sweet paprika

1 teaspoon dried marjoram

1 teaspoon caraway seeds

300 ml (10 fl oz) salt-reduced beef stock (page 14)

2 x 420 g (15 oz) cans white beans, rinsed and drained

Fresh sauerkraut

2 teaspoons vegetable oil

1 onion, thinly sliced

2 cloves garlic, sliced

1 cup (250 ml) white wine

6 cups (450 g) shredded savoy cabbage (1 small head)

1 bay leaf

3 cloves

2 tablespoons white wine vinegar

1 teaspoon sugar

¼ teaspoon salt

1 To make the sauerkraut, heat the oil in a large non-stick frying pan. Sauté the onion and garlic over medium heat for 5 minutes, until the onion is softened. Pour in the white wine and bring to a boil. Stir in the cabbage, bay leaf and cloves, then cover and simmer over medium-low heat for 20–30 minutes, until the cabbage is tender. Stir in the white vinegar, sugar and salt, and simmer for 10 minutes. Remove from the heat.

2 Heat the ghee in a large saucepan and cook the bacon, onions and garlic over medium heat, stirring frequently, for 3 minutes.

3 Add the sauerkraut and capsicums to the pan and sprinkle with the sugar, paprika, marjoram and caraway seeds. Pour in the stock and 600 ml (21 fl oz) water, and bring to a boil. Reduce the heat, then cover and simmer for 5 minutes.

4 Add the beans and simmer for a further 5 minutes, until heated through.

If you like, add a little low-fat sour cream to the hotpot before serving. Serve with crusty rye bread or baguette.

The cabbage retains its fresh flavour and much more of its nutritional power in this homemade fresh sauerkraut.

Sauerkraut, bean and bacon hotpot

Sauerkraut, bean and apple hotpot

Heat **2 tablespoons (40 g) butter** in a saucepan and fry **2 finely diced onions** and **100 g (3½ oz) slices rindless bacon (bacon strips)** until onions are translucent. Cut **2 tart apples** into thin wedges. Rinse and drain a **420 g (15 oz) can white beans.** Add the apples and beans to the saucepan together with the sauerkraut from the main recipe, and cook for 3 minutes. Season with **2 teaspoons sugar** and **freshly ground black pepper.** Add **2 bay leaves, 2 juniper berries** and **400 ml (14 fl oz) salt-reduced vegetable stock** (page 15), cover and cook over medium heat for a further 15 minutes.

Pork pot-au-feu with salsa verde

Serves 4

Preparation
20 minutes

Cooking
25 minutes

Per serving
*2164 kJ, 517 kcal,
40 g protein, 29 g fat
(5 g saturated fat),
23 g carbohydrate
(6 g sugars), 8 g fibre,
888 mg sodium*

*An Italian salsa
verde is perfect
to dollop into
pot-au-feu. It is
also lovely served
alongside roasted
meats, or as a
condiment for
chicken and
fish dishes.*

2 cups (500 ml) salt-reduced
beef stock (page 14)

6 black peppercorns

150 g (5 oz) baby carrots,
diagonally sliced

8 small new potatoes,
scrubbed, cut in half if large

1 celery stalk, thickly sliced

2 pork fillets, about 250 g
(8 oz) each, trimmed of fat

1 leek, white part only,
thickly sliced

3⅓ cups (200 g) small
broccoli florets

freshly ground black pepper

Salsa verde

1 bunch (80 g/3 oz) fresh
parsley, coarsely chopped

1 bunch (80 g/3 oz) fresh
basil, coarsely chopped

60 g (2 oz) gherkins (pickles)

1 clove garlic, crushed

2 French shallots (eschalots),
finely chopped

2 tablespoons capers, rinsed
and squeezed dry

100 ml (3½ fl oz) olive oil

2 tablespoons lemon juice

2 hard-boiled (hard-cooked)
eggs, finely chopped

freshly ground black pepper

1 Place the stock and peppercorns in a large saucepan. Add 2 cups (500 ml) water, cover and bring to a boil. Add the carrots, potatoes and celery to the hot stock, return to a boil, then reduce the heat, cover and simmer over low heat for 10 minutes.

2 Add the pork fillets to the pan and simmer, covered, for 12 minutes, until cooked. Add the leek and broccoli for the final 3 minutes of cooking.

3 Remove the poached pork fillets from the broth with a slotted spoon and allow to rest for 5 minutes, then cut into thick slices and season with freshly ground black pepper.

4 While the pork is resting, make the salsa verde. Place the herbs in a food processor or blender with the gherkins, garlic, shallots, capers, oil and lemon juice. Pulse until smooth, then fold in the eggs and season with pepper.

5 Place the pork in wide bowls and ladle in the vegetables and broth. Serve with a generous dollop of the salsa verde.

Pork and beans

1¼ cups (250 g) dried haricot (navy) beans

1 tablespoon sunflower or vegetable oil

4 thin lean pork chump chops, about 150 g (5 oz) each, trimmed of fat

1 onion, chopped

1 cup (250 ml) beer, such as dark ale

410 g (15 oz) can chopped tomatoes

2 teaspoons worcestershire sauce, or to taste

2 tablespoons dark brown sugar

3 allspice berries

2 tablespoons mild American or French mustard

2 slices rindless smoked lean back bacon (bacon strips), cut into bite-sized pieces

1 teaspoon cider vinegar, or to taste

Serves 4

Preparation
25 minutes, plus
8 hours soaking

Cooking
2 hours

Per serving
*1989 kJ, 475 kcal,
52 g protein, 11 g fat
(3 g saturated fat),
37 g carbohydrate
(13 g sugars), 13 g fibre,
587 mg sodium*

1 Put the dried beans in a large bowl and cover with plenty of water. Leave to soak for 8 hours or overnight.

2 Drain and rinse the beans, then place them in a large saucepan with enough water to come up to about twice the depth of the beans. Cover and bring to a boil. Skim off any scum, then reduce the heat, cover and cook the beans over low heat for 45–60 minutes, until they are just tender.

3 Meanwhile, heat the oil in a deep flameproof casserole dish, add the pork chops and onion, and fry until the chops are browned on both sides. Pour in the beer and tomatoes, then add the worcestershire sauce, sugar and allspice. Reduce the heat, cover and cook for about 1 hour, until the meat is very tender.

4 Drain the beans and add to the pork chops. Add the mustard, bacon and vinegar, and stir well. Cover and cook over low heat for a further 1 hour, until both the beans and the pork are tender.

5 Before serving, taste and add a dash or two more of worcestershire sauce or vinegar if needed.

Tomatoes contain lycopene, a valuable anti-oxidant that is thought to protect against pancreatic, prostate and bladder cancers. Lycopene is enhanced by cooking and so is most readily available in processed tomato products, such as canned tomatoes, tomato passata (puréed tomatoes) and tomato paste (concentrated purée).

Goulash in a hurry

This shortcut version of classic Hungarian goulash is rich and satisfying. Strips of lean pork, shredded red cabbage and capsicum cook quickly and work beautifully with the traditional flavourings of paprika and caraway seeds. Serve the goulash with rice or noodles and a simple green salad.

2 tablespoons extra virgin olive oil

1 large onion, finely chopped

2 cloves garlic, crushed

3 thick lean pork loin steaks, about 300 g (10 oz) in total, cut into thin strips

1 tablespoon plain (all-purpose) flour

800 g (28 oz) can tomatoes

1/2 cup (125 ml) extra dry white vermouth

2 tablespoons paprika, plus extra, to serve

1 teaspoon caraway seeds

1 teaspoon caster (superfine) sugar

1 chicken stock (bouillon) cube, crumbled

1 large green capsicum (bell pepper), chopped

2 2/3 cups (200 g) finely shredded red cabbage

pinch of salt

freshly ground black pepper

1/3 cup (90 g) thick (Greek-style) yogurt

fresh chives, to serve

1 Heat the oil in a large frying pan or saucepan. Add the onion, garlic and pork, and cook over high heat for about 3 minutes, until the meat has changed colour and become firm and the onion is slightly softened. Meanwhile, blend the flour with 1/3 cup (80 ml) of the juice from the canned tomatoes to make a smooth paste; set aside.

2 Add the vermouth, paprika, caraway seeds and sugar to the pan and stir, then add the tomatoes with the rest of their juice, breaking them up as you mix them in. Stir in the stock cube along with the flour and tomato juice mixture. Bring to a boil, stirring, and cook until the juices thicken.

3 Stir in the capsicum and red cabbage until thoroughly coated in the cooking juices. Reduce the heat, cover and simmer the goulash for 15 minutes, until the pork is cooked and the vegetables are just tender, but still slightly crisp.

4 Taste the goulash and season with salt and freshly ground black pepper, if needed. Ladle it into bowls and top each portion with yogurt and a sprinkle of paprika. Serve garnished with chives.

Serves 4

Preparation
15 minutes

Cooking
25 minutes

Per serving
1498 kJ, 358 kcal,
22 g protein, 18 g fat
(6 g saturated fat),
20 g carbohydrate
(14 g sugars), 7 g fibre,
493 mg sodium

Studies have shown that eating garlic can reduce the risk of heart attack and stroke by making the blood less sticky and likely to clot. Garlic can also help reduce high blood pressure.

Onions share garlic's healthy properties and they are also a natural decongestant. They are an excellent staple in your everyday cooking.

Moroccan-style lamb shank tagine

Serves 4

Preparation
10 minutes

Cooking
4 hours

Per serving
1407 kJ, 336 kcal,
35 g protein, 10 g fat
(3 g saturated fat),
25 g carbohydrate
(13 g sugars), 7 g fibre,
876 mg sodium

4 lamb shanks, about 250 g
(8 oz) each, French trimmed

410 g (15 oz) can chopped
tomatoes

1 apple, peeled and diced

1 onion, finely chopped

1 carrot, finely diced

400 g (14 oz) can chickpeas,
rinsed and drained

8 kalamata olives

8 pitted prunes

2 tablespoons chopped
preserved lemon

1 cinnamon stick

¼ teaspoon ground ginger

¼ teaspoon ground cumin

¼ teaspoon ground turmeric

green salad, to serve

1 Preheat the oven to 150°C (300°F/Gas 2).

2 Put the lamb shanks in a large casserole dish
with a tight-fitting lid, or in a tagine. Add the canned
tomatoes, apple, onion, carrot, chickpeas, olives,
prunes, preserved lemon and spices, and mix well.

3 Cover and bake for 4 hours, until the meat is
very tender. Serve hot, with a green salad.

To French trim lamb shanks, cut the meat
and fat away from the end of the shank to
expose the bone.

Tagines are usually high in fibre as they
feature legumes and dried fruits such as
prunes or figs; these ingredients also lower
the GI value of this dish. The herbs and
spices provide a range of anti-oxidants.

Lamb, fig and chickpea stew

1 lamb shoulder, about 1 kg (2 lb), or 1 kg (2 lb) lean lamb leg steaks, cut into 3 cm (1¼ inch) cubes

freshly ground black pepper

2 tablespoons extra virgin olive oil

1 large onion, chopped

2 cloves garlic, chopped

2 teaspoons ground coriander

2 teaspoons ground cumin

1 teaspoon ground ginger

1 tablespoon plain (all-purpose) flour

2 cups (500 ml) salt-reduced beef stock (page 14)

3 tomatoes, chopped

2 strips orange zest

1 cinnamon stick, broken

½ cup (95 g) chopped dried figs

300 g (10 oz) can chickpeas, rinsed and drained, or 1 cup (160 g) cooked chickpeas

¼ cup (7 g) chopped fresh parsley or coriander (cilantro) leaves

1 Preheat the oven to 180°C (350°F/Gas 4). Season the lamb with freshly ground black pepper. Heat 1 tablespoon of the oil in a large frying pan over medium heat. Add half the lamb and cook, stirring frequently, for 4–5 minutes, until browned, then transfer to a plate. Cook the remaining lamb, transfer to the plate and set aside.

2 Heat the remaining oil in a large flameproof casserole dish over medium-low heat. Cook the onion and garlic, stirring occasionally, for 2 minutes, until the onion is soft. Add the ground spices. Cook, stirring, for 1 minute. Add the flour and cook, stirring constantly, for 1 minute.

3 Stir in the stock, tomatoes and 1 cup (250 ml) water. Add the orange zest and cinnamon, and bring to a boil. Reduce the heat to low, add the lamb and stir to combine. Cover the casserole dish and transfer to the oven to cook for 1 hour.

4 Add the figs and chickpeas, cover and cook in the oven, stirring occasionally, for a further 30 minutes, until the lamb is tender. Add a little water during cooking if needed to keep the lamb just covered. Stir in the parsley or coriander and serve hot.

Serves 4

Preparation
20 minutes

Cooking
1 hour 50 minutes

Per serving
2386 kJ, 570 kcal, 59 g protein, 25 g fat (8 g saturated fat), 28 g carbohydrate (17 g sugars), 8 g fibre, 881 mg sodium

Taking the time to brown the lamb will result in a richly flavoured dish. Don't overcrowd the pan when you brown the meat, so that it colours to a deep golden brown rather than stewing.

This stew goes well with a side serve of wholegrain couscous.

Indian lamb with spiced lentils

Serves 4

Preparation
30 minutes

Cooking
1½ hours

Per serving
*2109 kJ, 504 kcal,
49 g protein, 20 g fat
(5 g saturated fat),
35 g carbohydrate
(6 g sugars), 11 g fibre,
853 mg sodium*

*Lentils are a
great source of
protein, dietary
fibre and a good
source of iron, as
well as vitamins
B_1 and B_6.*

6 black peppercorns

1 tablespoon cumin seeds

seeds from 8 green
cardamom pods

2 tablespoons sunflower
or vegetable oil

1 large onion, sliced

2 cloves garlic, crushed

5 cm (2 inch) piece fresh
ginger, peeled and finely
chopped

1 red chilli, seeded and
finely chopped

1 cinnamon stick

1 teaspoon ground turmeric

500 g (1 lb) lean boneless
leg of lamb or neck fillet,
trimmed of fat and cut
into cubes

600 ml (21 fl oz) hot salt-
reduced lamb stock (page 14)

1⅓ cups (250 g) green lentils

4 roma (plum) tomatoes,
cut into quarters

juice of ½ lemon

2 tablespoons chopped
fresh coriander (cilantro)
leaves

pinch of salt

freshly ground black pepper

1 Crush the peppercorns with the cumin and cardamom seeds in a mortar and pestle. Set aside.

2 Heat the oil in a large flameproof casserole dish and gently cook the onion over medium heat for 5 minutes, until softened. Add the garlic, ginger and chilli, and cook for a further 3 minutes, then add the crushed spices and the cinnamon stick and turmeric. Gently cook, stirring constantly, for 30 seconds.

3 Add the lamb and stir to coat with the spices. Gently cook for 4 minutes, until the meat is browned all over. Gradually pour in the stock, stirring well, and bring to a boil. Reduce the heat, cover and gently cook for 1 hour, until the lamb is tender and almost cooked.

4 Meanwhile, rinse and drain the lentils, then place them in a saucepan and cover with cold water. Bring to a boil and cook for 15 minutes, then drain.

5 Add the lentils and tomatoes to the curry and cook for 20 minutes, until the lamb and lentils are tender. Stir in the lemon juice and coriander, and season with salt and freshly ground black pepper. Serve hot.

Argentine beef stew

½ cup (125 ml) vegetable oil

1 tablespoon (20 g) butter

1 kg (2 lb) topside or round beef steak, cut into bite-sized pieces

2 onions, finely chopped

2 cloves garlic, finely chopped

1 dried bay leaf

½ teaspoon marinated green peppercorns

pinch of salt

freshly ground black pepper

½ teaspoon cayenne pepper

1 teaspoon dried basil

1 teaspoon dried marjoram

1 cup (250 ml) dry white wine

2 cups (500 ml) salt-reduced beef stock (page 14)

500 g (1 lb) boiling (waxy) potatoes, diced

2 cups (300 g) finely diced pumpkin (winter squash)

2 green capsicums (bell peppers), finely diced

410 g (15 oz) can corn kernels, drained

2 peaches

200 g (7 oz) red or black grapes, preferably seedless

1 cup (250 g) canned chopped tomatoes

Serves 6

Preparation
20 minutes

Cooking
1 hour 20 minutes

Per serving
2552 kJ, 610 kcal, 44 g protein, 30 g fat (7 g saturated fat), 35 g carbohydrate (16 g sugars), 6 g fibre, 706 mg sodium

1 Heat the oil and butter in a large saucepan. Brown the beef in batches on all sides over medium-high heat, removing each batch with a slotted spoon as it is done. Return all the meat to the pan, add the onions and garlic, and cook with the meat for 3 minutes.

2 Add the bay leaf and peppercorns, then season with salt, freshly ground black pepper, cayenne pepper, dried basil and dried marjoram. Pour in the wine and stock, then cover and simmer for 30 minutes.

3 Add the potatoes, pumpkin, capsicums and corn, then cover and simmer for a further 20 minutes.

4 Meanwhile, blanch the peaches in hot water. Peel off the skins, cut in half and remove the stones. Cut the peaches into thick wedges. Cut the grapes in half and remove any seeds using a small sharp knife.

5 Carefully mix the peaches, grapes and tomatoes into the stew, and cook for a further 5 minutes, until heated through. Taste, season further if necessary and serve.

If fresh peaches are not available, you can use canned peaches. Drain them well over a sieve before adding to the stew.

Many meals from one – ratatouille

A classic stew of summer vegetables, ratatouille is a splendid accompaniment to meat, chicken or fish. This simple version serves 8, so you can transform leftovers into enticing new meals.

Ratatouille

Serves 8   **Time** 45 minutes

2 tablespoons olive oil

1 large onion, chopped

3 cloves garlic, crushed

2 red capsicums (bell peppers), chopped

4 zucchini (courgettes), chopped

3 eggplant (aubergine), chopped

2 x 410g (15 oz) cans chopped tomatoes

pinch of salt

freshly ground black pepper

pinch of sugar

Heat the oil in a large heavy-based saucepan over medium heat. Add the onion and cook for 5 minutes, until soft and lightly golden. Add the garlic and cook for 1 minute, then add the capsicums and cook, stirring occasionally, for 2 minutes. Stir in the zucchini and eggplant.

Stir in the tomatoes and bring to a boil. Reduce the heat to low, partially cover the pan with a lid, then simmer, stirring occasionally, for 20 minutes, until the vegetables are tender. Season the ratatouille with salt, freshly ground black pepper and sugar.

Per serving
388 kJ, 93 kcal, 3 g protein, 5 g fat (<1 g saturated fat), 8 g carbohydrate (8 g sugars), 5 g fibre, 146 mg sodium

Tunisian ratatouille with eggs

Serves 4   **Time** 30 minutes

2 tablespoons olive oil

2 onions, thinly sliced

3 green capsicums (bell peppers), sliced

3 zucchini (courgettes), sliced

3 cloves garlic, crushed

1 teaspoon mild paprika

1 teaspoon ground cumin

large pinch of cayenne pepper, or to taste

pinch of salt

freshly ground black pepper

410 g (15 oz) can chopped tomatoes

8 eggs

Heat the oil in a very large, deep ovenproof frying pan. Gently cook the onions for 5 minutes. Add the capsicums, zucchini and garlic. Cover and cook over medium heat, stirring frequently, for 5 minutes, until beginning to colour.

Stir in the paprika, cumin and cayenne pepper. Season with salt and freshly ground black pepper. Stir in the tomatoes, cover and gently cook for 5 minutes.

Preheat the grill (broiler) to high. Make eight small hollows in the ratatouille mixture and crack an egg into each one. Gently cook over low heat for 2 minutes. Slide the pan under the grill and cook for 2-3 minutes, until the eggs are just set. Serve immediately.

Per serving
1180 kJ, 282 kcal, 17 g protein, 20 g fat (4 g saturated fat), 10 g carbohydrate (8 g sugars), 4 g fibre, 356 mg sodium

Ways to use ratatouille

The following recipes serve 2, and each uses two ratatouille portions. Halve the recipes to serve 1.

Spicy vegetarian chickpea stew

Rinse and drain **2 x 125 g (4 oz) cans chickpeas.** Gently heat the ratatouille and chickpeas in a saucepan. Stir in **1 cup (45 g) chopped baby spinach** and $\frac{1}{2}$ **teaspoon dried red chilli flakes.** Serve with a dollop of **yogurt** or **sour cream,** on a bed of **steamed rice,** if desired.

Tuna pasta bake

Preheat the oven to 200°C (400°F/Gas 6). Cook **100 g ($3\frac{1}{2}$ oz) short pasta** (such as penne, spirals or farfalle) until al dente. Drain well, then return to the pan. Drain and flake a **95 g (3 oz) can tuna** and stir into the pasta along with the ratatouille. Spread the pasta mixture into a 5 cup (1.25 litre) ovenproof dish. Top with $\frac{1}{2}$ **cup (75 g) grated mozzarella** or $\frac{1}{2}$ **cup (60 g) grated cheddar.** Bake for 15 minutes, until the cheese has melted and is bubbling.

Ratatouille tarts

Preheat the oven to 200°C (400°F/Gas 6). Cut **1 sheet frozen puff pastry** in half. Tightly wrap one pastry half in plastic wrap and return to the freezer. Thaw the other half, cut into two squares and place on a baking tray lined with baking (parchment) paper. Use a small sharp knife to score a border around each pastry square, 1 cm ($\frac{1}{2}$ inch) in from the edge. Prick the pastry inside the border with a fork, then bake for 15 minutes, until puffed and golden.

Meanwhile, reheat the ratatouille. Put each pastry square on a serving plate. If the centre has puffed up, gently press it down with a tea towel (dish towel). Pile the ratatouille in the centre, crumble some **fetta** over the top, sprinkle with **fresh thyme leaves** and serve immediately.

> *You can freeze portions of ratatouille in airtight containers or zip-lock bags for up to 3 months. Thaw in the microwave, or overnight in the fridge.*

Curried lentil pasties

Preheat the oven to 200°C (400°F/Gas 6). Reheat the ratatouille in a small saucepan. Stir in $\frac{1}{4}$ **cup (60 g) red lentils,** $\frac{1}{4}$ **cup (60 ml) water** and **1 teaspoon curry powder.** Cover and bring to a simmer, then reduce the heat to very low. Cook, stirring regularly, for 15 minutes, until the lentils are tender. Allow to cool completely.

Meanwhile, thaw **2 sheets frozen shortcrust pastry.** Using a bowl as a guide, cut a 15 cm (6 inch) circle from one corner of the pastry, then cut a round from the opposite corner: it will overlap where you have already cut, so use a scrap of pastry to patch the gap.

Spoon the cooled lentil mixture onto the pastry rounds. Gather up the pastry, pinch firmly to seal, then gently press down to give the pasties a flat base. Place the pasties on a baking tray lined with baking (parchment) paper and bake for 20 minutes, until golden brown.

Ratatouille with polenta

Reheat the ratatouille in a small saucepan. In another pan, heat $1\frac{1}{3}$ **cups (330 ml) salt-reduced chicken or vegetable stock** (pages 14-15) until boiling; add $\frac{1}{2}$ **cup (75 g) instant polenta** and stir over low heat for 3 minutes, until thick and soft. Stir in **2 tablespoons grated parmesan.** Serve the ratatouille over the polenta, sprinkled with **shredded fresh basil.** It is also good topped with a poached egg.

Ratatouille with baked fish

Preheat the oven to 200°C (400°F/Gas 6). Spread the ratatouille over a 20 x 15 cm (8 x 6 inch) ovenproof dish. Arrange **2 x 150 g (5 oz) salmon or white fish fillets** on top. Drizzle with **2 teaspoons olive oil** and **2 teaspoons lemon juice,** then season with **freshly ground black pepper.** Bake for 15 minutes, until the fish is cooked.

Aromatic beef curry

Serves 4

Preparation
20 minutes

Cooking
30 minutes

Per serving
*2629 kJ, 628 kcal,
35 g protein, 15 g fat
(5 g saturated fat),
88 g carbohydrate
(16 g sugars), 5 g fibre,
178 mg sodium*

1 tablespoon sunflower or vegetable oil

1 large onion, thinly sliced

150 g (5 oz) button mushrooms, sliced

400 g (14 oz) sirloin steak, trimmed of fat and cut into thin strips

1¹/₂ teaspoons bottled ginger in oil, drained

2 cloves garlic, crushed

¹/₂ teaspoon dried red chilli flakes

2 teaspoons ground coriander

¹/₄ teaspoon ground cardamom

¹/₂ teaspoon ground turmeric

¹/₄ teaspoon freshly grated nutmeg

410 g (15 oz) can chopped tomatoes

1 teaspoon cornflour (cornstarch)

1¹/₄ cups (310 g) natural (plain) yogurt

1 tablespoon honey

2 cups (90 g) baby spinach leaves

juice of ¹/₂ lime

2 tablespoons chopped fresh coriander (cilantro) leaves, plus extra sprigs, to garnish

Cardamom rice

1³/₄ cups (350 g) basmati rice, well rinsed

1 cinnamon stick

8 green cardamom pods, cracked

juice of ¹/₂ lemon

1 Heat the oil in a large saucepan and add the onion and mushrooms. Cook over high heat for 2 minutes, until the onion begins to colour, being careful it doesn't burn.

2 Add the beef with the ginger, garlic, chilli and spices. Cook for 2 minutes, stirring well, then add the tomatoes. Mix the cornflour with 1 tablespoon water and stir into the beef mixture. Bring to a boil, stirring. Stir in the yogurt and honey. Bring back to a boil, then reduce the heat, cover and gently simmer for 20 minutes.

3 Meanwhile, prepare the cardamom rice. Put 2 cups (500 ml) water in a saucepan and bring to a boil. Add the rice, cinnamon stick and cardamom pods. Bring back to a boil, then tightly cover and cook for 10 minutes, until the rice is tender. Drain off any water and return the rice to the saucepan. Stir in the lemon juice and keep covered until the curry is ready to serve.

4 Stir the spinach, lime juice and chopped coriander into the curry and allow the leaves to wilt down into the sauce. To serve, spoon the curry over the rice and garnish with coriander sprigs.

Along with its many other nutritional benefits, beef provides B group vitamins and is a useful source of selenium and copper.

Thai red curry paste is sold in most large supermarkets. Once opened, it will keep for several weeks in the fridge.

Thai red beef curry

Serves 2

Preparation
15 minutes

Cooking
10 minutes

Per serving
1554 kJ, 371 kcal, 33 g protein, 22 g fat (10 g saturated fat), 11 g carbohydrate (6 g sugars), 4 g fibre, 536 mg sodium

250 g (8 oz) rump (round) steak, trimmed of fat

3 teaspoons vegetable oil

½ small onion, sliced lengthwise

½ small red capsicum (bell pepper), cut into long strips

60 g (2 oz) snow peas (mangetout), trimmed, then halved lengthwise on the diagonal

2 cups (120 g) small broccoli florets

1 tablespoon Thai red curry paste

½ cup (125 ml) low-fat coconut milk

2 teaspoons fish sauce

juice of ½ lime

1 teaspoon soft brown sugar

4–5 sprigs fresh coriander (cilantro), to garnish

steamed jasmine rice (Thai fragrant rice), to serve

1 Cut the steak into very thin slices across the grain. Heat 1 teaspoon of the oil in a wok or large, deep non-stick frying pan over medium-high heat. Stir-fry half the meat and half the onion for 2 minutes, until just browned, then transfer to a plate. Heat another 1 teaspoon of the oil in the pan. Stir-fry the remaining meat and onion, then transfer to the plate.

2 Heat the remaining oil, then stir-fry the capsicum, snow peas and broccoli for 2 minutes. Add the curry paste and stir-fry for 1 minute. Return the meat and onion to the pan, then pour in the coconut milk. Bring to a boil, then reduce the heat and simmer for 2 minutes.

3 Stir in the fish sauce, lime juice and brown sugar. Sprinkle the curry with coriander leaves and serve with some steamed jasmine rice.

Irish stew

Traditional recipes for Irish stew use a tough, fatty cut of lamb and potatoes, onions and herbs. This up-to-date version with lamb leg steaks is leaner, and more colourful with the addition of carrots, but still retains its comforting, homely flavour.

4 boneless lean lamb leg steaks, about 500 g (1 lb) in total, trimmed of fat and each steak cut into 4 pieces

1 kg (2 lb) baking (floury) potatoes, thickly sliced

1 large onion, sliced

500 g (1 lb) carrots, thickly sliced

2 tablespoons chopped fresh parsley, plus extra, to serve

1 teaspoon fresh thyme leaves, plus extra, to serve

1 tablespoon snipped fresh chives

pinch of salt

freshly ground black pepper

2 cups (500 ml) hot salt-reduced lamb or vegetable stock (pages 14-15)

1 Preheat the oven to 160°C (320°F/Gas 2-3).

2 Layer the lamb, potatoes, onion and carrots in a large casserole dish, sprinkling each layer with parsley, thyme, chives, salt and freshly ground black pepper. Finish with a layer of potatoes, then pour in the stock.

3 Cover the casserole dish with a tight-fitting lid and bake for about 2 hours, until both the meat and vegetables feel tender when tested with a skewer.

4 Increase the oven temperature to 200°C (400°F/Gas 6). Remove the lid and cook for a further 20 minutes, until the potatoes on top are golden brown and crisp. Serve the stew hot, sprinkled with extra parsley and thyme.

Serves 4

Preparation
20 minutes

Cooking
2 hours 20 minutes

Per serving
1680 kJ, 401 kcal, 36 g protein, 8 g fat (4 g saturated fat), 45 g carbohydrate (12 g sugars), 8 g fibre, 812 mg sodium

Beef in red wine

Long, slow cooking gives this traditional casserole its inimitable flavour. The cooking liquid is reduced by removing the casserole lid, resulting in a rich, aromatic sauce that glazes the meat and vegetables. For a theatrical finale, the dish is flambéd with brandy.

2 tablespoons sunflower or vegetable oil

1 large onion, sliced

500 g (1 lb) lean stewing beef, cut into cubes

250 g (8 oz) baby carrots, trimmed

250 g (8 oz) baby parsnips, trimmed

250 g (8 oz) button mushrooms

1 clove garlic, finely chopped

1 bottle full-bodied red wine

grated zest and juice of 1 orange

1 sprig fresh thyme

1 sprig fresh rosemary

1 bay leaf

pinch of salt

freshly ground black pepper

1 cup (185 g) shelled fresh broad (fava) beans, or frozen broad beans, thawed

¼ cup (60 ml) brandy

2 tablespoons chopped fresh parsley, to serve

1 Preheat the oven to 150°C (300°F/Gas 2). Heat the oil in a large flameproof casserole dish. Add the onion and cook over medium-high heat for 5 minutes, until softened and beginning to brown. Add the beef and cook, stirring frequently, for about 5 minutes, until the pieces of meat are browned on all sides. Stir in the carrots, parsnips, mushrooms and garlic.

2 Pour in the wine, then stir in the orange zest and juice, thyme, rosemary and bay leaf. Season with salt and freshly ground black pepper. Bring to a boil, cover the casserole and transfer it to the oven to cook for 1¼ hours.

3 Remove the lid and cook the casserole for a further 30 minutes, stirring once or twice. Stir in the broad beans and cook for 30 minutes, stirring once or twice.

4 Taste and adjust the seasoning. Warm the brandy in a small saucepan and pour it over the casserole. Immediately set the brandy alight and carefully carry the casserole to the table while still flaming. When the flame goes out, sprinkle with the parsley and serve.

Serves 4

Preparation
20 minutes

Cooking
2½ hours

Per serving
2125 kJ, 508 kcal, 35 g protein, 18 g fat (4 g saturated fat), 17 g carbohydrate (11 g sugars), 9 g fibre, 303 mg sodium

Robust broad beans go well with beef and they bring valuable dietary fibre to this classic dish.

Red meat such as beef offers excellent value in a balanced diet – it is a good source of iron and zinc, as well as vitamins B_6 and B_{12}.

Slow-cooker Cajun chicken

Serves 4

Preparation
15 minutes

Cooking
4–8 hours

Per serving
*2132 kJ, 509 kcal,
76 g protein, 19 g fat
(6 g saturated fat),
7 g carbohydrate
(5 g sugars), 3 g fibre,
771 mg sodium*

4 boneless, skinless chicken breasts

$1/2$ teaspoon salt

$1/4$ teaspoon freshly ground black pepper

1–2 teaspoons Cajun seasoning, or to taste

410 g (14 oz) can chopped tomatoes

1 celery stalk, diced

1 green capsicum (bell pepper), diced

3 cloves garlic, crushed

1 onion, diced

$1^{1}/_{3}$ cups (120 g) sliced button mushrooms

1 green chilli, seeded and chopped

steamed rice, to serve

1 Place the chicken breasts in the slow cooker and add the salt, pepper and Cajun seasoning to taste. Stir in the remaining ingredients.

2 Cover and cook on low for 8 hours, or on high for 4–5 hours. Serve with steamed rice.

*This slow-cooker chicken is fantastic
for a busy weeknight meal. Simply
add your ingredients to the slow
cooker in the morning or afternoon,
turn it on and enjoy the aroma as
it fills the kitchen. When it's almost
dinnertime, all you need to do is
steam some rice.*

Slow-cooker honey ginger chicken

1 tablespoon vegetable oil

8 small boneless, skinless chicken thighs

$^1/_2$ cup (175 g) honey

$^1/_4$ cup (60 ml) light soy sauce

$^1/_4$ cup (60 ml) no added salt tomato sauce (ketchup)

440 g (15 oz) can pineapple pieces in juice, drained, juice reserved

2 cloves garlic, crushed

1 tablespoon grated fresh ginger

2 tablespoons cornflour (cornstarch)

steamed rice, to serve

coriander (cilantro) leaves, to garnish

1 Heat the oil in a large frying pan over medium heat. Add the chicken and cook for 4 minutes on each side, until golden brown. Set aside.

2 Pour the honey, soy sauce, tomato sauce and reserved pineapple juice into the slow cooker. Add the garlic and ginger, and mix well. Add the chicken and turn to coat all over with the sauce.

3 Cover and cook on high for 4 hours, stirring in the pineapple pieces during the final 20 minutes of cooking.

4 Remove the chicken from the slow cooker and keep warm. In a small bowl, mix the cornflour with $^1/_3$ cup (80 ml) water to make a smooth paste, then add to the remaining sauce and stir until it thickens.

5 Serve the chicken over steamed rice, drizzled with the sauce and garnished with the coriander.

Serves 4

Preparation
15 minutes

Cooking
4$^1/_4$ hours

Per serving
3023 kJ, 722 kcal, 62 g protein, 28 g fat (8 g saturated fat), 57 g carbohydrate (51 g sugars), 2 g fibre, 855 mg sodium

Coq au vin

Serves 4

Preparation
20 minutes

Cooking
1 hour 10 minutes

Per serving
1328 kJ, 317 kcal,
23 g protein, 15 g fat
(4 g saturated fat),
7 g carbohydrate
(5 g sugars), 4 g fibre,
542 mg sodium

12 French shallots (eschalots) or baby onions, unpeeled

1½ tablespoons olive oil

2 slices rindless bacon (bacon strips), cut into thin strips

12 Swiss brown or button mushrooms

1 clove garlic, crushed

4 bone-in chicken breast halves or thighs, about 625 g (1¼ lb) in total, skin removed

3 sprigs fresh parsley, stalks bruised

2 sprigs fresh thyme

1 bay leaf

150 ml (5 fl oz) salt-reduced chicken stock (page 14)

1½ cups (375 ml) full-bodied red wine, such as burgundy

1 teaspoon freshly ground black pepper

300 g (10 oz) carrots, cut into chunks

pinch of caster (superfine) sugar

1 tablespoon cornflour (cornstarch)

2 tablespoons chopped fresh parsley

1 Place the shallots in a heatproof bowl and cover with boiling water. Leave for 30 seconds, then drain. When cool enough to handle, peel and set aside.

2 Heat 1 tablespoon of the olive oil in a large heavy-based saucepan over medium heat. Cook the bacon, stirring often, for 3 minutes, until crisp. Remove and set aside. Add the peeled shallots to the pan. Cook over medium-high heat, stirring frequently, for 5 minutes, until golden brown. Remove and set aside.

3 Add the mushrooms and garlic to the pan along with the remaining olive oil. Cook, stirring often, for 4 minutes, until the mushrooms are golden.

4 Add half the bacon and half the shallots to the pan. Place the chicken on top and sprinkle with the remaining bacon and shallots. Tie the parsley, thyme and bay leaf into a bouquet garni, and add to the pan with the stock, wine and black pepper. Bring to a boil, then reduce the heat and simmer for 15 minutes. Add the carrots and simmer for a further 30 minutes, until the chicken is cooked through and the carrots are tender.

5 Transfer the chicken to a warmed serving platter, then add the bacon, mushrooms, shallots and carrots, reserving the bouquet garni. Keep the platter warm.

6 Strain the cooking liquid into a saucepan and add the bouquet garni and sugar. Bring to a boil and cook until the sauce has reduced to ½ cup (125 ml). Combine the cornflour with 1 tablespoon water to make a paste; add to the sauce, stirring constantly. Simmer for 2 minutes, until thickened. Discard the bouquet garni.

7 Spoon the sauce over the chicken and vegetables, sprinkle with the parsley and serve hot.

Coq au vin

Chicken with riesling

Instead of bone-in pieces, use **500 g (1 lb) boneless, skinless chicken breasts or thighs,** cut into large chunks. In step 4, substitute **riesling** for red wine; add the **carrots** with the chicken and simmer for 30 minutes, then add **1⅓ cups (200 g) frozen peas** and simmer for a further 5 minutes. Strain and reduce the cooking liquid as described in step 6, then thicken with ⅓ cup **(80 ml) reduced-fat cream or light sour cream.** Serve with boiled **pasta egg noodles,** tossed with **finely chopped fresh parsley** or **poppyseeds.**

Chicken mulligatawny stew

Serves 4

Preparation
20 minutes

Cooking
50 minutes

Per serving
2253 kJ, 538 kcal,
45 g protein, 17 g fat
(6 g saturated fat),
51 g carbohydrate
(7 g sugars), 7 g fibre,
785 mg sodium

1 tablespoon olive oil

2 teaspoons ground coriander

1 teaspoon ground cumin

1 teaspoon ground turmeric

4 bone-in chicken breast
halves, about 1.25 kg (2½ lb)
in total, skin removed, cut in
half crosswise

3 cups (375 g) small
cauliflower florets

2 cloves garlic, crushed

410 g (15 oz) can chopped
tomatoes

1 teaspoon ground cinnamon

½ teaspoon ground ginger

1 teaspoon salt

1 cup (200 g) long-grain
white rice

1½ cups (230 g) fresh or
frozen peas

⅓ cup (80 ml) reduced-fat
coconut milk

1 Heat the olive oil in a large heavy-based saucepan over medium heat. Add the coriander, cumin and turmeric, and cook for 1 minute. Add the chicken and fry for 4 minutes on each side, until golden brown. Transfer to a plate.

2 Add the cauliflower florets and garlic to the pan and cook for 1 minute, until the garlic is tender. Pour in ⅓ cup (80 ml) water, then cook for 3 minutes, until the water has evaporated.

3 Add the tomatoes, cinnamon, ginger and half the salt, and bring to a boil. Return the chicken pieces to the pan, reduce the heat, cover and simmer for 30 minutes, until the chicken is cooked and the cauliflower is tender.

4 Meanwhile, bring 2¼ cups (560 ml) water to a boil in a covered saucepan. Add the rice and the remaining salt. Reduce the heat to a simmer, then cover and cook for 17 minutes, until the rice is tender.

5 Stir the peas and coconut milk into the chicken mixture. Cook, uncovered, for 5 minutes, until the peas are heated through and the sauce is richly flavoured. Serve the stew on a bed of rice.

Mulligatawny originated in South India; its name means 'pepper water'. This interpretation is quite a hearty stew, with a touch of creaminess from the coconut milk.

Moroccan chicken with couscous

2 tablespoons extra virgin olive oil

400 g (14 oz) boneless, skinless chicken breasts, cut into 1 cm (½ inch) thick strips

1 large onion, finely chopped

2 cloves garlic, finely chopped

1 teaspoon ground cumin

1 teaspoon ground coriander

1 cinnamon stick

300 g (10 oz) zucchini (courgettes), halved lengthwise and sliced

410 g (15 oz) can chopped tomatoes

200 ml (7 fl oz) salt-reduced vegetable stock (page 15)

1⅓ cups (250 g) couscous

400 ml (14 fl oz) boiling water

200 g (7 oz) sugarsnap peas

400 g (14 oz) can chickpeas, rinsed and drained

2 teaspoons (10 g) butter

freshly ground black pepper

chopped fresh coriander (cilantro) leaves, to garnish

Serves 4

Preparation
15 minutes

Cooking
20 minutes

Per serving
2496 kJ, 596 kcal,
37 g protein, 19 g fat
(5 g saturated fat),
67 g carbohydrate
(9 g sugars), 8 g fibre,
509 mg sodium

Couscous is low in fat and scores low on the Glycaemic Index, meaning it breaks down slowly in the body, releasing energy gradually into the bloodstream.

1 Heat half the oil in a wok or heavy-based frying pan over medium-high heat. Cook the chicken, onion and garlic, stirring constantly, for 2 minutes, until the chicken starts to brown.

2 Reduce the heat to low and add the cumin, coriander and cinnamon stick. Cook, stirring, for 1 minute. Add the zucchini and stir well, then add the tomatoes and stock. Cook, stirring occasionally, for 5 minutes.

3 Meanwhile, put the couscous in a saucepan and pour in the boiling water. Add the remaining 1 tablespoon oil, stir well, then cover and leave to soak for 5 minutes.

4 Add the sugarsnap peas and chickpeas to the chicken mixture. Cook, stirring frequently, for a further 5 minutes.

5 Stir the butter into the couscous and cook over medium heat for 3 minutes, using a fork to separate the grains.

6 Pile the couscous on a platter, spoon the chicken mixture on top and sprinkle with freshly ground black pepper. Serve hot, garnished with chopped coriander.

Duck and vegetable ragout

Serves 4

Preparation
30 minutes

Cooking
1½ hours

Per serving
1179 kJ, 282 kcal,
21 g protein, 9 g fat
(2 g saturated fat),
17 g carbohydrate
(14 g sugars), 8 g fibre,
751 mg sodium

1 tablespoon extra virgin
olive oil

4 duck leg joints, about
800 g (1¾ lb) in total,
skin removed

250 g (8 oz) button
mushrooms

250 g (8 oz) baby onions or
French shallots (eschalots)

3 cloves garlic, finely chopped

½ teaspoon dried thyme

1 bay leaf

300 ml (10 fl oz) red wine

3 cups (750 ml) salt-reduced
chicken stock (page 14)

250 g (8 oz) baby carrots

250 g (8 oz) baby turnips,
halved if large

250 g (8 oz) sugarsnap peas

2 teaspoons redcurrant jelly

pinch of salt

freshly ground black pepper

sprigs fresh mint, to garnish

1 Heat the oil in a large flameproof casserole dish over medium heat. Cook the duck pieces for 10 minutes, turning until lightly browned. Transfer the duck to a plate. Add the mushrooms, onions, garlic, thyme and bay leaf to the pan. Slightly increase the heat and cook, stirring frequently, for 4 minutes, until the vegetables begin to colour.

2 Add the wine and let it bubble briefly. Return the duck and juices to the pan. Pour in the stock and bring to a boil. Reduce the heat, cover and simmer, stirring occasionally, for 30 minutes. Add the carrots and turnips, pushing them into the liquid, cover and simmer for 15 minutes. Add the sugarsnap peas and cook for a further 5-10 minutes, until the duck and vegetables are tender.

3 Use a metal spoon to skim off any fat from the surface of the casserole. Place a colander or strainer over a large saucepan. Strain the duck and vegetables, then return to the casserole, discarding the bay leaf. Cover and set aside. Vigorously boil the strained liquid for 10-12 minutes, until reduced by half. Stir in the redcurrant jelly until melted. Season with salt and freshly ground black pepper.

4 Arrange the duck and vegetables on plates. Spoon the sauce over the top, garnish with mint sprigs and serve.

Mustard croutes add crunch to the ragout. Mix 1 tablespoon extra virgin olive oil with 1 tablespoon dijon mustard, and spread over 12 thick baguette slices. Place on a baking tray and bake for about 10 minutes, until crisp and brown.

Turkey molé

2 tablespoons sunflower or vegetable oil

1 large onion, chopped

2 cloves garlic, crushed

1 red chilli, seeded and sliced (optional)

2 tablespoons sesame seeds

500 g (1 lb) skinless turkey breast steaks, cut into thin strips

1½ tablespoons mild chilli powder, or to taste

½ teaspoon ground cloves

410 g (15 oz) can chopped tomatoes

⅔ cup (85 g) raisins

150 ml (5 fl oz) salt-reduced chicken stock (page 14)

15 g (½ oz) dark chocolate, chopped

⅓ cup (30 g) flaked almonds, toasted

2 tablespoons chopped fresh coriander (cilantro) leaves, plus extra sprigs, to garnish

pinch of salt

freshly ground black pepper

Serves 4

Preparation
15 minutes

Cooking
25 minutes

Per serving
*1836 kJ, 439 kcal,
34 g protein, 24 g fat
(4 g saturated fat),
24 g carbohydrate
(22 g sugars), 6 g fibre,
363 mg sodium*

1 Heat the oil in a large wide saucepan over medium-low heat. Add the onion, garlic, chilli, if using, and sesame seeds. Cook, stirring frequently, for 10 minutes, until the onion is soft and golden.

2 Add the turkey strips and stir briefly to mix with the onion. Sprinkle with the chilli powder and cloves, and add the tomatoes and raisins. Stir until well combined. Pour in the stock. Bring to a boil, then reduce the heat to low, cover and gently simmer for 10 minutes.

3 Add the chocolate, almonds and chopped coriander, stirring until the chocolate has melted. Season with salt and freshly ground black pepper. Spoon into a serving dish, garnish with coriander and serve immediately.

This is a simplified version of the classic spicy-hot Mexican recipe, made with lean turkey, raisins and almonds. The bitter chocolate added towards the end of cooking is a traditional ingredient that enriches and darkens the sauce.

Chicken and potato curry

Marinating the chicken pieces in a turmeric, ginger and lemon mixture gives a wonderful flavour to this curry. Skinning the chicken not only does away with much of the fat, it also lets the marinade permeate the flesh.

1 chicken, about 1.35 kg (2¾ lb), jointed into 8 pieces

½ teaspoon ground turmeric

4 cm (1½ inch) piece fresh ginger, peeled and finely chopped

juice of ½ lemon

pinch of salt

2 tablespoons sunflower or vegetable oil

1 dried red chilli, broken into 2-3 pieces

1 teaspoon brown or black mustard seeds

½ teaspoon fennel seeds

¼ teaspoon cumin seeds

¼ teaspoon ground cumin

¼ teaspoon ground cinnamon

1 tablespoon besan (chickpea flour)

3 cloves garlic, roughly crushed

½ green capsicum (bell pepper), thinly sliced

1 large onion, sliced

410 g (15 oz) can chopped tomatoes

250 g (8 oz) potatoes, peeled

¼ green cabbage, about 150 g (5 oz), thinly sliced

1 cup (150 g) frozen peas, thawed in boiling water and drained

1 Remove the skin from the chicken pieces. Cut three or four slashes in the flesh of each piece, cutting right to the bone. Rub the turmeric, ginger, lemon juice and salt all over the chicken pieces, then leave to marinate for about 30 minutes.

2 Heat the oil in a large heavy-based frying pan. Add the dried chilli, mustard seeds, fennel seeds and cumin seeds, and let them sputter and pop for a few minutes. Stir in the ground cumin, cinnamon and besan. Watch carefully so that you do not burn the spices.

3 Add the garlic, capsicum and onion to the spice mixture and cook, stirring, for a few minutes. Add the chicken and tomatoes, and stir to mix. Cover and cook for 15 minutes.

4 Meanwhile, cook the potatoes in boiling water for 5 minutes, then drain and cut into bite-sized pieces. Blanch the cabbage in a separate pan of boiling water for 1 minute, then drain.

5 Add the potatoes and cabbage to the curried chicken and stir to combine. Cover the pan again and simmer over medium-low heat for 20-25 minutes, until the chicken is cooked through and tender. Add the peas to warm through for a few minutes.

Serves 4

Preparation
30 minutes,
plus 30 minutes
marinating

Cooking
45 minutes

Per serving
2041 kJ, 487 kcal,
43 g protein, 25 g fat
(6 g saturated fat),
22 g carbohydrate
(8 g sugars), 7 g fibre,
378 mg sodium

The vitamin C provided by the peas, tomatoes and potatoes will increase the absorption of iron from the chicken.

Fish casserole with spicy yogurt

Serves 4

Preparation
15 minutes

Cooking
20 minutes

Per serving
*1754 kJ, 419 kcal,
33 g protein, 19 g fat
(3 g saturated fat),
29 g carbohydrate
(5 g sugars), 5 g fibre,
279 mg sodium*

2 tablespoons olive oil

1 leek, white part only, sliced

2 celery stalks, sliced

1 carrot, chopped

700 g (1 lb 9 oz) boiling (waxy) potatoes, cut into chunks

100 g (3$\frac{1}{2}$ oz) button mushrooms

600 ml (21 fl oz) hot salt-reduced fish stock (page 15)

250 g (8 oz) skinless white fish fillets, cut into chunks

250 g (8 oz) skinless salmon fillets, cut into chunks

1 tablespoon chopped fresh tarragon

2 tablespoons chopped fresh flat-leaf (Italian) parsley

toasted baguette slices, to serve

Spicy yogurt

2 tablespoons natural (plain) yogurt

2 tablespoons mayonnaise

1 clove garlic, crushed

$\frac{1}{2}$ teaspoon paprika

pinch of chilli powder

Try fresh sardine or mackerel fillets instead of the salmon fillets.

1 Heat the oil in a large saucepan over high heat. Add the leek, celery and carrot, reduce the heat to medium, cover and cook for 3 minutes.

2 Add the potatoes and mushrooms to the pan and stir in the hot fish stock. Bring to a boil, cover and simmer for 10 minutes, until the potatoes are tender. Stir the white fish and the salmon into the casserole. Bring back to simmering point, cover and cook for a further 5 minutes, until the fish is cooked through.

3 Meanwhile, to make the spicy yogurt, put the yogurt, mayonnaise, garlic, paprika and chilli powder in a small bowl. Mix until well combined.

4 Stir the tarragon and parsley into the casserole before transferring it to four large bowls. Serve with the spicy yogurt and some toasted baguette slices.

Malay-style braised fish

1 tablespoon sunflower
or vegetable oil

6 spring onions (scallions),
chopped

1 red chilli, seeded and
thinly sliced

2 celery stalks, thinly sliced

1 red capsicum (bell pepper),
thinly sliced

1 clove garlic, crushed

$1/2$ teaspoon fennel seeds

2 teaspoons ground coriander

$1/2$ teaspoon ground cumin

$1/4$ teaspoon ground turmeric

1 cup (250 g) canned chopped
tomatoes

$1/2$ cup (125 ml) coconut milk

300 ml (10 fl oz) salt-reduced
fish stock (page 15)

1 tablespoon fish sauce or
light soy sauce

225 g (8 oz) can sliced
bamboo shoots, rinsed
and drained

700 g (1 lb 9 oz) thick
skinless white fish fillets,
cut into chunks

16 raw prawns (uncooked
shrimp), peeled

juice of $1/2$ lime

steamed rice, to serve

1 tablespoon chopped fresh
coriander (cilantro) leaves,
to serve

Serves 4

Preparation
15 minutes

Cooking
20 minutes

Per serving
*1705 kJ, 407 kcal,
55 g protein, 17 g fat
(8 g saturated fat),
9 g carbohydrate
(6 g sugars), 4 g fibre,
832 mg sodium*

1 Heat the oil in a large frying pan. Add two-thirds of
the spring onions, the chilli, celery and capsicum. Cook,
stirring constantly, for 5 minutes, until the vegetables
are slightly softened.

2 Add the garlic, fennel seeds, ground coriander, cumin
and turmeric, and cook for 1 minute. Stir in the tomatoes,
coconut milk, stock and fish sauce or soy sauce, and bring
to a boil. Reduce the heat, cover and simmer for 5 minutes.

3 Stir in the bamboo shoots, fish and prawns. Cover
the pan and simmer for 5-7 minutes, until the fish is just
cooked and the prawns are pink. Stir in the lime juice.

4 Serve the braised fish with steamed rice, topped with
the reserved spring onions and fresh coriander.

*Some studies
have shown that
chillies can help
to reduce blood
cholesterol levels.
There are reports
suggesting that
chillies can help
protect against
gastric ulcers.*

Thai green fish curry

Serves 4

Preparation
25 minutes

Cooking
20 minutes

Per serving
1547 kJ, 370 kcal,
32 g protein, 16 g fat
(5 g saturated fat),
26 g carbohydrate
(12 g sugars), 4 g fibre,
888 mg sodium

2 tablespoons vegetable oil

600 ml (21 fl oz) salt-reduced fish stock (page 15)

1$\frac{1}{2}$ tablespoons fish sauce

2 tablespoons sugar

300 g (10 oz) small new potatoes, halved

1 red capsicum (bell pepper), cut into strips

500 g (1 lb) firm white fish fillets, cut into chunks

125 g (4 oz) sugarsnap peas

100 ml (3$\frac{1}{2}$ fl oz) low-fat coconut milk

juice of 1 lime

chopped fresh coriander (cilantro) leaves, to serve

steamed rice, to serve

Green curry paste

2 tablespoons finely grated fresh galangal

2 teaspoons finely chopped fresh lemongrass

4 makrut (kaffir lime) leaves, shredded

$\frac{1}{2}$ cup (25 g) finely chopped fresh coriander (cilantro) leaves

6 Asian shallots, very finely chopped

4 cloves garlic, crushed

1 teaspoon ground coriander

1 teaspoon ground cumin

1 red chilli, seeded and finely chopped

finely grated zest of 1 lime

1 To make the green curry paste, combine all the ingredients and stir in 100 ml (3$\frac{1}{2}$ fl oz) water. (If you have a food processor, you can save chopping time by using the machine to process all of the paste ingredients with the water until smooth.)

2 Heat the oil in a non-stick saucepan. Fry the green curry paste, stirring frequently, for 5 minutes, until the liquid has evaporated and the shallots have softened and are starting to colour.

3 Pour the fish stock and fish sauce into the pan and stir in the sugar, potatoes and capsicum. Bring to a boil, then cover and cook for 10 minutes, until the potatoes are almost tender.

4 Add the fish, sugarsnap peas and coconut milk, then cover again and gently cook for 5 minutes, until the fish flakes easily. Remove from the heat, stir in the lime juice and scatter over the coriander leaves. Serve hot with steamed rice.

Fresh coconut milk is a key ingredient in Caribbean and some Asian cooking. The canned version is high in saturated fat, but low-fat coconut milk is available.

Italian seafood stew

Serves 4

Preparation
20 minutes

Cooking
1 hour

Per serving
*2437 kJ, 582 kcal,
41 g protein, 17 g fat
(3 g saturated fat),
51 g carbohydrate
(9 g sugars), 8 g fibre,
620 mg sodium*

*Fish and seafood
are among the
most reliable
sources of iodine
because of the
consistent iodine
level in sea water.
Other foods rely
on the iodine
content of soil,
which can vary
considerably.*

2½ tablespoons extra virgin olive oil

1 leek, white part only, coarsely chopped

1 onion, chopped

4 cloves garlic, chopped

½ green capsicum (bell pepper), chopped

½ bulb fennel, diced

350 ml (12 fl oz) dry white wine

300 ml (10 fl oz) salt-reduced fish stock (page 15)

410 g (15 oz) can chopped tomatoes

pinch of salt

freshly ground black pepper

2 tablespoons tomato paste (concentrated purée)

¼ teaspoon dried herbes de Provence

1 zucchini (courgette), sliced

1½ cups (225 g) instant cornmeal or polenta

½ cup (80 g) fresh or frozen peas

2 cups (90 g) baby beetroot (beet) leaves

200 g (7 oz) skinless firm white fish fillets, cut into chunks

400 g (14 oz) peeled or shelled mixed shellfish

¼ cup (15 g) coarsely chopped fresh parsley

1 Heat 2 tablespoons of the oil in a large saucepan and cook the leek and onion for 2 minutes, until starting to soften. Add the garlic, capsicum and fennel, and cook for a further 5-10 minutes, until softened.

2 Add the wine, stock and tomatoes, and season with salt and freshly ground black pepper. Simmer for 30 minutes, until slightly thickened. Stir in the tomato paste, herbes de Provence and zucchini, and simmer for 10 minutes, adding a little water if the mixture becomes too thick.

3 Meanwhile, cook the polenta according to the packet instructions until it is thick. Season with salt and pepper. Pour the polenta into a lightly oiled 18 x 28 cm (7 x 11 inch) shallow cake tin. Leave until cool and firm, then cut into triangles. Preheat the grill (broiler) to high.

4 Stir the peas, beetroot leaves, fish and shellfish into the tomato mixture. Cover and gently simmer for about 5 minutes, until all the seafood is just cooked.

5 Lightly brush the polenta triangles with the remaining oil and grill until lightly browned. Serve the stew in bowls with the polenta triangles, topped with the parsley.

Prawn gumbo

1 tablespoon extra virgin olive oil

2 onions, chopped

1 red capsicum (bell pepper), chopped

2 celery stalks, chopped

3 cloves garlic, chopped

75 g (2½ oz) rindless bacon (bacon strips), diced

1 tablespoon plain (all-purpose) flour

1 tablespoon paprika

4 cups (1 litre) salt-reduced fish stock (page 15)

1 teaspoon chopped fresh thyme

1 cup (250 g) canned chopped tomatoes

2 tablespoons chopped fresh parsley

2 bay leaves

2 teaspoons worcestershire sauce

Tabasco sauce, to taste

100 g (3½ oz) okra, sliced crosswise

350 g (12 oz) peeled raw prawns (uncooked shrimp)

50 g (1¾ oz) green beans, cut into short lengths

pinch of salt

freshly ground black pepper

steamed rice, to serve

3 spring onions (scallions), thinly sliced

1 Heat the oil in a large saucepan and cook the onions, capsicum and celery for 5–6 minutes, until lightly browned. Stir in the garlic and bacon, and cook for 3 minutes. Stir in the flour, slightly increase the heat and cook, stirring, for 2 minutes. Stir in the paprika and cook for 2 minutes. Gradually add the stock, stirring well.

2 Add the thyme, tomatoes, parsley, bay leaves and worcestershire sauce. Bring to a boil, then reduce the heat to a simmer and add Tabasco sauce to taste. Add the okra and simmer for 15 minutes, until the okra is tender and the gumbo mixture has thickened.

3 Add the prawns and beans, and cook for 3 minutes, until the prawns turn pink and the beans are tender.

4 Remove the bay leaves and season the gumbo with salt and freshly ground black pepper. Serve with steamed rice, sprinkled with spring onions.

Serves 4

Preparation
25 minutes

Cooking
35 minutes

Per serving
1025 kJ, 245 kcal, 28 g protein, 8 g fat (2 g saturated fat), 15 g carbohydrate (7 g sugars), 5 g fibre, 777 mg sodium

Chicken cacciatore, page 272

Bakes and roasts

Prepared in advance, then popped in the oven and left to cook, healthy bakes and roasts make great comfort food at any time of the year. They are ideal for family meals or informal entertaining.

Spicy apple and sausage gratins

Serves 4

Preparation
10 minutes

Cooking
15 minutes

Per serving
*1268 kJ, 303 kcal,
10 g protein, 18 g fat
(8 g saturated fat),
24 g carbohydrate
(18 g sugars), 4 g fibre,
594 mg sodium*

4 red apples

2 tablespoons lemon juice

1 small red onion, cut into thin wedges

$\frac{1}{2}$ teaspoon sugar

200 g (7 oz) spicy pork sausages

$\frac{1}{4}$ cup (60 ml) dry white wine

pinch of salt

freshly ground black pepper

6 crostini or melba toasts

1 teaspoon dried thyme

$\frac{1}{3}$ cup (40 g) grated gruyère

2 teaspoons chilled butter

sprigs fresh thyme, to garnish

1 Preheat the oven to 220°C (425°F/Gas 7). Grease four ovenproof ramekins or small, shallow baking dishes.

2 Quarter and core the apples. Slice the quarters into thin wedges and immediately drizzle with the lemon juice. Divide the apple and onion wedges among the ramekins and sprinkle with the sugar.

3 Squeeze the sausage meat from the skins and divide it into bite-sized pieces. Place the pieces on top of the apple wedges, drizzle with the wine and season with salt and freshly ground black pepper.

4 Finely crumble the crostini or melba toasts. Combine the crumbs with the dried thyme and cheese. Sprinkle the gratins with the crumb mixture, and dot with the butter.

5 Bake the gratins for 15 minutes, until the cheese has melted and the tops are golden. Garnish with sprigs of fresh thyme and serve immediately.

Use any variety of raw pork sausages in this recipe. Simply squeeze the sausage meat from its skin and use as in the recipe above.

These gratins are lovely served with sliced walnut bread spread with butter.

Spicy apple and sausage gratins

Sausage-stuffed apples

Preheat the oven to 220°C (425°F/Gas 7). Core and hollow out **4 large red apples,** leaving a 2 cm (³/₄ inch) wall. Finely dice the apple pulp and combine with **150 g (5 oz) spicy pork sausage, 1 teaspoon dried thyme, ¹/₂ teaspoon sugar** and **¹/₂ cup (50 g) grated parmesan.** Season and stuff the apples with the sausage mixture. Transfer the apples to four small greased ramekins and dot with **1 tablespoon (20 g) butter.** Combine **100 ml (3¹/₂ fl oz) dry white wine** with **2¹/₂ tablespoons vegetable stock** (page 15) and pour into the ramekins. Bake in the middle of the oven for 25 minutes.

Chicken and capsicum calzone

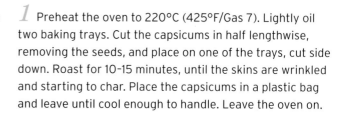

Serves 4

Preparation
35 minutes, plus
15 minutes rising

Cooking
30 minutes

Per serving
2265 kJ, 541 kcal,
40 g protein, 30 g fat
(14 g saturated fat),
26 g carbohydrate
(8 g sugars), 3 g fibre,
896 mg sodium

2 red capsicums (bell peppers)

1 tablespoon extra virgin
olive oil

1 large onion, sliced

3 cloves garlic, crushed

300 g (10 oz) boneless,
skinless chicken breast, diced

12 sun-dried tomato halves
in oil, drained and chopped

⅓ cup (20 g) chopped
fresh basil

12 pitted black olives, halved

pinch of salt

freshly ground black pepper

1 packet pizza base mix,
about 290 g (10 oz)

1 cup (150 g) diced mozzarella

1 egg, beaten

1 tablespoon sesame seeds

1 Preheat the oven to 220°C (425°F/Gas 7). Lightly oil two baking trays. Cut the capsicums in half lengthwise, removing the seeds, and place on one of the trays, cut side down. Roast for 10-15 minutes, until the skins are wrinkled and starting to char. Place the capsicums in a plastic bag and leave until cool enough to handle. Leave the oven on.

2 Meanwhile, heat the oil in a frying pan. Cook the onion and garlic over medium-low heat, stirring frequently, for 10 minutes, until softened and starting to turn golden.

3 Add the chicken to the pan and cook for 2 minutes, until the chicken changes colour (it will not be cooked through). Remove from the heat. Stir in the sun-dried tomatoes, basil and olives, and season with salt and freshly ground black pepper. Set aside.

4 Make up the pizza dough according to the packet instructions. Briefly knead the dough until smooth, then cut it into four portions. Roll out each piece on a lightly floured work surface to a 20 cm (8 inch) round.

5 Peel the skins from the roasted capsicums and roughly chop the flesh. Stir the capsicums and mozzarella into the chicken mixture. Pile one-quarter of the chicken filling in the centre of each dough round.

6 Brush the edge of each dough round with some of the beaten egg, then fold over into a half-moon. Seal the edges by firmly folding them over and crimping together. Place the calzones on the prepared trays and loosely cover with plastic wrap. Leave to rise in a warm place for 15 minutes.

7 Brush the calzones with the remaining egg and sprinkle with the sesame seeds. Bake for 15 minutes, until golden brown. Serve warm or at room temperature.

Baked rigatoni with eggplant

2 tablespoons extra virgin
olive oil

1 large onion, chopped

2 cloves garlic, crushed

$\frac{1}{3}$ cup (80 ml) red wine

1 eggplant (aubergine), cut
into small cubes

2 x 410 g (15 oz) cans
chopped tomatoes

5 sun-dried tomatoes in oil,
drained and chopped

2 tablespoons chopped
fresh oregano

250 g (8 oz) rigatoni or other
large chunky pasta tubes,
such as penne

pinch of salt

freshly ground black pepper

$\frac{1}{3}$ cup (25 g) fresh wholemeal
(whole-wheat) breadcrumbs

$\frac{1}{3}$ cup (35 g) grated parmesan

Serves 4

Preparation
20 minutes

Cooking
50 minutes

Per serving
*1831 kJ, 437 kcal,
15 g protein, 14 g fat
(3 g saturated fat),
59 g carbohydrate
(11 g sugars), 8 g fibre,
459 mg sodium*

1 Heat the oil in a large saucepan. Gently cook the onion,
stirring frequently, for 4-5 minutes, until softened and
lightly golden. Add the garlic and cook for 1-2 minutes.

2 Pour in the wine and allow it to bubble for 3 minutes,
then add the eggplant cubes, canned tomatoes, sun-dried
tomatoes and oregano. Bring to a boil, then reduce the
heat, cover and gently simmer, stirring occasionally, for
15-20 minutes.

3 Meanwhile, cook the rigatoni in a large saucepan of
boiling water for 10-12 minutes, or according to the packet
instructions, until al dente. Drain well.

4 Preheat the oven to 200°C (400°F/Gas 6). Season the
tomato sauce with salt and freshly ground black pepper.
Tip the pasta into a large, lightly greased ovenproof dish.
Pour in the sauce and stir until the pasta is well coated.

5 Combine the breadcrumbs and parmesan in a bowl, and
sprinkle this mixture evenly over the top of the pasta. Bake
for 15-20 minutes, until the sauce is bubbling and the top is
golden brown and crisp. Serve hot.

*Pasta is a versatile
starchy carbohydrate
food, providing
protein, particularly
if wholemeal (whole-
wheat) varieties are
used, B vitamins and
minerals. It is also
low in fat – it is the
fattening sauces often
served with pasta
that push up the
kilojoule and fat
content of a dish.*

Lentil macaroni cheese

2 tablespoons olive oil

1 brown (yellow) onion, finely chopped

2 cloves garlic, crushed

5 ripe tomatoes, about 750 g (1½ lb) in total, peeled and diced

400 g (14 oz) can brown lentils, rinsed and drained

½ cup (15 g) roughly chopped fresh flat-leaf (Italian) parsley

400 g (14 oz) macaroni

1 tablespoon (20 g) olive oil spread

¼ cup (35 g) plain (all-purpose) flour

1¾ cups (435 ml) skim milk

1 cup (125 g) grated reduced-fat cheddar

½ cup (50 g) grated parmesan

freshly ground black pepper

1 Heat 1 tablespoon of the oil in a large non-stick frying pan over medium heat. Cook the onion for 3 minutes, until softened. Add the garlic and cook for 1 minute. Stir in the tomatoes and 1 cup (250 ml) water. Bring to a boil, then reduce the heat and simmer for about 10 minutes, until thickened. Stir in the lentils and half the parsley, and cook for a further 10 minutes. Spoon the mixture into a shallow 6 cup (1.5 litre) ovenproof dish.

2 Meanwhile, cook the macaroni in a large saucepan of boiling water for 10 minutes, or according to the packet instructions, until just tender. Drain and return to the pan.

3 Preheat the oven to 200°C (400°F/Gas 6).

4 Heat the olive oil spread and the remaining oil in a saucepan over medium heat. When sizzling, add the flour and stir until well combined. Cook, stirring continuously, for 1 minute, until the mixture is bubbling. Remove from the heat and slowly pour in the milk, whisking continuously until well combined. Return to the heat and whisk until the mixture comes to a boil. Reduce the heat and simmer for 2 minutes. Add half the cheddar and half the parmesan, and stir until melted.

5 Add the cheese sauce to the macaroni. Season with freshly ground black pepper and stir until well combined. Spoon the macaroni mixture over the lentil mixture and sprinkle the remaining cheddar and parmesan over the top. Bake for 20-25 minutes, until the cheese on top is melted and golden.

6 Sprinkle the remaining parsley over the macaroni cheese and serve hot.

Serves 4

Preparation
25 minutes

Cooking
50 minutes

Per serving
2988 kJ, 714 kcal, 38 g protein, 21 g fat (6 g saturated fat), 91 g carbohydrate (12 g sugars), 8 g fibre, 663 mg sodium

Baked eggplant with yogurt

Serves 4

Preparation
20 minutes

Cooking
1¼ hours

Per serving
1443 kJ, 345 kcal,
18 g protein, 21 g fat
(5 g saturated fat),
18 g carbohydrate
(17 g sugars), 8 g fibre,
480 mg sodium

¼ cup (60 ml) extra virgin olive oil

1 red onion, finely chopped

2 cloves garlic, finely chopped

410 g (15 oz) can chopped tomatoes

2 teaspoons tomato paste (concentrated purée)

100 ml (3½ fl oz) dry red wine

1 bay leaf

2 tablespoons chopped fresh parsley

pinch of salt

freshly ground black pepper

3 eggplant (aubergine)

3 zucchini (courgettes)

½ teaspoon ground cumin

1⅔ cups (410 g) low-fat natural (plain) yogurt

2 eggs, beaten

⅓ cup (35 g) grated parmesan

1 Heat 1 tablespoon of the oil in a saucepan and cook the onion for 8 minutes, until softened. Add the garlic and cook, stirring, for 1 minute. Stir in the tomatoes, tomato paste, wine and bay leaf. Cover and gently simmer for 10 minutes. Uncover the pan and cook the sauce, stirring occasionally, for a further 10 minutes, until thickened. Remove the bay leaf. Stir in the parsley and season with salt and freshly ground black pepper.

2 While the sauce is cooking, preheat the grill (broiler) to medium. Cut the eggplant into 1 cm (½ inch) slices. Thinly slice the zucchini. Lightly brush the eggplant and zucchini with remaining oil. Grill in batches for 3-4 minutes on each side, until browned and very tender.

3 Preheat the oven to 180°C (350°F/Gas 4).

4 Stir the cumin into half of the yogurt. Arrange one-third of the eggplant slices, in a single layer, in a large ovenproof dish about 10 cups (2.5 litres) in capacity. Spoon over half of the tomato sauce. Arrange half of the zucchini slices on top, in a single layer, then drizzle with half of the cumin-flavoured yogurt. Repeat the layers, then finish with a layer of the remaining eggplant slices.

5 Mix the remaining yogurt with the beaten eggs and half of the parmesan. Spoon the yogurt mixture over the top of the eggplant, spreading with the back of the spoon to cover the eggplant. Sprinkle the remaining parmesan over the top.

6 Bake for 40-45 minutes, until the top is lightly browned and set, and the sauce is bubbling. Serve hot.

Ratatouille with fetta gratin

2 tablespoons olive oil

1 onion, chopped

1 clove garlic, crushed

1 eggplant (aubergine), about 300 g (10 oz), cut into 1 cm (½ inch) cubes

2 zucchini (courgettes), cut into 1 cm (½ inch) cubes

4 large tomatoes, diced

2 tablespoons tomato paste (concentrated purée)

⅓ cup (20 g) chopped fresh parsley

fresh basil, to serve

freshly ground black pepper

Topping

2 slices wholemeal (whole-wheat) bread, cut into 1 cm (½ inch) cubes

1 cup (150 g) crumbled fetta

1 tablespoon olive oil

Serves 4

Preparation
20 minutes

Cooking
20 minutes

Per serving
1177 kJ, 281 kcal,
12 g protein, 20 g fat
(7 g saturated fat),
14 g carbohydrate
(9 g sugars), 7 g fibre,
550 mg sodium

1 Heat the oil in a large saucepan and cook the onion and garlic over high heat for 1 minute. Add the eggplant, reduce the heat to medium and cook, stirring occasionally, for 5 minutes, until softened. Add the zucchini and cook, stirring occasionally, for a further 2 minutes, until the vegetables start to brown.

2 Add the tomatoes along with the tomato paste to the pan. Stir in ⅓ cup (80 ml) of cold water. Heat the mixture until simmering, then cover and cook for 8–10 minutes.

3 Stir in the parsley and transfer the ratatouille to a shallow ovenproof dish or gratin dish. Preheat the grill (broiler) to the hottest setting.

4 To make the topping, combine the bread cubes and crumbled fetta in a bowl, then pour over the olive oil and toss to coat.

5 Sprinkle the topping over the ratatouille and grill for 1–2 minutes, until the cheese softens and the bread browns. Sprinkle the basil and some freshly ground black pepper over the ratatouille before serving.

There is no need to salt the eggplant before use. In the past, eggplant cultivars were bitter and had to be salted (known as degorging) to draw out the sour juices, but the varieties available in supermarkets today have been bred to avoid this and can therefore be added straight to the ratatouille.

Tofu and vegetable gratin

Serves 4

Preparation
20 minutes,
plus 10 minutes
marinating

Cooking
20 minutes

Per serving
*1537 kJ, 367 kcal,
16 g protein, 28 g fat
(4 g saturated fat),
15 g carbohydrate
(10 g sugars), 7 g fibre,
508 mg sodium*

400 g (14 oz) firm tofu

1½ tablespoons peanut
(groundnut) oil

400 g (14 oz) Chinese
cabbage, thinly sliced

400 g (14 oz) carrots, cut
into thin matchsticks

pinch of salt

freshly ground black pepper

1 teaspoon mild curry powder

2 spring onions, thinly sliced

2 tablespoons cornflakes,
lightly crushed

1½ tablespoons sesame
seeds

1½ tablespoons sesame oil

snipped fresh chives, to serve

Marinade

1½ tablespoons soy sauce

1½ tablespoons lemon juice

3 teaspoons sesame oil

1 teaspoon honey

2 cm (¾ inch) piece fresh
ginger, grated

1 clove garlic, crushed

pinch of cayenne pepper

1 To make the marinade, combine the soy sauce, lemon juice, sesame oil and honey in a bowl, stir in the ginger and garlic, and season with cayenne pepper.

2 Cut the tofu into slices and toss with the marinade. Cover and set aside for 10 minutes to allow the flavours to mingle.

3 Preheat the oven to 200°C (400°F/Gas 6) and lightly oil a shallow ovenproof dish.

4 Drain the tofu in a sieve over a bowl, reserving the marinade. Heat the peanut oil in a large, deep non-stick frying pan or wok. Stir-fry the tofu slices for 2 minutes over medium heat. Remove from the pan and set aside.

5 Add the Chinese cabbage and carrots to the pan, and stir-fry for 2 minutes. Season with salt and freshly ground black pepper, then add the curry powder and reserved marinade. Add the spring onions and toss to combine.

6 Transfer the vegetables to the prepared dish and top with the tofu. Sprinkle with the combined cornflakes and sesame seeds, and drizzle with the sesame oil. Bake in the middle of the oven for 15 minutes. Serve sprinkled with snipped chives.

Cook a packet of instant noodles according to the packet instructions, toss with fresh, crunchy sprouts and serve with the gratin, together with a bowl of sweet chilli sauce.

You could replace the chives with chopped parsley or coriander (cilantro) leaves for a different flavour.

Tofu and vegetable gratin

Smoked tofu with cabbage

Preheat the oven to 200°C (400°F/ Gas 6). Cut **400 g (14 oz) smoked tofu** into bite-sized pieces and toss with the marinade as described in the main recipe. Stir-fry **500 g (1 lb) sliced cabbage** in **2 tablespoons vegetable oil**. Add **400 g (14 oz) chopped tomatoes,** cover and simmer for 3 minutes. Season with **salt, freshly ground black pepper** and **1 teaspoon red curry paste.** Transfer to an oiled ovenproof dish and top with the tofu and marinade. Sprinkle with **1½ tablespoons chopped peanuts (groundnuts)** and **2 tablespoons cornflakes.** Bake as described in the main recipe.

Baked polenta with tomatoes and fetta

Baked polenta rounds with fontina cheese

Prepare the polenta as directed in the main recipe. Rinse a shallow 20 x 40 cm (8 x 16 inch) ovenproof dish with cold water, add the polenta and smooth the top. Leave to cool and set, then use a cookie cutter to cut out circles. Preheat the oven to 200°C (400°F/Gas 6). Grease a baking tray and place the polenta rounds on top. Slice **500 g (1 lb) tomatoes** and arrange two slices on each of the polenta rounds. Top with **250 g (8 oz) sliced fontina or other mild cheese.** Drizzle with **2 tablespoons olive oil** and sprinkle with **2 teaspoons dried oregano.** Bake for 15 minutes, until the cheese is starting to brown.

Baked polenta with tomatoes and fetta

1 cup (250 ml) salt-reduced vegetable stock (page 15)

400 ml (14 fl oz) low-fat milk

1²/₃ cups (250 g) instant polenta or cornmeal

freshly ground black pepper

freshly grated nutmeg

¼ cup (20 g) grated parmesan

¼ cup (60 ml) olive oil

600 g (1¼ lb) small tomatoes, sliced

180 g (6 oz) reduced-fat fetta, sliced

2 teaspoons dried oregano

1 Preheat the oven to 200°C (400°F/Gas 6). Lightly oil a shallow ovenproof dish, about 20 x 40 cm (8 x 16 inches).

2 Bring the stock, milk and 350 ml (12 fl oz) water to a boil in a saucepan. Add the polenta, stirring constantly, and cook according to the packet instructions.

3 Season the cooked polenta with freshly ground black pepper and grated nutmeg. Stir in the parmesan and half the olive oil. Transfer the polenta to the prepared dish and smooth the top.

4 Arrange the tomato slices in overlapping rows on top of the polenta, and season with black pepper. Top with the sliced fetta, sprinkle with the oregano and drizzle with the remaining olive oil. Bake in the middle of the oven for about 20 minutes, until the fetta is starting to brown.

Serves 4

Preparation
15 minutes

Cooking
30 minutes

Per serving
2242 kJ, 536 kcal, 25 g protein, 24 g fat (7 g saturated fat), 55 g carbohydrate (11 g sugars), 4 g fibre, 894 mg sodium

Polenta, which is finely milled corn or maize meal, is a good gluten-free source of starchy carbohydrate.

Fish and mushroom pie

Serves 4

Preparation
20 minutes

Cooking
55 minutes

Per serving
1578 kJ, 377 kcal,
38 g protein, 10 g fat
(5 g saturated fat),
34 g carbohydrate
(11 g sugars), 3 g fibre,
502 mg sodium

500 g (1 lb) potatoes, cut into chunks

$\frac{1}{3}$ cup (90 g) thick (Greek-style) yogurt or fromage frais

1 tablespoon (20 g) butter

1 small onion, sliced

400 g (14 oz) piece firm white fish fillet

2 cups (500 ml) low-fat milk

2 bay leaves

4 stalks fresh parsley

$\frac{2}{3}$ cup (100 g) small pasta shells

$\frac{1}{4}$ cup (30 g) cornflour (cornstarch)

$\frac{1}{2}$ teaspoon mustard powder

freshly grated nutmeg

125 g (4 oz) peeled cooked prawns (shrimp)

85 g (3 oz) mushrooms, thinly sliced

$\frac{1}{4}$ cup (15 g) chopped fresh parsley

pinch of salt

freshly ground black pepper

1 Preheat the oven to 180°C (350°F/Gas 4). Put the potatoes in a saucepan, cover with boiling water and cook for 15–20 minutes, until tender. Drain well, then mash the potatoes with the yogurt or fromage frais; keep warm.

2 While the potatoes are cooking, melt the butter in a flameproof casserole dish and gently cook the onion for 5 minutes, until soft. Place the fish on top, pour in 400 ml (14 fl oz) of the milk and add the bay leaves and parsley stalks. Cover and poach in the oven for 15 minutes, until the fish flakes easily.

3 Meanwhile, cook the pasta shells in a saucepan of boiling water for 10 minutes, or according to the packet instructions, until barely tender. Drain and set aside.

4 Put the cornflour, mustard and remaining milk in a saucepan, and mix to a smooth paste. Strain the poaching liquid from the fish into the pan, reserving the onion, and season with nutmeg. Stir well, then bring to a boil, stirring. Reduce the heat and simmer for 5 minutes, until thick.

5 Flake the fish, discarding the skin and bones. Stir into the sauce with the reserved onion, prawns, mushrooms, chopped parsley and pasta. Season with salt and freshly ground black pepper, then transfer to the casserole dish.

6 Spread the mashed potatoes over the filling, right to the edge of the dish. Use a fork to rough up the surface. Bake for 20 minutes, until bubbling and brown. Serve hot.

Juicy prawns and mushrooms transform this simple fish pie into a special meal. Serve the pie with some steamed seasonal vegetables.

Herbed fish crumble

Serves 4

Preparation
20 minutes

Cooking
50 minutes

Per serving
1346 kJ, 321 kcal,
32 g protein, 12 g fat
(7 g saturated fat),
23 g carbohydrate
(6 g sugars), 4 g fibre,
782 mg sodium

200 g (7 oz) whiting fillets

200 g (7 oz) smoked
haddock fillets

1 leek, white part only,
thinly sliced

300 ml (10 fl oz) low-fat milk

2 bay leaves

pinch of salt

freshly ground black pepper

$^1/_2$ cup (75 g) wholemeal plain
(whole-wheat all-purpose)
flour

2 tablespoons (40 g) butter

$^1/_4$ cup (25 g) grated parmesan

2 tablespoons chopped
fresh marjoram

1 tablespoon cornflour
(cornstarch)

100 g (3$^1/_2$ oz) button
mushrooms, thinly sliced

2 tablespoons chopped fresh
flat-leaf (Italian) parsley

steamed peas, to serve

1 Preheat the oven to 190°C (375°F/Gas 5). Put the fish in a single layer in a large saucepan or frying pan and add the leek, milk and bay leaves. Season with salt and freshly ground black pepper. Heat until just boiling, then reduce the heat and gently simmer for 5 minutes. Remove the pan from the heat and stand for about 5 minutes.

2 Meanwhile, put the flour in a bowl and rub in the butter with your fingertips to make fine crumbs. Stir in the grated parmesan and marjoram, and season with salt and pepper.

3 Using a fish slice, transfer the fish to a plate, reserving the milk in the pan. Remove the skin and flake the flesh, discarding any bones.

4 Mix the cornflour with a little water to make a smooth paste, add to the milk in the pan and bring to a boil, stirring until the sauce has thickened. Discard the bay leaves. Stir in the mushrooms and cook for 1 minute. Gently stir in the flaked fish and chopped parsley.

5 Pour the fish mixture into a 5 cup (1.25 litre) shallow ovenproof dish, and spoon the crumble mixture over the top. Bake for 35-40 minutes, until the top is golden. Serve hot, with some steamed peas on the side.

Milk is an excellent source of several important nutrients – protein, calcium, phosphorus (for strong bones and teeth) and many of the B vitamins.

Mushrooms contain useful amounts of the B vitamins B₂ and niacin. They are also a good source of copper, which is needed for bone growth.

This healthy dish is quick to prepare but takes a while to cook. You could bake some potato slices or wedges in the oven along with the fish.

Add some sliced black olives and capers to the lentil mixture.

Fish baked with lentils

400 g (14 oz) can lentils, rinsed and drained

1 tomato, roughly diced

¹/₂ cup (80 g) sliced roasted red capsicum (bell pepper)

2 bay leaves

2 sprigs fresh thyme

¹/₄ cup (60 ml) salt-reduced chicken stock (page 14) or white wine

2 x 200 g (7 oz) perch or other firm white fish fillets

1 tablespoon chopped fresh parsley

freshly ground black pepper

1 Preheat the oven to 180°C (350°F/Gas 4). Put the lentils, tomato, capsicum, bay leaves, thyme and stock or wine in a 4 cup (1 litre) ovenproof dish, and gently stir to combine. Tightly cover with foil and bake for 20 minutes.

2 Remove the dish from the oven and remove the foil. Lay the fish on top of the lentils and bake for a further 20 minutes, until the fish is cooked through.

3 Serve the fish on a bed of lentils, drizzled with the baking juices and sprinkled with the parsley and some freshly ground black pepper.

Serves 2

Preparation
10 minutes

Cooking
40 minutes

Per serving
1107 kJ, 265 kcal,
41 g protein, 3 g fat
(<1 g saturated fat),
13 g carbohydrate
(4 g sugars), 5 g fibre,
485 mg sodium

Fish fillets with mustard crust

Serves 4

Preparation
30 minutes

Cooking
10 minutes

Per serving
*1031 kJ, 246 kcal,
16 g protein, 13 g fat
(8 g saturated fat),
15 g carbohydrate
(3 g sugars), 5 g fibre,
697 mg sodium*

45 g (1½ oz) butter, softened, plus 2 teaspoons (10 g) chilled butter

2 tablespoons wholegrain mustard

1½ tablespoons dry packaged breadcrumbs

8 sprigs fresh parsley, leaves finely chopped

1½ tablespoons lemon juice

pinch of salt

freshly ground black pepper

pinch of grated lemon zest

4 firm white fish fillets, such as pike or perch, about 200 g (7 oz) each, skin removed

2 x 400 g (14 oz) cans brown lentils, rinsed and drained

200 g (7 oz) red cherry tomatoes, halved

3 spring onions (scallions), finely chopped

1 dried red chilli, crushed

1 Preheat the oven to 250°C (480°F/Gas 9). Grease a shallow ovenproof dish.

2 Put the softened butter in a small bowl and whisk in the mustard, breadcrumbs, half of the parsley and 1 teaspoon of the lemon juice until creamy. Season with salt, freshly ground black pepper and lemon zest.

3 Season the fish fillets with salt and pepper, and drizzle with 2 teaspoons of the lemon juice. Spread the mustard butter on one side of each fish fillet. Cover and refrigerate for about 10 minutes to allow the butter to firm.

4 Meanwhile, combine the lentils, tomatoes, spring onions, chilli, remaining parsley and remaining lemon juice in a bowl, then transfer the mixture to the prepared dish. Finely dice the chilled butter and sprinkle it on top of the lentil mixture.

5 Arrange the fish fillets on top of the lentils and bake in the middle of the oven for about 8 minutes. Change the oven to the grill (broiler) setting and crisp for about 2 minutes, until the mustard crust is crunchy.

Finely chop some fresh tarragon leaves and add them to the mustard and butter mixture instead of the parsley.

Fish fillets with mustard crust

Fish fillets with sesame crust

Preheat the oven to 250°C (480°F/Gas 9). Cook **200 g (7 oz) red lentils**
in **2 cups (500 ml) salt-reduced vegetable stock** (page 15) for 10 minutes,
until soft. Drain and season with **2 tablespoons chopped fresh parsley**,
1/2 teaspoon hot curry powder and **1 tablespoon cider vinegar**. Whisk
**3 tablespoons (60 g) softened butter, 2 tablespoons dijon mustard,
1 tablespoon sesame seeds, 2 tablespoons dry packaged breadcrumbs,
1 teaspoon lemon juice** and **a pinch of lemon zest** until creamy. Season the
fish and spread with the sesame butter as directed in the main recipe, then
chill for 10 minutes. Spoon the lentils into an ovenproof dish and dot with
butter. Top with the fish, bake and crisp as in the main recipe.

Fish and tomato gratin

Fish on tomatoes and leeks

Preheat the oven to 250°C (480°F/Gas 9). Season **4 firm white fish fillets, about 175 g (6 oz) each,** with **freshly ground black pepper, sweet paprika** and **1 tablespoon lemon juice.** Cook **400 g (14 oz) sliced leeks** in boiling water for 5 minutes, then drain. Combine the leeks with **400 g (14 oz) sliced tomatoes** in a shallow ovenproof dish, and season with **freshly ground black pepper.** Arrange the fish on top. Combine $^1/_3$ **cup (35 g) grated parmesan, 2 tablespoons dry packaged breadcrumbs** and **1 teaspoon each of dried oregano and thyme.** Sprinkle over the fish and drizzle with **2 tablespoons olive oil.** Bake as directed in the main recipe.

Fish and tomato gratin

⅓ cup (80 ml) olive oil

1 teaspoon dried oregano

pinch of cayenne pepper

grated zest of ½ lemon

1 tablespoon lemon juice

1 clove garlic, crushed

1 tablespoon thinly sliced
fresh mint

4 cod or other firm white fish
fillets, about 175 g (6 oz) each

pinch of salt

freshly ground black pepper

800 g (1¾ lb) tomatoes,
sliced

2 tablespoons finely chopped
fresh parsley

2 tablespoons fresh or dry
packaged breadcrumbs

⅓ cup (35 g) grated parmesan

1 Preheat the oven to 250°C (480°F/Gas 9). Lightly oil an ovenproof dish.

2 Combine ¼ cup (60 ml) of the oil with the oregano, cayenne pepper, lemon zest and lemon juice. Stir in the garlic and mint.

3 Pat the fish dry with paper towels and season with salt and freshly ground black pepper. Place the fish in a large shallow bowl. Drizzle the fish with the lemon mixture, then turn to coat. Cover and set aside for 5 minutes to allow the flavours to develop.

4 Meanwhile, arrange the tomato slices over the base of the prepared dish and season with salt and pepper.

5 Combine the parsley, breadcrumbs and parmesan in a small bowl.

6 Place the fish fillets on top of the tomatoes, reserving the liquid. Sprinkle the fish fillets with the breadcrumb mixture, then drizzle with the reserved marinating liquid and the remaining olive oil. Bake for 10 minutes, until the fish is cooked through. Serve hot.

Serves 4

Preparation
15 minutes

Cooking
10 minutes

Per serving
1653 kJ, 395 kcal,
37 g protein, 24 g fat
(5 g saturated fat),
8 g carbohydrate
(4 g sugars), 4 g fibre,
484 mg sodium

If you are running very short of time, marinate the fish in ready-made olive oil seasoned with herbs or lemon.

For a quick and easy side dish, combine some cooked rice with cooked frozen peas. Season with salt, pepper and 1 tablespoon chopped fresh mint, and fold in a small piece of butter.

Fish medallions with fennel

Serves 4

Preparation
25 minutes

Cooking
25 minutes

Per serving
2167 kJ, 518 kcal,
43 g protein, 30 g fat
(6 g saturated fat),
19 g carbohydrate
(14 g sugars), 8 g fibre,
897 mg sodium

⅓ cup (50 g) sun-dried tomatoes

⅓ cup (80 ml) orange juice

2 tablespoons lemon juice

¼ cup (60 ml) olive oil

grated zest of ½ lemon

grated zest of ½ orange

8 fish medallions, about 75 g (2½ oz) each

freshly ground black pepper

3-4 small bulbs fennel, about 700 g (1½ lb) in total

1½ cups (375 ml) salt-reduced vegetable stock (page 15)

8 slices prosciutto, about 80 g (2½ oz) in total

½ teaspoon fennel seeds

⅓ cup (50 g) chopped almonds

¼ cup (25 g) dry packaged breadcrumbs

You can use thinly sliced ham to wrap the fish medallions instead of prosciutto if you like.

1 Preheat the oven to 200°C (400°F/Gas 6). Lightly oil a shallow ovenproof dish that is large enough to hold the fennel and fish medallions in a single layer.

2 Rinse the sun-dried tomatoes under cold water and drain in a sieve. Cut into fine strips, transfer to a bowl and combine with the orange juice.

3 Combine the lemon juice, 1 tablespoon of the olive oil, the lemon zest and orange zest. Pat the fish medallions dry with paper towels, season with freshly ground black pepper and add to the marinade, turning to coat. Cover and refrigerate for about 10 minutes.

4 Meanwhile, trim and cut the fennel bulbs lengthwise into quarters. Reserve some of the fennel fronds. Bring the stock and 2½ cups (625 ml) water to a boil in a large saucepan, add the fennel, cover and simmer over medium heat for 8-10 minutes. Drain the fennel and season with pepper. Discard the stock.

5 Remove the fish medallions from the marinade and wrap each one in a prosciutto slice. Reserve the marinade.

6 Coarsely grind the fennel seeds and combine them with the almonds and breadcrumbs. Arrange the wrapped fish medallions and fennel quarters, cut side up, in the prepared dish. Top with the sun-dried tomato strips and drizzle with the orange juice.

7 Sprinkle the fennel and fish with the almond mixture and drizzle with the remaining oil and reserved marinade. Bake for 15 minutes, until the fish is cooked and the fennel is tender. Garnish with the reserved fennel fronds.

Moroccan-style fish gratin

Fish gratin with tomato couscous

Preheat the oven to 220°C (425°F/Gas 7). Prepare and marinate the fish as described in the main recipe (steps 2 and 3). Meanwhile, cook **1⅓ cups (250 g) couscous** in **2 cups (500 ml) boiling salt-reduced vegetable stock** (page 15) for about 5 minutes, or according to the packet instructions. Stir in **¼ cup (60 ml) orange juice**, a **410 g (15 oz) can diced tomatoes** and **2 tablespoons chopped fresh coriander (cilantro) or parsley.** Season with **cayenne pepper.** Transfer to an oiled ovenproof dish and top with the fish. Sprinkle with **¼ cup (25 g) dry packaged breadcrumbs.** Bake as directed in the main recipe.

Moroccan-style fish gratin

2 tablespoons lemon juice

90 ml (3 fl oz) olive oil

1 onion, finely chopped

2 cloves garlic, crushed

6 sprigs fresh coriander
(cilantro) or parsley, leaves
chopped, plus extra, to serve

1/2 teaspoon ground cumin

1/2 teaspoon sweet paprika

2 pinches of cayenne pepper

pinch of salt

600 g (1 1/4 lb) firm white fish
fillets, such as pollock

50 g (1 3/4 oz) pitas or
white bread

450 g (15 oz) green capsicum
(bell pepper), cut into thin
strips

410 g (15 oz) can diced
tomatoes

freshly ground black pepper

1 Preheat the oven to 220°C (425°F/Gas 7). Lightly oil a shallow ovenproof dish.

2 Combine the lemon juice and 1/3 cup (80 ml) of the olive oil with the onion, garlic and chopped herbs. Season with the cumin, paprika, cayenne pepper and salt.

3 Pat the fish fillets dry with paper towels and cut into bite-sized pieces. Toss the fish with the lemon mixture, cover and set aside for 10 minutes.

4 Cut the bread into small pieces, transfer to a food processor and chop into fine crumbs.

5 Heat the remaining olive oil in a frying pan and sauté the capsicum strips for 2 minutes. Add the tomatoes and cook until heated through. Season with salt and freshly ground black pepper.

6 Transfer the vegetables to the prepared dish, top with the fish and drizzle with the left-over marinade. Sprinkle with the fresh breadcrumbs and bake for 15 minutes, until golden and bubbling. Serve garnished with extra herbs.

Serves 4

Preparation
20 minutes

Cooking
20 minutes

Per serving
*1796 kJ, 429 kcal,
35 g protein, 26 g fat
(4 g saturated fat),
15 g carbohydrate
(7 g sugars), 3 g fibre,
419 mg sodium*

Make a quick dip from sour cream, lemon juice, crushed garlic and harissa (a Moroccan spice paste), and serve the gratin with fresh pitas.

The breadcrumbs can be made using day-old bread, or use packaged breadcrumbs.

Sweet bakes

A hot pudding or pie makes a lovely finish to a meal. Prepare one of these comforting desserts while your roast is cooking, then pop it into the hot oven when you serve the main course.

Orange and rosemary soufflés

Serves 4   **Time** 30 minutes

butter and sugar, for brushing

2 eggs, separated

1 eggwhite

1 tablespoon cornflour (cornstarch)

⅓ cup (75 g) sugar

grated zest and juice of 1 orange

100 g (3½ oz) quark (20% fat) or low-fat sour cream

1 tablespoon chopped fresh rosemary

Add 1–2 tablespoons orange liqueur to the soufflé mixture for an even richer flavour.

Substitute the orange with a lemon and the rosemary with basil, lemon thyme or lavender.

Preheat the oven to 180°C (350°F/ Gas 4). Grease four ½ cup (125 ml) ramekins with butter and sprinkle with sugar.

Whisk the three eggwhites until stiff, then whisk in the cornflour.

Whisk the egg yolks and sugar until thickened and increased in volume. Stir in the orange zest and orange juice, then whisk in the quark and rosemary until well combined.

Fold the eggwhites into the orange mixture and divide it among the ramekins. Bake for 15 minutes. Remove from the oven and serve immediately, as the soufflés will collapse quickly.

Per serving
764 kJ, 183 kcal, 7 g protein, 6 g fat (3 g saturated fat), 26 g carbohydrate (22 g sugars), 1 g fibre, 83 mg sodium

Baked apples

Serves 6   **Time** 1 hour

6 cooking apples, such as granny smith

50 g (1¾ oz) butter, melted

⅓ cup (60 g) soft brown sugar

¼ cup (30 g) sultanas (golden raisins)

¼ cup (35 g) currants

¼ cup (40 g) chopped raisins

1 teaspoon mixed (pumpkin pie) spice

custard, cream or vanilla ice-cream, to serve

Preheat the oven to 170°C (340°F/ Gas 3). Remove the cores from the apples using an apple corer. Use a small sharp knife to score a line through the skin around the centre of each apple.

Mix the butter, sugar, sultanas, currants, raisins and mixed spice in a large bowl until well combined. Press the mixture into the cavities in the apples. Place the apples in a large ovenproof dish and bake for 45 minutes, until tender.

Drizzle the apples with the cooking juices. Serve warm, with custard, cream or vanilla ice-cream.

Per serving
929 kJ, 222 kcal, 1 g protein, 7 g fat (5 g saturated fat), 40 g carbohydrate (39 g sugars), 4 g fibre, 72 mg sodium

Spiced apple and blueberry pie

Serves 6   **Time** 1½ hours

500 g (1 lb) apples

⅔ cup (100 g) blueberries

¼ cup (45 g) soft brown sugar

1 teaspoon ground cinnamon

½ teaspoon freshly grated nutmeg

1 eggwhite, lightly whisked

vanilla frozen yogurt or thick (Greek-style) yogurt, to serve (optional)

Pastry

½ cup (75 g) plain (all-purpose) flour

½ cup (75 g) wholemeal plain (whole-wheat all-purpose) flour

1¼ teaspoons mixed (pumpkin pie) spice

75 g (2½ oz) unsalted butter, diced and chilled

¼ cup (30 g) icing (confectioners') sugar, sifted

1 egg yolk

To make the pastry, sift the flours and mixed spice into a bowl, tipping in the bran left in the sieve. Using your fingertips, rub in the butter until the mixture resembles fine breadcrumbs. Stir in the sugar.

Mix the egg yolk with 1 tablespoon cold water, and stir into the flour mixture until it forms a soft dough, adding a few more drops of water if needed. Wrap the dough in plastic wrap and chill for at least 30 minutes.

Preheat the oven to 190°C (375°F/ Gas 5). Peel and slice the apples, and mix with the blueberries. Stir together the sugar, cinnamon and nutmeg. Reserve 1 tablespoon of the sugar mixture, and stir the rest into the fruit.

Thinly roll out the pastry on a large non-stick baking tray to make a 30 cm (12 inch) round. Brush the pastry all over with the eggwhite.

Pile the fruit in the middle of the pastry, then draw up the sides over the fruit, leaving the centre open. Brush the outside of the pastry with the remaining eggwhite and sprinkle with the reserved spiced sugar mixture.

Bake the pie for 30-35 minutes, until the pastry is golden brown and the apples are tender. Serve warm, with vanilla frozen yogurt or thick yogurt, if liked.

Per serving
1169 kJ, 279 kcal, 4 g protein, 12 g fat (7 g saturated fat), 40 g carbohydrate (22 g sugars), 4 g fibre, 15 mg sodium

Plum cobbler

Serves 6   **Time** 1 hour

800 g (1¾ lb) plums, halved or quartered

grated zest and juice of 1 large orange

1 cinnamon stick

2 tablespoons soft brown sugar

Scone topping

1⅓ cups (200 g) self-raising flour

pinch of salt

1 teaspoon baking powder

1½ tablespoons (30 g) unsalted butter, diced and chilled

2 tablespoons soft brown sugar

1 tablespoon chopped walnuts

100 ml (3½ fl oz) low-fat milk, plus 1 tablespoon, extra, for brushing

Use any other seasonal fruit, such as peaches, nectarines or apricots. You can replace the orange with a lemon.

Preheat the oven to 180°C (350°F/ Gas 4). Put the plums in a 5 cup (1.25 litre) ovenproof dish. Add the orange zest and juice, cinnamon stick and sugar, and mix thoroughly.

To make the scone topping, sift the flour, salt and baking powder into a bowl. Using your fingertips, rub in the butter until the mixture resembles fine breadcrumbs. Stir in the sugar and walnuts. Make a well in the centre, add the milk and mix to a soft but not sticky dough.

Transfer the dough to a lightly floured work surface and briefly knead. Roll out to a rectangle about 1 cm (½ inch) thick and the length of the ovenproof dish. Using a sharp knife or a pastry wheel, cut the dough into strips about 1.5 cm (⅝ inch) wide.

Dampen the rim of the dish with water, then arrange the scone strips over the fruit in a lattice pattern, pressing each end of the strips onto the rim of the dish and neatly trimming the ends. Brush the lattice with the extra milk.

Bake the cobbler for 25-30 minutes, until the scone topping is golden and the fruit is tender. Serve hot or warm.

Per serving
1686 kJ, 403 kcal, 6 g protein, 21 g fat (13 g saturated fat), 47 g carbohydrate (22 g sugars), 4 g fibre, 517 mg sodium

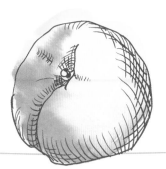

Baked basil and tapenade chicken

The generous use of herbs is a feature of the cuisines of the Mediterranean. Here, fresh basil combines with tapenade, the Provençal condiment made with ripe olives, capers, anchovies, olive oil and lemon juice.

Serves 4

Preparation
15 minutes

Cooking
40 minutes

Per serving
1718 kJ, 411 kcal,
32 g protein, 29 g fat
(6 g saturated fat),
4 g carbohydrate
(2 g sugars), 4 g fibre,
770 mg sodium

2½ tablespoons olive oil

6 cloves garlic, crushed

500 g (1 lb) frozen artichoke hearts, thawed, or canned artichokes, drained

500 g (1 lb) asparagus spears, trimmed

1 bay leaf

½ teaspoon dried rosemary

½ teaspoon salt

¼ cup (60 g) tapenade (olive paste)

¼ cup (15 g) chopped fresh basil

4 bone-in chicken breast halves, about 1.25 kg (2½ lb) in total

lemon wedges, to serve

1 Preheat the oven to 200°C (400°F/Gas 6). Combine the oil and garlic in a 23 x 33 cm (9 x 13 inch) ovenproof dish. Heat the dish in the oven for 5 minutes, until the oil begins to sizzle. Stir in the artichokes, asparagus, bay leaf, rosemary and half the salt. Bake for 10 minutes.

2 Meanwhile, in a small bowl, combine the tapenade and basil. With your fingers, gently loosen the skin from the chicken breasts without removing it, then spoon the tapenade mixture under the skin.

3 Place the chicken breasts, skin side up, on top of the roasted vegetables, and sprinkle with the remaining salt. Bake for 25 minutes, until the chicken is cooked through and the vegetables are tender. Discard the bay leaf and serve with lemon wedges.

You can buy jars of ready-made tapenade from delicatessens, specialist grocers and some larger supermarkets.

Chicken and blue cheese gratin

750 g (1½ lb) boiling (waxy) potatoes, thinly sliced

300 g (10 oz) celeriac (celery root), thinly sliced

350 g (12 oz) leeks, white part only, sliced

250 g (8 oz) boneless, skinless chicken breast, cut into thin strips

1 tablespoon chopped fresh thyme or 1½ teaspoons dried thyme

freshly ground black pepper

1 cup (250 ml) hot salt-reduced chicken stock (page 14)

75 g (2½ oz) firm blue cheese, crumbled

1 tablespoon (20 g) butter, chilled and diced

1 Preheat the oven to 200°C (400°F/Gas 6). Put the potatoes and celeriac in a saucepan of water, cover and bring to a boil over medium heat. Remove the lid and simmer for 3 minutes, until starting to soften. Remove from the heat and drain well.

2 Arrange about one-third of the potato and celeriac slices in a greased 8 cup (2 litre) ovenproof dish, allowing the slices to overlap. Scatter about half of each of the leek, chicken strips and thyme over the vegetable layer. Season with plenty of freshly ground black pepper.

3 Continue layering the potatoes and celeriac with the remaining leek, chicken and thyme. Finish with a layer of potatoes and celeriac.

4 Pour the hot stock over the top, then sprinkle with the cheese and dot with the butter. Cover with foil and bake for 20 minutes. Remove the foil and bake for a further 20 minutes, until the cheese has melted and the top is golden and bubbling. Serve hot.

Serves 4

Preparation
20 minutes

Cooking
50 minutes

Per serving
1560 kJ, 373 kcal, 26 g protein, 16 g fat (8 g saturated fat), 31 g carbohydrate (7 g sugars), 10 g fibre, 472 mg sodium

This simple but hearty Greek casserole, known as 'pastitsio', calls for tubular pasta, such as ditalini ('little thimbles'). The chicken is cooked in a spicy tomato sauce, then layered with the pasta and white sauce, creating a comforting, hearty meal.

Chicken pasta bake

Serves 4

Preparation
20 minutes

Cooking
1 hour 5 minutes

Per serving
2309 kJ, 552 kcal, 35 g protein, 22 g fat (8 g saturated fat), 54 g carbohydrate (12 g sugars), 5 g fibre, 666 mg sodium

1 tablespoon olive oil

1 large onion, finely chopped

2 cloves garlic, crushed

400 g (14 oz) minced (ground) chicken

2 cups (500 g) canned chopped tomatoes

1 teaspoon ground cinnamon

$\frac{1}{2}$ teaspoon salt

$\frac{1}{2}$ teaspoon freshly ground black pepper

$\frac{1}{4}$ teaspoon ground allspice

small pinch of ground cloves

200 g (7 oz) ditalini, penne or ziti

$1\frac{1}{2}$ tablespoons (30 g) butter

$\frac{1}{4}$ cup (35 g) plain (all-purpose) flour

2 cups (500 ml) skim milk

$\frac{1}{4}$ cup (25 g) grated parmesan

1 Heat the oil in a large frying pan over medium heat. Add the onion and garlic, and cook, stirring frequently, for 4 minutes, until the onion is soft. Stir in the chicken, tomatoes, cinnamon, salt, pepper, allspice and cloves. Reduce the heat and simmer for 20 minutes, until the mixture is thick and almost dry.

2 Meanwhile, cook the pasta in a large saucepan of boiling water for 10-12 minutes, or according to the packet instructions, until al dente. Drain well.

3 Preheat the oven to 180°C (350°F/Gas 4). Melt the butter in a saucepan over low heat. Whisk in the flour until combined. Gradually whisk in the milk, stirring until smooth. Cook, stirring, for 5 minutes, until thickened.

4 Spoon $\frac{1}{4}$ cup (60 ml) of the sauce into a 23 cm (9 inch) square ovenproof dish. Spoon half the pasta over the top, then half the chicken mixture, and sprinkle with half the parmesan. Top with the remaining pasta, chicken mixture and white sauce. Sprinkle with the remaining parmesan.

5 Bake for 35 minutes, until the topping is crusty and golden brown. Serve hot.

Chicken pot pie

2 tablespoons olive oil

3 leeks, white and pale green parts only, roughly chopped

2 celery stalks, roughly chopped

2 large carrots, thickly sliced

1 large red-skinned potato, such as desiree or pontiac, unpeeled and cut into bite-sized chunks

1 cup (90 g) thickly sliced button mushrooms

$^1/_4$ cup (35 g) plain (all-purpose) flour

$^1/_2$ teaspoon dried thyme

$^1/_4$ teaspoon salt

400 ml (14 fl oz) salt-reduced chicken stock (page 14)

1$^2/_3$ cups (250 g) diced cooked chicken breast or thighs

1 cup (150 g) fresh or frozen peas

1 large egg

1 tablespoon milk

1 sheet frozen puff pastry large enough to cover a 23 cm (9 inch) pie dish, thawed

1 Heat the oil in a large saucepan and cook the leeks, celery, carrots and potato over medium heat, stirring occasionally, for 5 minutes. Add the mushrooms and cook, stirring occasionally, for 5 minutes. Stir in the flour, thyme and salt until blended, then stir in the stock. Increase the heat to medium-high and cook, stirring, for 2 minutes. Stir in the chicken and peas. Transfer the pie filling to a deep, 23 cm (9 inch) pie dish. Allow to cool to room temperature.

2 Meanwhile, preheat the oven to 200°C (400°C/Gas 6). Whisk together the egg and milk, and brush over the pastry. Place the pastry, glazed side down, over the filling in the pie dish. Trim the edge of the pastry, and crimp or mark decoratively with a fork if desired. Brush the top with the remaining egg mixture. Cut four 2.5 cm (1 inch) slits in the centre of the pastry to allow steam to escape.

3 Bake the pie for 25–30 minutes, until the filling is bubbling and the top is golden brown. Remove from the oven and stand for at least 10 minutes before serving.

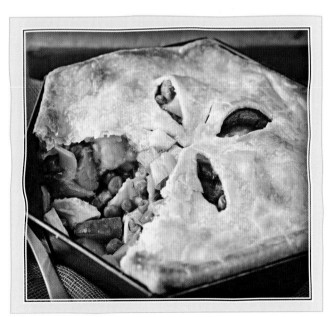

Serves 6

Preparation
25 minutes

Cooking
45 minutes,
plus 10 minutes
standing

Per serving
*1398 kJ, 334 kcal,
19 g protein, 17 g fat
(6 g saturated fat),
25 g carbohydrate
(5 g sugars), 5 g fibre,
476 mg sodium*

Topped with flaky puff pastry, this popular one-pot dish takes classic comfort food and gives it a healthy modern twist: it contains a higher ratio of vegetables to poultry.

Chicken cacciatore

Serves 2

Preparation
15 minutes

Cooking
45 minutes

Per serving
1400 kJ, 334 kcal,
29 g protein, 17 g fat
(4 g saturated fat),
12 g carbohydrate
(9 g sugars), 6 g fibre,
554 mg sodium

1 tablespoon olive oil

4 bone-in skinless chicken thighs

freshly ground black pepper

1 small onion, chopped

1 celery stalk, thinly sliced

1 carrot, finely chopped

125 g (4 oz) button mushrooms, cut into quarters

1 slice rindless bacon (bacon strips), finely diced

¼ cup (60 ml) dry red wine or salt-reduced chicken stock (page 14)

410 g (15 oz) can crushed tomatoes

1 bay leaf

1 sprig fresh rosemary

3 stalks fresh parsley, plus extra chopped parsley, to garnish

pinch of paprika

crusty bread, to serve

1 Heat the oil in a heavy-based saucepan or flameproof casserole dish over medium-high heat. Season the chicken with freshly ground black pepper. Cook the chicken until golden all over, about 3 minutes on each side. Transfer to a plate.

2 Reduce the heat to medium and add the onion, celery, carrot, mushrooms and bacon to the pan. Cook for about 5 minutes, until the mushrooms are soft.

3 Pour in the wine or stock, reduce the heat to medium-low and simmer for 1 minute. Stir in the tomatoes, bay leaf, rosemary, parsley stalks and paprika.

4 Return the chicken to the pan. Cover and simmer for 30 minutes, until the juices run clear when tested with a skewer. Remove the bay leaf, rosemary and parsley.

5 Sprinkle the chicken with chopped parsley and serve with some crusty bread.

Use chicken drumsticks instead of thighs, and pancetta instead of bacon. Toss some baby spinach leaves through the stew just before serving.

Eat any left-over chicken within the next two days, perhaps on a bed of rice or pasta. Alternatively, freeze the chicken mixture in a small airtight container for up to 2 months.

Chicken and mushroom pot pies

Serves 2

Preparation
20 minutes

Cooking
30 minutes

Per serving
1768 kJ, 422 kcal,
36 g protein, 20 g fat
(8 g saturated fat),
24 g carbohydrate
(6 g sugars), 4 g fibre,
633 mg sodium

1 teaspoon vegetable oil

250 g (8 oz) boneless, skinless chicken thighs, trimmed and chopped

1 slice rindless bacon (bacon strips), chopped

2 spring onions (scallions), chopped

100 g (3^1/$_2$ oz) button mushrooms, chopped

1 teaspoon butter

2 teaspoons plain (all-purpose) flour

100 ml (3^1/$_2$ fl oz) low-fat milk, plus extra, for brushing

^{1}/$_3$ cup (50 g) frozen peas and corn, thawed slightly

freshly ground black pepper

^{1}/$_2$ sheet frozen puff pastry, thawed and cut in half

1 Preheat the oven to 200°C (400°F/Gas 6). Heat the oil in a non-stick frying pan over medium-high heat. Cook the chicken, stirring often, for 5 minutes, until brown and cooked. Place in a large bowl.

2 Reduce the heat to medium. Cook the bacon, spring onions and mushrooms for 3 minutes, stirring often, until the bacon is cooked and the vegetables have softened. Add to the chicken.

3 Melt the butter in the frying pan, then add the flour. Cook, stirring, for about 30 seconds. Gradually add the milk, stirring constantly. Bring to a boil and cook for 1 minute, until thickened.

4 Add the white sauce to the chicken mixture, along with the peas and corn. Season with freshly ground black pepper, and mix well.

5 Spoon the mixture into two 1 cup (250 ml) ramekins and place on a baking tray. Cover with the pastry, press it down around the side of each ramekin and trim the edges. Lightly brush with extra milk and bake for 15-20 minutes, until golden. Serve hot.

You can find mixed packets of frozen peas and corn in the freezer section of your supermarket. Alternatively, use 2 tablespoons fresh or frozen peas and 2 tablespoons corn kernels.

Substitute the chopped olives with ¼ cup (60 g) tapenade (olive paste). Combine with the breadcrumb mixture and coat the chicken as directed in the recipe.

Chicken with olive crust

250 g (8 oz) red capsicums (bell peppers), cut into strips

250 g (8 oz) yellow capsicums (bell peppers), cut into strips

⅓ cup (80 ml) olive oil

2½ tablespoons lemon juice

1 clove garlic

pinch of salt

½ teaspoon fennel seeds

½ cup (60 g) pitted black olives, finely chopped

1 eggwhite

¼ cup (25 g) dry packaged breadcrumbs

2 sprigs fresh rosemary, leaves finely chopped

freshly ground black pepper

4 boneless, skinless chicken breasts, about 150 g (5 oz) each

2 teaspoons wholegrain mustard

1 Combine the capsicums with 2 tablespoons of the olive oil and 2 tablespoons of the lemon juice in a bowl.

2 Peel the garlic, sprinkle with salt and crush with the blade of a knife. Grind the fennel seeds using a mortar and pestle.

3 Preheat the oven to 200°C (400°F/Gas 6). Lightly oil a shallow ovenproof dish that is large enough to hold the chicken and capsicum strips.

4 Combine the chopped olives, eggwhite, breadcrumbs, rosemary, crushed garlic and ground fennel seeds with the remaining olive oil and lemon juice. Season the mixture with freshly ground black pepper.

5 Pat the chicken dry with paper towels and season with salt and black pepper. Spread one side with mustard and top with the olive mixture, pressing it into the chicken.

6 Arrange the chicken in the centre of the prepared dish and the capsicums around the sides. Bake for 25 minutes. Change the oven to the grill (broiler) setting and crisp for 2–3 minutes, until the crust is crunchy. Serve immediately.

Serves 4

Preparation
20 minutes

Cooking
30 minutes

Per serving
1933 kJ, 462 kcal, 37 g protein, 30 g fat (6 g saturated fat), 12 g carbohydrate (6 g sugars), 3 g fibre, 586 mg sodium

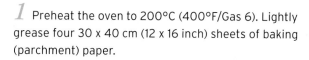

Beef with mushrooms en papillote

Serves 4

Preparation
25 minutes

Cooking
25 minutes

Per serving
1580 kJ, 377 kcal,
28 g protein, 25 g fat
(5 g saturated fat),
10 g carbohydrate
(6 g sugars), 4 g fibre,
414 mg sodium

4 small beef fillet steaks, about 120 g (4 oz) each, trimmed of fat

⅓ cup (80 ml) olive oil

pinch of salt

freshly ground black pepper

8 sprigs fresh rosemary

8 sprigs fresh thyme

200 g (7 oz) button mushrooms, sliced

200 g (7 oz) fresh shiitake mushrooms, stems removed, sliced

2 cloves garlic, crushed

100 g (3½ oz) pickled small white onions, drained

1 Preheat the oven to 200°C (400°F/Gas 6). Lightly grease four 30 x 40 cm (12 x 16 inch) sheets of baking (parchment) paper.

2 Pat the steaks dry with paper towels and flatten them with the heel of your hand. Heat 1 tablespoon of the oil in a non-stick frying pan over medium heat and cook the steaks for 1 minute on each side. Remove from the pan and briefly drain on paper towels. Season with salt and freshly ground black pepper.

3 Chop half the rosemary and half the thyme. Combine with the mushrooms, garlic, onions and 2 tablespoons of the oil. Season with salt and pepper. Divide the mushroom mixture among the baking paper sheets.

4 Put the steaks on the mushrooms and place a sprig of rosemary and a sprig of thyme on top of each steak. Drizzle the remaining oil over the steaks. Carefully wrap each parcel, bringing the short edges to the centre and folding down firmly to secure the top and sides, then firmly twist both long ends together.

5 Place the parcels on a cold baking tray and bake for 20 minutes. Arrange the parcels on serving plates and slice open with kitchen shears. Serve immediately.

When you are opening the cooked beef parcels, be careful not to burn yourself as the steam escapes.

Cottage pie

500 g (1 lb) lean minced (ground) beef

1 onion, finely chopped

1 large carrot, grated

1 celery stalk, finely chopped

1 tablespoon tomato paste (concentrated purée)

1 teaspoon worcestershire sauce

1 teaspoon mixed dried herbs

1½ cups (375 ml) hot salt-reduced beef stock (page 14)

1 tablespoon plain (all-purpose) flour

pinch of salt

freshly ground black pepper

1 kg (2 lb) boiling (waxy) potatoes, such as long white, diced

100 ml (3½ fl oz) low-fat milk, warmed

30 g (1 oz) butter

Serves 4

Preparation
20 minutes

Cooking
30 minutes

Per serving
1893 kJ, 452 kcal, 36 g protein, 15 g fat (8 g saturated fat), 42 g carbohydrate (6 g sugars), 5 g fibre, 752 mg sodium

1 Heat a large heavy-based frying pan until hot, then add the beef, onion, carrot and celery. Fry, stirring occasionally to break up any lumps, for 5 minutes, until the beef is lightly browned all over.

2 Stir the tomato paste, worcestershire sauce and dried herbs into the stock. Sprinkle the flour over the beef and vegetables, then stir in the stock mixture. Bring to a boil, then reduce the heat, cover with a lid and cook over low heat for 15 minutes. Season with salt and freshly ground black pepper.

3 Meanwhile, cook the potatoes in a saucepan of boiling water for 10 minutes, until tender. Drain, then mash with the warmed milk and butter. Season with salt and pepper.

4 Preheat the grill (broiler) to medium. Spoon the beef mixture into a large warmed ovenproof dish. Spread the mashed potatoes over the top and fluff up with a fork. Put under the grill to brown and crisp the top.

If you prefer, you can bake the pie at 200°C (400°F/ Gas 6) for about 20 minutes, until the topping is golden brown.

Index

WEIGHTS AND MEASURES

Australian metric cup and spoon measurements are used throughout this book: 1 cup = 250 ml; 1 tablespoon = 20 ml and 1 teaspoon = 5 ml. If using the smaller imperial measures (where 1 cup = 235 ml and 1 tablespoon = 15 ml), some adjustments may need to be made. A small variation in the weight or volume of most ingredients is unlikely to adversely affect a recipe. All cup and spoon measures are level, unless stated otherwise. Ingredients are listed by weight or volume with cup measurements given for convenience, unless the conversion is imperfect; then ingredients are listed by weight or volume only.

Sometimes conversions within a recipe are not exact but are the closest suitable measurement for each system. Use either the metric or the imperial measurements; do not mix the two systems. Can sizes vary between countries and manufacturers; if the stated size is unavailable, use the nearest equivalent.

NUTRITIONAL ANALYSIS

Each recipe is accompanied by a nutrient profile showing kilojoules (kJ), calories (kcal), protein, fat (including saturated fat), carbohydrate (including sugars), fibre and sodium. Serving suggestions, garnishes and optional ingredients are not included in the nutritional analysis. For the recipe analyses, we used FoodWorks ® based on Australian and New Zealand food composition data. In line with current nutritional recommendations, use salt-reduced stock wherever possible.

ALTERNATIVE TERMS

Where the recipe calls for 'cream' and doesn't specify which type, it refers to pure (single/light) cream.

More Healthy
One-Dish Cooking

Project Editor Justine Harding
Senior Editors Jessica Cox, Bronwyn Sweeney
Project Designer Melanie Young
Senior Designer Joanne Buckley
Nutritional Analysis Toni Gumley
Proofreader Susan McCreery
Indexer Diane Harriman
Senior Production Controller Martin Milat

Reader's Digest General Books

Editorial Director Lynn Lewis
Managing Editor Rosemary McDonald
Design Manager Donna Heldon

CREDITS

All images © Reader's Digest, except the following:
Shutterstock 14, 49, 64, 92, 216; all fruit and vegetable
illustrations; coloured backgrounds (throughout),
coloured circles (throughout).

More Healthy One-Dish Cooking contains material first
published in the following Reader's Digest books:
5 Ingredient Cookbook; *30 Minute Cookbook*;
Anti-Ageing Diet Cookbook; *Beautiful Baking*; *Cooking
for 1 or 2*; *Cooking the Classics*; *Delicious and Healthy
Meals for the Over 50s*; *Eggs, Milk and Cheese*; *Fish and
Seafood*; *Food in a Flash*; *Grandma's Quick and Thrifty
Cookbook*; *The Great Chicken Cookbook*; *Light Bites
and Lunches*; *Low Fat No Fat Asian*; *Meat Classics*;
Meat Favourites; *Perfect Poultry*; *Pies, Tarts and
Puddings*; *Rice, Beans and Grains*; *Quick and Easy
Cooking*; *Soups and Casseroles*; *Super Foods Super
Easy*; *Vegetables for Vitality*.

More Healthy One-Dish Cooking is published by
Reader's Digest (Australia) Pty Limited
80 Bay Street, Ultimo NSW 2007
www.readersdigest.com.au
www.readersdigest.co.nz
www.rdasia.com

First published 2014
Copyright © Reader's Digest (Australia) Pty Limited 2014
Copyright © Reader's Digest Association Far East Limited 2014
Philippines Copyright © Reader's Digest Association Far East
Limited 2014

National Library of Australia Cataloguing-in-Publication entry:
  Title: More healthy one-dish cooking.
  ISBN: 978-1-922085-71-9 (paperback)
  Notes: Includes index.
  Subjects: One-dish meals.
  Casserole cooking.
  Dewey Number: 641.82

Prepress by Colourpedia Bros, Sydney
Printed and bound by Leo Paper Products, China

We are interested in receiving your comments on the
contents of this book. Write to:
The Editor, General Books Editorial,
Reader's Digest (Australia) Pty Limited,
GPO Box 4353, Sydney, NSW 2001,

or email us at
bookeditors.au@readersdigest.com

To order additional copies of *More Healthy One-Dish Cooking*,
please contact us as follows:
www.readersdigest.com.au, 1300 300 030 (Australia);
www.readersdigest.co.nz, 0800 400 060 (New Zealand);
or email us at customerservice@readersdigest.com.au

Concept code: AU 0959
Product number: 041-5436 (pbk)